# EXPLORATION ON EXPRESSIONS

## A COLLECTION OF SHAKESPEAREAN PHRASES

DR. M A MOHAMED SAHUL HAMEED

*To my belov'd parents*

# Contents

# Tribute To Shakespeare

Others abide our question. Thou art free
We ask and ask – Thou smilest and art still,
Out-topping knowledge. For the loftiest hill,
Who to the stars uncrowns his majesty,

Planting his steadfast footsteps in the sea,
Making the heaven of heavens his dwelling place,
Spares but the cloudy border of his base
To the foiled searching of mortality;

And thou, who didst the stars and sunbeams know,
Self-schooled, self-scanned, self-honoured, self-secure,
Didst tread on earth unguessed at - Better So!

All pains the immortal spirit must endure,
All weakness which impairs, all griefs which bow,
Find their sole speech in that victorious brow.

- Mathew Arnold

# Acknowledgements

A favour done, not as return for another, is more valuable than heaven and earth put together. - Thirukkural

Being a believer myself, I offer my sincere prayers to God for His greatest blessings upon me!

At the outset, I wish to express my heartfelt thanks to my beloved parents Janab Abdur Rahman and Janaba Hajaral Beevi, who, I do feel, are with me for ever, praying for me even after their leaving this earth. My dedicating this book to my beloved parents is nothing before their care and concern that they were bestowing upon me till the end of their life.

I place on record my heartfelt thanks to our Hon'ble Chancellor Dr G.Viswanathan, our respected Vice-Presidents Mr Sankar Viswanathan, Dr Sekar Viswanathan and Mr G.V.Selvam and to our respected Vice-Chancellor Dr Rambabu Kodali and Pro Vice-Chancellor Dr S.Narayanan and Registrar Dr K.Sathiyanarayanan for their constant support and encouragement in bringing this book to light.

I am thankful to Dr M.Manoharan, Dean, SSL, Dr G. Velmurugan, former Dean, Dr Sarika Gupta, Head and all my belov'd colleagues, Dept of English for their greatest support, help and motivation.

I am greatly indebted to my belov'd colleagues Dr R.Srinivasan, Dept of English and Dr R.Calaivanane, Dept of Languages for their kind consent to be the co-authors of this book and for their commendable contributions to this book.

I thank Dr Muthukrishnan, former Professor of English, Bharathiar University, Coimbatore and Dr R.V.Baskar, former professor of

English, VIT for their valuable input.

I express a great deal of gratitude to my wife Yasmin and my belov'd daughter Sajitha Hajr for sparing their time with me, motivating me to bring this book to light.

My heartfelt thanks are due to my belov'd son M.S.Abdur Rahman for designing the cover page of the book, making all page alignments and helping me in bringing this book expeditiously to light.

I thank all my friends, well-wishers, relatives and students for encouraging me a lot to bring this book out. It is the fondness of my students for unique expressions in English that made me think of writing this book.

M.A.MOHAMED SAHUL HAMEED

# Introduction

William Shakespeare is an ever glittering star in the world of literature. Among all languages, English continues to enjoy a proud and prestigious status for which the contributions of William Shakespeare are highly commendable. His expressions are the greatest treasures that the whole world is proud to be in possession of. The beauty of English can be felt by heart while reading William Shakespeare. He is one of the greatest dramatists that the world has ever produced. Reading of Shakespearean plays makes one feel that Shakespeare is yet to be discovered and rediscovered.

William Shakespeare's expressions, besides enriching one's language skills, create some sort of linguistic spirit that can be felt by passionate readers. He has expressions for all ages and for all occasions. English without Shakespearean expressions is like a garden without flowers. We got freedom from the English in 1947, but we never wish to get freedom from Shakespeare, for his expressions uniquely enslave us and enable us to use words and expressions so freely, so creatively that boundaries cannot be thought of. Greatest stalwarts in every field and greatest leaders everywhere have never failed to quote William Shakespeare. Authors in thousands have paid rich tributes to William Shakespeare.

Self-schooled, self-scanned, self-honoured, self-secure, William Shakespeare still remains as an amazing mystic in the world of literature. The world of Science is nothing without outstanding scientists like Isaac Newton, Thomas Alva Edison and Albert Einstein; the world of philosophy is nothing without outstanding philosophers like Socrates and Aristotle and the world of literature is nothing without outstanding literary figures like William Shakespeare and John Milton. He stands tall in the annals of history with his unique expressions in English.

Great wits must never get wasted in the street. The perfumes of Arabia must never lose its flavour. The expressions of William Shakespeare must not stay just on the pages of books unread or rarely read or read for securing some grade in examinations, but must be got imprinted in minds. The edge of appetite cannot be cloyed by bare imagination of a royal feast, and use of beautiful expressions in English cannot be just thought of or imagined without having a taste for Shakespearean expressions.

Though the advancements of technology are highly remarkable, and have their own advantages in acquisition of knowledge, too much impact of the same in acquisition of language skills poses threat to the use of King's or Queen's English that was highly glorified in the days gone. Frequent use of SMS language even in formal contexts and use of e-language have made communication easy, but the beauty of language can be felt only while reading books on literature.

"Old is gold" is a proverb. The authors have collected some of the most quoted and most quotable expressions from all Shakespeare's comedies with the passionate desire to get the minds of young learners filled with Shakespearean expressions and to enable them to explore more such expressions. The authors have given readers sample sentences following Shakespearean expressions. This attempt has been made to kindle the linguistic spirit of young learners in the hope that at least a few among many would further explore expressions not only from Shakespeare, but also from other great writers of English.

# About The Authors

xiii

Dr M.A.Mohamed Sahul Hameed, Dr R.Srinivasan and Dr R. Calaivanane are Members of Faculty in the School of Social Sciences and Languages, VIT, Vellore. They have great love for teaching and research. They have publised a number of research papers on language teaching-learning, pedagogical strategies, psychological research, teaching of literature and language skills in international journals of repute and delivered guest lectures on Language Teaching and Learning and Development of Life Skills in various institutes. They have received Research Awards from VIT for their contributions to the field of research. Though their area of specialization is language teaching, they have great passion and love for literature. They strongly believe that literature is a unique tool for enhancing language skills.

# CHAPTER ONE

# THE COMEDY OF ERRORS

- *First Merchant: My present business calls me from you now.*

He has no business at all, but he speaks as if his business calls him often.

Joe remains jobless for years, but he is so showy and self-boasting that he says that Time itself schedules his business.

("Everybody's business is nobody's business" is a proverb.)

If my business does not call me, I shall attend your sister's marriage.

I myself do not know when my business will call me.

Everybody's business calls my dad, except his.

- *Antipholus of Syracuse: I am not in a sportive humor now.*

*Tell me, and dally not:*

(sportive mood-joking mood) (dally not-stop fooling)

To be in a sportive humour relieves one of any stress.

Tom could not be in a sportive humour, when he fell a prey to false accusations.

I am not in a sportive mood to keep my eyes and ears engaged in entertainment.

Mind filled with dark clouds cannot be in a sportive mood.

Tell me now, dally me later.


- *Antipholus of Syracuse: ..........I'll break that comical head of yours for goofing*

  *Or I shall break that merry sconce of yours*
  *That stands on tricks when I am undisposed.*

Every doctor needs a merry sconce, since half of the disease gets cured throughmerry.

Our English classes are quite interesting as our teacher has merry sconce.

The merry sconce of yours lazily sits on happy occasions but actively stands on tricks on sad occasions.

The clown's comical head was tragically broken by someone for reasons unknown.

His merry sconce was broken into pieces for goofing all the time.


- *Luciana: A man is master of his liberty;*

  *Time is their master, and when they see time*
  *They'll go or come.*

The problem with some of us is that want tobecome masters of others' liberty.

After marriage, Jacob became a servant of his own liberty.

My wish to be at my own liberty has chained me be at the liberty of others.

He is a master of his liberty, but a slave of his wife's.

The liberty of the cowards is only in words.

I have left everything to time, being my master.

He has made good time his servant, but bad time his master, and time continues to be bad for him.

- *Luciana: .........headstrong liberty is lashed with woe.*

(Too much liberty leads to woe.)

It is your headstrong liberty that has landed you in troubles.

She misused all her powers with headstrong liberty, but now she is not able to show anyone her head.

Your headstrong liberty one day or other will be lashed with woe.

He has been a slave all these years and he needs now headstrong liberty.

Roger became a saint only after his headstrong liberty was lashed with woe.

- *Luciana: How many fond fools serve mad jealousy!*

(Many infatuated fools go mad with jealousy)

Suji is not a fool to serve mad jealousy.

His serving all vices has removed from his all virtues.

He does not mind becoming mad out of jealousy.

I am competitive, but not jealousy.

The fool that serves jealousy shall become mad out of mad jealousy.

To serve jealousy may give one pleasure, but not profit.

- *Antipholus of Syracuse: When the sun shines, let foolish gnats make sport,*

***But creep in crannies when he hides his beams.***

(Foolish gnats come out in the sunshine, but they creep back into their holes when it is dark.) (gnat- a small insect)

"Make hay while the sun shines" is a proverb.

They are so lazy and foolish that they are looking for light under the shadow of darkness.

You creep in crannies when the sun hides his beams.

He becomes a foolish gnat creeping in crannies, when the sun hides his beams.

She has lost all her hopes that she feels that even the sun intends to hide her beams.

My hope will continue to shed its light even when my beams are hidden by the entire sky.

- ***Dromio of Syracuse:*** ...........................................***I shall***

***seek my wit in my shoulders.***

(To seek wit in shoulders- to seek brain in chest)

Mithun is so brilliant that he seeks his wit in his shoulders.

Let him seek his wit at least in his shoulders.

The soldiers were so witty that they easily won the war by displaying their fleshy shoulders.

He is so witty that he seeks his wit in shoulders, that too in someone;s shoulders.

You seek your wit in your shoulders and claim yourself to be ignorant.

She has flesh in head and wit in shoulder.

- ***Dromio of Syracuse: There's no time for a man to recover his hair that grows bald by nature.***

(There may be a time for everything, but no man who has gone bald naturally can get his hair back.)

Come to Naturals and recover your hair that grows bald by nature. (Advertisement?)

He is wasting his time by trying to recover every hair that he has lost by nature.

"You may recover your health, not your hair", said the doctor to the cancer patient.

Some of us spend a lot on online products to recover their hair that grows bald by nature and become financially bald too.

She is so beauty-conscious that she has applied for leave for one year to recover her hair that grew bald by nature.

Many of us become bald not by nature, but by stress.

- *Antipholus of Syracuse: ............there's many a man hath more hair than wit.*

(Ladies and Gentlemen! I am happy to say that the Chief Guest of today's programme hath more hair than wit.) (???)

Do not judge anyone by his/her bald head.

Lily has neither hair nor wit.

He has more hair than wit.

He has as much hair as wit.

He has as much wit as his hair. (an intelligent person with good hair)

You can take pride in saying that you have more hair.

- *Adriana: .........wrong not that wrong with a more contempt.*

(The word 'wrong' is used both as a verb and as an adjective. )

What you say is wrong. (Adjective)

You try to wrong me in every issue. (Verb))

Don't make things worse by treating me with a more contempt.

You go wrong with your wrong notions about the policy and continue to do wrong by wrongly treating the employees with contempt.

I may be wrong, but I need not be treated with contempt.

Treating others with contempt is wrong.

- *Dromio of Syracuse: If we obey them not, ..............................*

   *They'll suck our breath, or pinch us black and blue.*

('To pinch one black and blue' is an idiomatic expression that means 'to beat one severely.)

He is so angry with her that he will suck her breath and pinch her black and blue, if he happens to see her somewhere.

The very breath of the labourers in some workplaces is being sucked from sunrise to sunset for low wages.

They do not want to work in a place where "obedience to the core" is the only policy and "Do or Die; Don't ask why" is the only slogan.

Obey our commands or we shall suck your breath and pinch you black and blue.

I, as the poor father of many children living in abject penury, don't mind having my breath sucked and getting myself pinched black and blue, with reasons or without reasons, as I cannot leave my children without bread at least once day.

The imperialistic attitude of the British made them suck the breath of many of our freedom fighters.

- *Antipholus of Syracuse: My wife is shrewish when I keep not hours.*

(shrewish-angry)

    (to keep not hours- to keep not time, to come late)

    (Robert: My wife is shrewish when I keep not hours.

    Peter: My wife is shrewish when I keep hours. )

    The teacher became shrewish, as his students kept not hours.

    My boss is so strict and punctual that he would become shrewish if hours are not kept.

    Bio-metric attendance comes to effect, as employees keep not hours.


- *Antipholus of Syracuse: ...............................either at flesh or fish*

    *A table full of welcome make scarce one dainty dish.*

(All the welcome in the world cannot be compared to a good meal, whatever kind of food it

    might be.) (dainty-esteem or honour)

    Every table in our house is full of welcome.

    Only tables in your house are full of welcome.

    Besides our minds and hearts, our tables are full of welcome.

    When did you sell your table that was full of welcome?

    He welcomes his guests in such a manner that any guest may get the doubt whether his house is made up of full of walls or full of welcome.

    You welcome me with your words, not with your heart.

    Flesh or fish, my guests will have some dainty dish.

    The girl says, "Though I am a vegetarian, I can marry one fond of fish, but not of mere flesh".

    It is most unfortunate that she sold her flesh to get her son one dainty dish.

    He is so poor that the bread in his house never looks fresh and the dining table never looks used, but his house is full of welcome and guests with empty stomachs get them filled with warm welcome.

Avvaiyar, a renowned Tamil poetess, who lived during the reign of Athiyaman, a powerful king and one of the great 7 patrons of arts and literature in Tamilakam, was once invited by a friend to dinner. Noticing the sign of hatred on the face of his friend's wife while her serving food, Avvaiyar sang the following song in Tamil

"Kaana kan (eye) koosuthey. Kai edukka naanuthey
Maanokka vaai thirakka mattathey-veenukkena
Enbellam patri erihinra thaiyaiyo
Anbilaal itta amuthu". (Courtesy: Daily Malar- June 17, 2016)
My eyes refuse to see the food.
Hand refuses to take the food.
Mouth does not open to taste the food, for
It is served without love.


- ***Balthasar: Small cheer and great welcome makes a merry feast.***


Feast is delicious, but it is without even small cheer and welcome.

Feast without great welcome is not feast at all, however delicious it is.

You make merry feast but with no smile in face, with no sweet in words.

Mirth does not lie in a merry feast.

The way my uncle welcomes his guests is more than a merry feast.

Kind words mean more than a merry feast.


- ***Dromio of Ephesus: ........................There was blow for blow.***


(Believers of violence take pride in saying 'Eye for eye'. Mahatma Gandhi used non-violence as the most powerful weapon and said aptly as follows

'Eye for eye' will make the whole world blind. )

Even a piece of peace is not possible, as long as there are words for words and blows for blows.

'Blow for blow' is not the solution to any problem.

'Blow for blow' is the only way in which some can be answered.

'Blow for blow' may be your policy, but you get blows from somebody, but give blows to somebody else.

- ***Dromio of Ephesus: A man may break a word with you, sir, and words are but wind.***

I will break words with you. As words are just like wind, I will break wind.

The lover, with his honey-tongue, poured words so sweet and so appealing, but after marriage, all his words became but wind.

Most of the promises made by politicians at the time of elections are but wind.

You have broken words with a number of people that you have created a record in breaking words with people.

(Teacher: I asked you to write an essay in about 350 words, but........

Student: Sir, words are but wind.

Teacher:???)

- ***Dromio of Syracuse: ...........when fowls have no feathers and fish have no fin.***

(When birds have no feathers and fish have no fin, ...................................)

She is so rude and arrogant that she cannot mend her attitude even if fowls lose feathers and fish lose fin.

They are my so close friends that I, without them, will feel like fowls without feathers and fish without fin.

I will not give up my efforts, even if fowls lose their feathers and fish their fin.

(People: Sir, you gave us promises in hundreds and fifties before the election!

Politician: You will get everything when fowls are born without feathers and fish without fin.

People: We will also cast our votes for you when fowls are born without feathers and fish without fin.

Politician: !!!!!!!!! )


• *Luciana: Be not thy tongue thy own shame's orator;*

*Look sweet, be fair, become disloyalty;*
*Apparel vice like virtue's harbinger.*
*Bear a fair presence, though your heart be tainted.*
*Teach sin the carriage of a holy saint. ......................*
*What simple thief brags of his own attaint?*

(Be not thy tongue thy own shames's orator- Mind your words

....Apparel vice like virtue's harbinger....................your heart be tainted.

(harbinger- a person or thing that foreshadows)

Disguise your misbehaviour as integrity, and behave properly even if your heart is tainted.

Teach sin the carriage of a holy saint- Though you are sinful, carry yourself like a holy saint.

What simplethief brags of his own attain?- What foolish thief brags abouthis crimes?

It is histongue that brings him shame.

All know that he is a criminal, but he looks sweet, fair and appears to be virtue's harbinger whenever he talks to the girls, who are in madly love with him.

No thiefbrags of his ownattain and no saint brags of his own sins.

(Former Chief Justice, Govt of India says, "Every saint had his past and every criminal his future". )


• *Dromio of Syracuse: .........................Noah's flood could not do it.*


Noah's flood would not be enough water to clean it.

When she was shedding tears out of depression, I wondered whether her eyes were filled with Noah's flood.

Expecting Noah's flood during heavy rain, the Govt took all precautionary steps to rescue the people near seashore areas.

The state is so scarce that even Noah's flood could not do it.

The street is so dirty that Noah's flood could not do it.


• *Angelo: Both wind and tide stays for this gentleman.*


("Time and tide wait for none" is a proverb.)

He is such a great orator that even wind and tide will stay for long to listen to his speech.

He is so gentle that even wind and tide will stay for him.

When you are so lazy that even your wife and children will not wait for you, how could you expect wind and tide wait for you.

Wind and tide stay for none.

The have nots laments that even the wind and the tide stay only for the haves.

It becomes a great pain when wind and tide stay for luck, not for diligence.

Politicians can influence even wind and tide and make them wait for them.

- ***Dromio of Syracuse: Not that Adam that kept the Paradise, but that Adam thatkeeps the prison;***

He wishes to marry any Eve that converts his home into a paradise

After marriage, he, for quite a short period, was the Adam that kept the Paradise, but after that, he became the Adam that kept the prison.

She was in deep love with his Eve in the hope that he would be the Adam that keeps the Paradise, but she never expected that he would become the Adam that keeps the prison.

His wife is so powerful that she will convert her Adam into Lucifer.

Adam lost Paradise because of his Eve and you lost your life because of your Eve.

He has been looking for his Eve for the past 10 years.

He has given his consent to marry his Eve, hoping that she will not force him to eat any forbidden fruit.

- ***Dromio of Syracuse: ..................................................they appear to men***

***like angels of light. Light is an effect of fire, and fire will burn:***

White married her, as she appeared to him like an angel of light, but without knowing that the light with an effect of fire would burn him.

Even if I am burned to death, I shall marry my angel of light, whether the light has the effect of fire or the fragrance of a flower.

Though his wife has the effect of fire, she has never burned him even once in life.

She appears only to Romeos like an angel of light, but to others, she is the devil.

See Diana from a distance. If you go near her on her being like an angel of light, she, with the effect of fire, will burn you.

- ***Antipholus of Ephesus: Thou art sensible in nothing but blows, and so is an ass.***

***Dromio of Ephesus: I am an ass, indeed; you may prove it by my long ears.***

Though he is sensible in nothing, he senses everything.

You prove yourself to be an ass by sensing only the blows and punches.

One cannot inherit the characteristics of an ass just with long ears.

She has long ears, but she is not an ass.

An ass is an ass, whether it has long or short ears.

(When an ass is summoned to a wedding, it is carry some luggage. )

By carrying his daughter's heavy school bag every day, he feels having almost become an ass.

- ***Angelo: I knew he was not in his perfect wits.***

Though he has never been in his perfect wits, he is always by the side of perfect wind.

He is an imperfect person with perfect wits.

Though you are not witty, your projection of being so is perfect.

John might have made this inflammatory statement when he was not in his perfect wits.

Your perfect wits alone will not get you your bread and butter.

Nothing is perfect in him, except his wits.

• ***Abbess: The venom clamors of a jealous woman***

***Poisons more deadly than a mad dog's tooth.***

(A jealous woman's poisonous ranting is worse than the bite of rapid dog.)

Jealousy hurts one severer than a mad dog's tooth.

She smiles with the teeth of a mad dog.

He may be a mad dog, but he has no tooth.

Lucy's every word is more poisonous than a mad dog's tooth.

Why are you so furious? Have you replaced your teeth with those of a mad dog?

# THE TAMING OF THE SHREW

• *Christopher Sly: ................................I'll answer him*

*by law.*

("The law-maker should not be a law breaker" is a proverb in English.

The equivalent proverb for the above in Tamil is "Veiliye payirai meikkalaama?".)

(The quintessence of the Indian Constitution is "All are equal before law". )

(For ignorance of law, there is no excuse.)

"The accused was forced to answer all questions by law, but the investigation was against law", says the lawyer.

Though he always speaks by law, he never abides by law.

Law must not only on paper, but in practice.

Some lawyers are so efficient that they can illegally break a law and legally justify that.

He answered the questions of his wife and children by law as if he were a great lawyer and so he is in an orphanage now.

We may not answer all questions by law, but we must obey law.

Justice cannot be expected from one who bends or breaks law.

(Professor: Why didn't you complete your assignment?
Student: I will answer you in the court, sir.
Professor: Which court?
Student: Foodcourt.
Professor: !!!)


- *Lord: O monstrous beast, how like a swine he lies!*


(It is quite common among human beings to, while burning with uncontrollable anger, call each other by the names of animals. You dog.........You pig.........You bull...........are some ofthe phrases used by human beings to pour out their feelings of anger. Here Shakespeare makes his characters use such phrases. 'Sweating like a pig' is a phrase to mean 'over-sweating'. Man proudly claims himself to be a unique creature blessed with six senses. Though man is considered a social animal, man becomes an animal when he involves himself in serious crimes such as murder and rape, posing threats to the society he lives in. Mr Vairamuthu has written a poem titled Ai(n)thu Perithu Aaru Sirithu, in which he describes certain characteristics of animals (with only five senses) and compares them with those of human beings with six senses. Some of the most catchy lines of the poem are translated into English and highlighted as follows

"Oh Man!
You find not any animal anywhere
Developing extra belly
Have you ever seen anywhere
Any bellied parrot?
Any bellied rabbit?
No animal has diabetes
No bird is found sweating
No bird lets its nest
No animal possesses land of its own

Oh Man! Keep your senses open
Joint family system-
Still in practice among birds and animals
No animal suffers from leprosy-the disease
That buries body into the body
Time of pregnancy- not the time for any bull
To have intercourse
Monogamy!
For you
It is a word
For doves
It is life (principle).
Tsunamis-storms are
Well-predicted by animals by movements
Well-predicted by birds by swift flights
(Without any technical instrument used by man)
Oh Man!
Analyse and Admit now.
Greater in number!
Six? Or Seven?
Death
It is inevitable.
Death
It is Life's Gift
If dead,
Deer's skin turns out to be a seater
Feathers of peacock serve as fans
Tooth of elephant reflects its strength
Bones of camel turn out to be ornaments
Man!!!
If dead,
Ignored even by flames of fire,
Thus came the custom of burial.
Scold not Man in the name of any animal
Hush...... Hush.........

Lend thine ears
Some sound of fury from forest!
An animal scolds some fellow animal
"You bloody Man! )
(Outstanding Tamil poet Kannadasan writes a poem as follows
Oh God!
Thou created Man and Animal
Man is now becoming an animal!
In course of time,
If Animal becomes Man,
I shalt be delighted.......
If Man becomes Animal.....? )
He is wasting his precious time, lying like a swine.
He is a monstrous beast, but never lies like a swine.
'Lying like a pig in mud' means 'being as happy as a pig in mud'.
Hog, Pig, Brute, Beast, Sow, Boar, Porker and Peccary are the words related to swine.

If someone is called a swine, it is to express aversion or dislike.
Water tank is not a mud for you to lie like a swine happily.


- *Lord: .................................a watery eye.*


The following have been identified as causes for watery eyes

a. weather conditions such as dusty weather, wind, cold and sunshine
b. eye strain
c. environmental factors such as bright light and smog
d. cold, sinus problems and allergies
e. inflammation of the eyelid (blepharitis)
f. eyelid turned outward (ectropion) or inward (entropion)
g. ingrown eyelash (trichiasis) (Source: http://www.healthline.com)

His eyes being watery are neither because of any pleasure or pain, but because of intoxication.

The farmerdoesn't mind spending money like water on his daughter's marriage and he never wants to see his daughter's eyes watery.

The student says that his natural watery eyes provide him non-verbal excuses for all his mischievous deeds.

His eyes are so watery that his mind and heart must be burdened with worries.

My watery eyes hide my visibility.

Sunlight makes his eyes watery in day times and alcohol makes his eyes red eyes in the evenings.

He is stony-hearted, but he cheats all with his watery eyes.

People said to their MLA, "You cannot quench our thirst with your watery eyes".

- *Hortensio: ........................He that runs fastest gets the ring.*

"Theearly bird catches its worm" is a proverb in English.

(In Tamil, 'Bundikku munthu; Padaikku pinthu' is a proverb. That means 'Be the first to feast, but be the last to the battle'. )

(Tom: He did not run fast, but he got the ring!

Sam: His father must be either a goldsmith or apolitician.)

Runfast as you have your ring close to hands.

Never give in; never stop running just because the ring seems closer. (Never give up your efforts just because success seems closer. )

John ran fast, but Peter married Lucy.

He runs fastest, but his misfortune runs faster than he.

He ran fastest, but he could not get the ring, as the rule was changed at the drop of a hat.

These labourers have been running for years, but no ring is visible to their eyes.

- *Lucentio: ........I saw her coral lips to move,*

  *And with her breath she did perfume the air.*
  *Sacred and sweet was all I saw her.*

(Coral-yellowish pink colour)

I love her so much that I feel the air breathed by her perfuming my life.

Her lips are so attractive that I move along with her lips.

The poet says that his mind gets intoxicated between her coral lips and glittering teeth.

The beauty of her lips is more intoxicating than the power of all sorts of liquor taken at a time.

She is so sweet that I am afraid that I might get diabetes.

All the perfumes of Arabia fail to perfume me when I breathe the air that she perfumes.

- *Petruchio: My best beloved and approved friend.*

He is my best, but not approved friend.

Approval certificate for true friendship is not obtained from any govt office.

His friendship is true, but it is yet be approved.

She could not tolerate such harsh words from her best beloved and approved friend.

Our General Manager is my beloved and approved friend, but he never approves my leave.

- *Petruchio: .........she as foul as was Florentius' love,*

*As old as Sibyl, and as curst and shrewd*
*Socrates' Xanthippe,.........................*

(Florentius's love means 'foul love'. The knight Florentius, by force, married an old woman, as she saved his life. She was supposed to be as old as Sibyl, also known as Sibylla, a prophetess in Greek legend and literature. Tradition represents her as a woman of prodigious old age uttering predictions in ecstatic frenzy. There have been thus prophetesses in Greek mythology.

In Islam, it is believed that Allah has so far sent down to the earth one lakh and twenty four thousand Prophets (124000), thefirst of whom is Prophet Adam (PBUH) and the last of whom is Prophet Muhammad (PBUH), but no prophetess (female prophet) has been sent down to earth.

Xanthippe known as a great shrew was an ancient Athenian. The Greek philosopher Socrates, being impressed with her argumentative skills, married her. They had three sons Lamprocles, Sophroniscus and Menexenus. Xanthippe was much younger than Socrates. Though Plato said that Xanthippe was a dedicated wife to Socrates and dedicated mother to her three sons, she is traditionally known as a shrew. 'Xanthippe' means now 'any nagging scolding person' or 'a shrewish wife'. Xanthippe was said to be so disagreeable with her husband Socrates that she once poured the contents of a chamber pot over her husband's head. Once when Socrates was going on continuing his philosophical discussions with his friends or comrades, sitting outside his house, Xanthippe shouted at him with harsh words and threw here and there whatever objects she got in hand. Socrates described the noise as "thunder'. Unable to control her anger, Xanthippe poured over Socrates' head the contents of a chamber and Socrates coolly described it as 'rain followed by thunder'. The argumentative skills for which Socrates married Xanthippe turned out to be for him a 'great headache' in his life. Socrates could easily converse and convince any person in Athens, except his wife. Neither her heart nor her ears were with her husband. But it is said that Xanthippe, during the eleventh hour of Socrates, when he was forced to consume the hemlock poison, was crying uncontrollably. Her tears may be the indication of her hidden and never-shown or rarely-shown love for Socrates, but as she was very argumentative with Socrates, literature portrays her as a shrew.

The cordial relationship between husband and wife is of vital importance for a peaceful life. It is said that one, who is not happy in his personal life, may not be happy in his professional life. The good relationship between husband and wife is emphasized by all religions. About the relationship between husband and wife, Holy Quran (30:21) says as follows

"And among His signs is this that He created for you wives from among yourselves, that you may find repose in them, and He has put between you affection and mercy. Verily, in that are, indeed, signs for people who reflect".

Imam Ali, son-in-law, of Prophet Muhammad (PBUH) records as uttered by the latter the following points regarding attainment of peace and prosperity in life.

a.  Piety that keeps one away from prohibitions
b.  Good temperament with which one lives among people
c.  Forbearance which wards off the ignorance of the ignorant
d.  A good wife who assists him in the affairs of this world and the hereafter.

Thiruvalluvar in the chapter Vaalkkai Thunai Nalam" of Thirukkural says as follows
"Petraanperin peruvar pendir perumchirappu
Putheilir vaalum vulahu". (in Tamil)
"When to her groom she stays true
Heaven's glory becomes her due". (in English)
(If you get a good wife, you will be a man.
If you get a bad wife, you will be a philosopher. )
(Lord Rama is noted for his strict adherence and practice of monogamy. Lord Rama was for Sita and Sita was for Lord Rama.

Couples are advised to live like Rama and Sita. )

(Friend I: What happened to you? After marriage, you speak only philosophy!

Friend 2: My Xanthippe has made me speak like that. )

My wife is so argumentative that my life has become worse than that of Socrates.

Though Mithun has married a woman as old as Sibyl, he is happy because she is not as argumentative of Xanthippe.

His wife is not only as old as Sibyl, but also as argumentative as Xanthippe.

I am neither a Florentius to marry a Sibyl and olden my young life, nor a Socrates to marry a Xanthippe and perish my peace with unwanted arguments.

She is a Sibyl in age, but not in appearance.

He has lost his peace of mind because of his Xanthippe.

I am not too patient like Socrates to live with Xanthippe.

(Mother: What sort of girl would you like to marry?

Son: I don't like to marry any girl as old as Sibyl, because I am not a Florentius and I don't like to marry any girl as argumentative as Xanthippe because I am not a Socrates. I like to marry a girl as patient as Grizzel and as chaste as Lucrece.)

- ***Hortensio: Renowned in Padua for her scolding tongue.***

Tongue becomes one's enemy on many occasions.

It is because of your filthy tongue that your words are naked.

She is renowned in our street for her scolding tongue.

She silences the whole street with her scolding tongue.

Words lose steadiness on a scolding tongue.

Her tongue is soft, but her words are thorny.

The neighbour vacated the house because of the scolding tongues of both the husband and the wife.

Her tongue can withstand any heat, for every word of hers is hotter than the fire.

I wish I were deaf whenever her scolding tongue becomes energetic.

Love has become dry on your scolding tongue.


• *Gremio: ........she is sweeter than perfume itself*


She is sweeter than perfume, because perfume is sweet in the presence of its fragrance, but she is sweet even in her total absence.

I consider her sweeter than perfume that even the fragrance of all perfumes is not sweet.

Perfume loses its sweetness in her very presence.

(Girl: Am I sweeter than perfume itself?

Boy: Yes, but I am allergic towards all perfumes.

Girl:???)


• *Gremio: ........such a life with such a wife*


('.........such a life with such a wife' has positive andnegative meanings. The way it isexpressed conveys the meaning.)

Manaithakka maanbudaiyaval aahithar kondaan

Valathakkal vaalkkaithunai- Thirukural (in Tamil)

"In the careful use of her husband's means

She is her home's queen of queens" .-Kural (in English)

He is leading such a life without a such wife. (both positive and negative meanings)

It is his wife who has made him lead "such a life'.

Roger needs neither 'such a wife' nor 'such a life'.

"Better to be wifeless and lifeless than to live with 'such a wife' and to lead 'such a life'", says the patient to the psychiatrist.

"Such a wife' only can give one 'such a life'.

- *Petruchio: Think you a little din can daunt mine ears?*

  *Have I not in my time heard lions roar?*
  *Have I not heard the sea, puffed up with winds,*
  *Rage like an angry boar chafed with sweat?*
  *Have I not heard great ordnance in the field*
  *And heaven's artillery thunder in the skies?*

  ...................................................................
  *And do you tell me of a woman's tongue.*

(daunt-to discourage, to overwhelm

puff up- to swell

chafe- to excite, to feel irritated

ordnance- military equipment

artillery- large cannon-like weapons)

When the sounds of roaring lions, puffing up of winds, raging boar chafed with sweat and of military weapons in operation cannot daunt my ears, how can you daunt my ears?

I am not afraid of lions, but of their roaring sounds; I am not afraid of the sea, but of its windy sounds; I am not afraid of a boar, but of its very appearance in anger; and I am not afraid of the weapons, but of their sounds.

He roars like a lion in the street, but mews like a cat at home.

My heart is puffed up with unbearable and untold miseries as the sea is puffed up with winds.

Whenever he goes home late, his wife stands before him like an angry boar chafed with sweat.

None can sleep beside him, because he snores like a thunder in the sky.

- *Bianca: ................wrong me not, nor wrong yourself,*

("To belittle is to be little" is a proverb in English.)

Do not wrong any, as you may be wronged by some.

He wrongly wronged all and finally he by habitual practice wrongly wronged himself.

Some politicians wrongly wait for right occasions and wrongly wrong their political rivals just for some political gains.

What is wrong with him is that he wrongs everyone.

The right never wrong any.

- *Baptista: A thousand thanks.................................*

*.............................................May I*
*be so bold to know the cause of your coming?*

(Millions thanks)

The people asked their MLA whether they might be so bold to ask him how he had become an MLA.

I express a thousand thanks to my boss for his having helped me more than thousand times.

May I be so bold to know your response to my love proposal?

His tongue pours out a thousand thanks, but his face looks ungrateful.

A word of gratitude means more than any other way of repayment.

My mind and heart are filled with a thousand thanks.

- *Petruchio: ..............................two raging fires meet together,*

*.......................................................*

*Though little fire grows great with little wind,*
*Yet extreme gusts will blow out fire and all*

(gusts-a strong, abrupt of rush of wind)

When the two politicians were exchanging harsh words, I felt two raging fires meeting together.

Don't allow Tom to poke his nose into the issue because his every word is little fire that might grow great with little wind.

I caught fire by her eyes that no wind can blow it out.

Fire is not needed to burn into ashes one's body, but her eyes do.

Don't consider little fire just little, it leaves little, if little wind blows.

She has the guts to face extreme gusts in life.

None can work peacefully between two raging fires.

(Man 1: Two raging fires meet together.

Man 2: I do not understand what you say.

Man 1: My wife and my mother meet together. )

(Some are so interested in adding fuel to the fire that if they happen to be the third persons in any casual conversation even between two real saints, they will convert them into two raging fires meeting together.)

- *Petruchio: ..............................mounts are for winds,*

   *That shakes not, though they blow perpetually.*

No wind could shake him, but her love has totally shaken him and his life altogether.

He is like a mountain that cannot be shaken by winds.

Strong winds blow perpetually, but I never feel perplexed.

Mounts can be shaken, but not the minds of ideologists.

After marriage, Ajip has become too fat to be shaken even by tsunami.

- *Petruchio: She sings as sweetly as a nightingale.*

   *..............................she looks as clear*
   *As morning roses newly washed with dew.*

I love her because she sings as sweetly as a nightingale and looks as clear as morning roses newly washed with dew.

I love her so much that her every word, though her voice is not so sweet, echoes rhythmic in my ears and I love her so much that she, though not fair, looks more beautiful than morning roses washed with dew.

Morning roses are washed with dew, but she washes her face with roses.

Her voice is so sweet that I can't just compare hers with that of the nightingale.

She sings so sweetly that even the nightingale could lend her its ears.

She just becomes a nightingale while singing songs.

The poor girl says that even the roses in her little garden are never washed with dew. (Even Nature doesn't pity her poverty. )

- *Petruchio: ............thou art pleasant, gamesome.............*

*........slow in speech, yet sweet as springtime flowers*

(gamesome-playful, energetic, lively, enthusiastic, sexually aroused)

When my baby speaks, I am reminded of springtime flowers.

You are swift in thoughts, but slow in speech.

He has not seen spring even once in his whole life, but he describes springtime flowers in the summer of his life.

When shall my summer become spring?

His birth was as pleasant as spring, but his greediness has made his life as hot as summer.

He is slow in speech? Or does he slow down his speech due to fear?

Nights make him gamesome and lights make him saintly.

- *Petruchio: Thou must be married to no man but me.*

Thou must be married to any man, not me.

You must be married to no man, but me.

(After marriage, Mulla Nazruddin's wife asked her husband before whom she could and before whom she could not come. Mulla Nazruddin said, "You can come before anyone except me". )

- **Petruchio: For patience she will prove a second Grissel,**

**And Roman Lucrece for her chastity.**

My mother is so patient that Grisselcould learn patience from her.

He is so irritating that he will make even Grissel lose her patience.

He is mad after flesh, but he expects his wife to be a Lucrece.

He is so a doubting Thomas that even Lucrece would develop aversion towards chastity.

There is nothing wrong that a bachelor expects Grissels and Lucreces, but he too must have such virtues.

Rohit says that his life has become miserable, as his wife is neither a Grissel nor a Lucrece.

(In Roman mythology, Lucrece is noted for her chastity. Here the authors are reminded of a scene in one of the Tamil movies 'Munthaanai Mudhichi" directed and acted by K.Baagyaraj. When people of a village gather during a Panjayat meeting to penalize a lady on allegation of some illegal sex affair, K.Baagyaraj analyzing and identifying the innocent and unintentional act of the girl, will ask the Panjayat leaders the following question

Who comes to your mind when you think of chastity?

The Panjayat leaders would think for a while and pronounce the names of Kannahi and some more characters from Tamil literature.

K.Baagyaraj after patiently getting different names will again ask them, "Didn't your mother and wife come to your mind on the very thought of chastity? This question would just make the leaders blink with great embarrassment and their vigilant wives would chase them angrily, as their chastity disappeared from the minds of their 'so called' life partners. )

- *Tranio: ..........................I am one that love Bianca more*

*Than words can witness or your thoughts can guess.*

I love you more than words can witness or your thoughts can guess.

My love for my nation can be bound neither by words or nor by thoughts.

He loves her so much that words are beyond any dictionary and thoughts are beyond any guess.

I love her so much that word power becomes powerless before the power of my love for her.

His love for her is only in words, not in thoughts.

- *Gremio: .........................my house within the city*

*Is richly furnished with plate and gold.*

His house is richly furnished with plate and gold, but his heart is rusted withdirt.

Your house is poorly covered with roof, but your heart is richly furnished with gold.

He loves her because her father's house within the city is richly furnished with plate and gold. (He says that he could not have a rich father, but could at least get a rich father-in-law. )

I do not have a house, but my mind is a home richly furnished with love and affection.

I do not need a house richly furnished with plate and gold, but a home filled with love and affection.

What is the use of owning a house richly furnished with plate and gold, when the mind is filled with dark clouds?

- *Tranio: That's but a cavil.*

(cavil- a petty or trivial objection or criticism)

I care not about any cavil.

That's but a cavil, but it hurts me a lot.

The govt considers all objections of the opposite party a cavil and continues its run.

That might be a cavil, but it hurts me.

- *Bianca: Old fashions please me best. I am not so nice*

*To change true rules for odd inventions.*

The modern girl refuses to marry Peter as old fashions please him best.

Old may be gold, but old styles and fashions never please me.

I can't change true rules for odd inventions.

The company is changing rules at the drop of a hat.

Rules are framed not to be followed, but to be recorded for the sake of record.

Our Manager is fond of framing and breaking rules.

Only true rules are being changed these days.

- *Petruchio: ..........................to kill a wife with kindness.*

He kindly killed his wife, but the police brutally arrested him.

His tongue intends to please his wife, but his mind intends to kill.

He is so hospitable that he will kill his guests with his kindness.

The professor kills his students with his lectures.

Both the husband and the wife kill each other with kindness.

- *Biondello: Master, a marcantant, or a pedant,*

*I know not what, but formal in apparel.*

*In gait and countenance surely like a father.*

(pedant- a teacher, a person who emphasizes the use of vocabulary, a person who is overly concerned with formal rules and trivial points of learning.

Apparel –way of dressing

Gait- manner of walking

Countenance- facial expression, superficial appearance)

(It is generally said, perhaps after carefully observed by someone just out of some curiosity, that the sister of the bridegroom, during marriage ceremonies) can be easily identified from the ways in which she behaves. Keeping costly mobile phones near ears (with or without calls) displaying fingers ornamented either with well-designed gold rings glittering (to attract the eyes of relatives, friends and visitors), walking, wearing footwear of maximum height, here and there, with her nose in the air, unnecessarily giving the workers and cooks instructions already given umpteenth times, looking down upon the innocent parents (scapegoats of the day) of the bride every now and then as if they were the most cursed slaves on earth, behaving despotically, but expecting them to behave saintly, waiting eagerly for every opportunity to pick holes in their pockets and behaving like the Queen of Egypt in the presence of the dear and near ones of the bride are all some of the symptoms for one to identify the bridegroom's sister.)

I know not who she is, but formal in apparel, irrelevant in attitude,

in gait and countenance surely like bridegroom's sister.

He is formal in apparel, but informal in language.

In gait, he reminds me of a duck and in countenance, of a clown.

- *Merchant: I know him not, but I have heard of him;*

*A merchant of incomparable wealth.*

He is a merchant of incomparable wealth, but with deteriorating health.

I neither know him nor have I heard of him.

His incomparable wealth has become comparable after his paying school fees for his LKG child.

You are a professor of incomparable knowledge.

Mr Shashi Tharoor is a powerful orator with incomparable knowledge of vocabulary.

The girl I am in love with is an angel of incomparable beauty.

It is better that I know you not, as I have heard of you enough.

Having heard of you a lot, he wishes to meet you.

- *Katherine: My tongue will tell the anger of my heart,*

  *Or else my heart, concealing it, will break,*

My tongue looks red because of the anger it has.

My heart conceals my anger, but my tongue reveals it.

His tongue tells (pours out) the anger of his heart.

My heart will break, unless my tongue tells the anger of my heart.

Her face will get pimples out of heat not by the hot sun, but by the suppressed anger.

- *Petruchio: Our purses shall be proud, our garments poor,*

  *For 'tis the mind that makes the body rich,*
  *And as the sun breaks through the darkest clouds,*

When I proposed my love to her, she got hotter than the sun and broke my heart.

Though our garments are poor, our ATM cards are proud.

She is poor, but conceals her poverty by wearing rich garments.

Do not judge him by the garment he wears, but the weight of his pocket with debit and credit cards.

This news breaks through his heart as the sun breaks through the darkest clouds.

Will the sun break through my mind that is filled with darkest clouds?.

She is not proud of her husband, but of his purses.

(Sir M.Vishveshvariah once went to meet Gandhiji. He sat down on the chair offered to him. Gandhiji chuckled. Sir M.Vishveshvariah asked him why. Gandhiji replied that he (Sir M.V) was wearing a suit carrying a gold handled cane and a gold watch in his pocket. He added that he was like the poor in the country with just one cloth to wear and without a chair to sit on.

Sir M.Vishveshvariah said to Mahatma Gandhi, "I am the son of a poor temple priest who could hardly make two ends meet. I saw an Englishman ride in a carriage drawn by horses with a gold handled stick with all the people looking at him in awe. I decide that I should be better than him. Therefore, I toiled hard, studied hard and earned hard to reach this position. If all our countrymen think like you in future, we will sit on the floor and others will rule us".

Though Mahatma Gandhiji continued to be simple and humble, he would have certainly agreed with Sir M.V on the point that we must not be ruled by others. )

- *Katherine: ..............................mistaking eyes*

*...........everything I look on seemeth green.*

His mistaking eyes concern his wife a lot.

There is no problem with his eye-sight, but with his eyes.

A jaundiced person finds everything yellow.

A physician cures jaundice, but the jaundiced (the prejudiced by nature)with mistaking eyes can be cured by a psychiatrist.

He lost his wife and life because of his mistaking eyes.

(Boy: Everything I look on seemeth beautiful, as and when you are with me, my sweet darling.

Lady: First consult some ophthalmologist. I am your girl friend's grandmother.

Boy: !!!!)

There are some who see the right people with mistaking eyes and don't see the wrong people with their eyes at all.

- *Gremio: ..................................................................be cony-*

  *catched in this business.*

('cony-catch' means 'cheat')

He was cony-catched in this business. –He was cheated in this business. )

She is unfit to do any business because she can be easily cony-catched by any Tom, Dick and Harry.

She cannot be cony-catched by any on earth, except by her near and dear ones.

- *Katherine: It blots thy beauty as frosts do bite the meads,*

  *Confounds thy fame as whirlwinds shake fair buds,*
  *...................................................................*
  *Thy husband is thy lord, thy life, thy keeper,*
  *Thy head, thy sovereign, one that cares for thee,*
  *And for thy maintenance commits his body*
  *To painful labor both by sea and land,*
  *-------------------------------------------------------*
  *And craves no other tribute at thy hands*
  *But love, fair looks, and true obedience-*

(to blot – to cause a stain, to damage, to obscure, to mar)

(meads- meadows)

You are just an angel on earth, but all your vices and evil thoughts blot your beauty as frosts do bite the meads.

When he lost his mother, he felt himself being a bud violently shaken by atrocious whirlwind.

Such acts will confound your name and fame as whirlwinds shake fair buds.

We are not fair buds to be shaken by whirlwinds.

It is corruption that confounded his fame as fair buds are shaken by whirlwinds.

She hates her husband because he wishes to be her lord, life, keeper, head and sovereign with no love, care and concern for her.

Fisher man's life is laborious both by sea and land.

I crave no other tribute at your hands, but love, fair looks and true obedience.

# CHAPTER THREE

# TWO GENTLEMEN OF VERONA

- *Proteus: I leave myself, my friends and all, for love.*

  *Thou, Julia, thou hast metamorphosed me,*
  *Made me neglect my studies, lost my time,*
  *War with good counsel, set the world at naught:*
  *Made wit with musing weak, heart sick with thought.*

(to metamorphose- to undergo some transformation
  Naught-nothingness
  Musing- absorbed in thought, contemplative)
The difference between a true saint and a true lover is that the former leaves everything for peace and the latter for love.

Failure in love converts one either into a saint or into a philosopher.

A saint lacks worldly pleasures when all pleasures seem to him meaningless, and a lover lacks his senses when his love becomes too blind.

The girl I am in love with has metamorphosed me and made me neglect my studies.

Before marriage, Cruso lost his time in love with her and after marriage lost everything in his life with her.

She had made his wit with musing weak and his heart sick with thought.

The cardiologist says, "The patient's heart is functioning well, but the problem is that his heart is sick with evil thoughts".

Many teenagers in love encounter wars with good counsel.

His blind love for her has set his life at naught.

(A poet converts whatever he/she captures in eyes /in mind into a poem. Karl Vilhelm of Germany loved his wife so much that he wrote a poem in about 100 words for his wife every day. Terribly upset over the death of his wife, Karl Vilhelm started writing poems for his wife every day. He used to read loud his poems, sitting beside the graveyard of his wife every day. He did this not for a few days or for a few months, but for 44 years, till he breathed his last. True love lives even after lovers' death.)


- *Proteus: Indeed, a sheep doth very often stray,*

   *An if the shepherd be a while away.*

He wishes to be a good shepherd, but his sheep (son) doth very oftenstray.

The sheep with no a shepherd may go to the hands of the butchers.

He is not a straying sheep, but a sacrificial goat.

I am a sheep, but invisible to the eyes of the butchers.

The sheep can stray freely, as long as they fall a prey to the eyes of butchers.

How can you expect the sheep to be safe in the hands of butchers?

He may be a straying sheep, but not a barking dog.

I am expecting my shepherd to be a while away so that I could stray.

Many of the youngsters have become straying sheep without shepherds.

- *Speed: The shepherd seeks the sheep, and not the sheep*

  *the shepherd; but I seek my master, and my master seeks*
  *not me: therefore I am no sheep.*

The aged forsaken parents seek their rich and well-settled sheep.

I am not a sheep to be sought by a shepherd.

I am neither a shepherd to seek the sheep nor a sheep to be sought by a shepherd.

The nation has innumerable suffering, starving, struggling sheep without a good shepherd.

- *Proteus: Go, go, be gone, to save your ship from wreck,*

In his attempts to save someone's ship from wreck, he lost his own ship.

In many poor families, father goes, goes, is gone, to save his ship from wreck.

You cannot save your ship from wreck unless you have courage and confidence.

Just to save his skin, he is saving his ship from wreck.

To get his family bread and butter, every fisherman is drowning his life into oceans.

- *Lucetta: Fire that's closest kept burns most of all.*

He is talking to her without knowing that he has fire in his own pocket.

She is the fire that is closest to you, waiting to burn you.

High posts convert even soft petals into fires, don't they?

The fire that is closest to your neighbour is closer to you.

The fire that has injured your chest takes not much time to injure your face.

Flatterers near us are like fire close to us.

Judo says to his girl friend, "Oh! my sweet heart! I don't mind fire that's closest burning me, but not your eyes piercing through my heart".

- ***Antonio: Experience is by industry achieved***

   ***And perfected by the swift course of time.***

Experience is achieved by labour, but perefected by the swift course of time.

I achieved experience by industry, but time has never given me an opportunity to perfect it.

Though his experience was achieved by industry, it has not been perefected by the swift course of time.

He is highly experienced, but not perefected by the swift course of time.

- ***Proteus: O, how this spring of love resembleth***

   ***The uncertain glory of an April day,***
   ***Which now shows all the beauty of the sun,***
   ***And by and by a cloud takes all away!***

(One's glory is as uncertain as the days of April. Even though the weather these days is quite unpredictable, the days of April are generally will be sunny and all of a sudden we can find the sunshine being taken away by clouds. It is known as 'confusing month'. The month is full of surprises and contradictions. April 1 is celebrated as 'All Fools' Day'. People used to make fun of their friends, dear and near ones on April 1 with jokes, hoaxes and pranks. However, April is the month when tress and flowers begin to bloom.

April, the fourth month of every year, it is believed, is named after Aphrodite (Aphros) the Greek goddess. )

My love may be as uncertain as an April day, but I will love you till some cloud takes me away.

She showed me all the beauty of the sun till she loved me, but by and by a cloud in the name of marriage (with someone) took all away.

Love is as uncertain as the glory of an April day.

Your words and deeds are as confusing and as contradictory as the month of April.

Some girl may show all the beauty of the sun, but when you go near, you will get affected by its rays.

His mind is too cloudy for anyone to read.

He is so foolish that April 1 can be made his birthday.

- *Valentine: ..................her beauty is exquisite, but her favour*

  *infinite.*

(exquisite- Fine, pleasing, exceptional

Infinite-Boundless, endless)

He loves her for her beauty being exquisite and her father's favour being infinite.

(Just for fun, it is said that one's father may be poor, but certainly not one's father-in-law.)

Her exquisite beauty and infinite favour have bedded him for ever.

I am pleased with your exquisite beauty and infinite favour.

Your exquisite beauty maddens me and your infinite favour mesmerizes me.

He loves her neither because of her exquisite beauty nor because of her infinite favour, but because of her good heart.

- *Valentine: I have loved her ever since I saw her; and still I see*

  *her beautiful.*

*Speed: If you love her, you cannot see her.*
*Valentine: Why?*
*Speed: Because Love is blind.*

He has loved her ever since he saw her.

You have seen her face and you love her. Had you known her mind and heart, you would have become a misogynist.

Love at the first sight makes many blind.

His love has become so blind that his own parents look invisible to him.

Not her love, but her beauty has blinded you and your senses.

Love is blind and so are the lovers.

No optometrist or no ophthalmologist can cure his eye defects, as love has blinded his eyes beyond any medical treatment.


• *Valentine: To clothe mine age with angel-like perfection,*


........................................................

*His years but young, but his experience old;*
*His head unmellow'd, but his judgment ripe;*
*And, in a word, for far behind his worth*
*Comes all the praises that I now bestow,*
*He is complete in feature and in mind*
*With all good grace to grace a gentleman.*

Diana clothes herself during all ceremonies with angel-like perfection.

He has an old head on young shoulders. (He is young, but experienced)

Our leader is complete in feature and in mind with all good grace to grace a gentleman.

Many of us clothe their age with hair-dye.

He is complete in body, but not in mind.

He is a gentleman with all good grace to grace.

He is a gentleman, but without any grace.

- *Valentine: ..................Love hath twenty pair of eyes.*

(Boy: Love hath twenty pair of eyes

   Girl: First check your two eyes.

   Boy: Oh sorry, you are my girlfriend's sister!)

(The eye sight of a boy was quite doubtful to the girl he was in love with. The girl told him that all her friends said that he had had some problem with his eyes. Terribly upset over this, the boy planned a trick to prove to his girl friend that his eye sight was perfect. He hit a nail on a tree that evening and met his girl friend at night. Showing the tree from a distance, he asked her what she could see. The girl replied that she could see the tree. He asked her what else she could see and she replied that she could also see the branches of the tree and some birds sitting on the branches. The boy asked her whether she could see the nail hit on the tree. The girl wondered and asked her whether a nail was visible to his eyes from such a distance. Getting overjoyed, the boy went towards the tree to bring the nail from the tree, but the fate against his love played with him so violently that he fell down over a slip on a bull of half elephant-size on his move towards the tree. The girl roared with laughter and commented that a nail was visible to his eyes, but not a bull. )

   Love hath twenty pair of eyes, but hath not even a single brain.

   (Boy: Love hath twenty pair of eyes.

   Girl: But you are not able to see my heart with all your twenty pair of eyes. )

- *Valentine: Love hath chased sleep from my enthralled eyes*

*And made them watchers of mine own heart's sorrow.*

*..................................................................*

*Now can I break my fast, dine, sup and sleep,*

*Upon the very naked name of love.*

(Enthral- to hold spellbound)

Is there any lover without a smart phone? Smart phones also chase lovers' sleep.

Love has chased sleep from his enthralled eyes and I doubt whether he has nights or not.

He is unable to break his fast and his love.

Broken love can be renewed, but broken heart?

Love, while budding, makes one's heart a dwelling place of joys, but while blossoming, becomes a dwelling place of sorrows.

It is his blind love that has made his whole life naked.

Love has intoxicated him so much that his breakfast has become his dinner and dinner his breakfast, days have become nights and night days. The earth revolves round the sun and he round her.

Love looks well-dressed in the beginning, but becomes utterly naked in the end.

(Patient: My love has made me unable to have my breakfast, lunch, supper and sleep.

Doctor: You are too fat to be cured by medicine. Cure yourself by love. )

- *Valentine: O, flatter me; for love delights in praises.*

(Boy: you are synonymous with beauty.

You are an angel on earth.

You are a mobile statue.

Girl: O, flatter me; for love delights in praises.)

Love makes one an excellent flatterer.

One who does not know how to flatter is unfit to love.

Flattery in words is flattery in love.

Love that delights in debit and credit cards is not love at all.

(Speaking lies becomes inevitable, while flattering. Can speaking a lie just to keep one's heart warm be considered a 'white lie'?. In Mahabharata, Lord Krishna favours the following situations for speaking lies, while his talking to Arjuna.

1.  When marriage arrangements are on (Good intention is to unite two hearts.)
2.  When someone's soul is in peril (Nothing is more important than saving a soul. )
3.  When one speaks something just for fun (Humour gives one some mental relief. )
4.  When one talks to his wife on being alone. (Any house becomes a home filled with love and affection. )

Lord Krishna's utterance in favour of lies when someone's soul is in peril reminds the author of a short story. There was a small country, where the citizens spoke innumerable languages. Once when there was a rebellion against the King of the country, soldiers brought before the King a rebel. The King asked his soldiers to cut off his (the rebel's) head. He angrily shouted 'Labothi bo' 'Labothi bo', the meaning of which was not known to any there. The King asked a minister what the meaning of 'Labothi bo' was. The minister said, "'Labithi bo' means 'why should I be killed for a small crime of mine?. Have mercy on me'". The King showed mercy on him. When the rebel was about to leave that place happily, another minister told the king that 'Labothi bo' was a filthy word used against him (the King). The King said, "I appreciate the minister who gave me a wrong meaning, because of which a rebel's life was saved. )

(Flatterers are supposed to be the worst enemies. Appreciation is good, but certainly not flattery. Flattering someone for cheap reasons/gains is equal to killing him/her. But appreciation means a lot. Friends can be appreciated in their absence, teachers and parents in their presence and absence, wife under circumstances, people in minds and servants immediately after their completing the works assigned. But flattery is more beneficial than appreciation, when it comes to love, for love delights in flattery. )

- *Proteus: Even as one heat another heat expels,*

   *Or as one nail by strength drives out another,*
   *So the remembrance of my former love*
   *Is by a newer object quite forgotten.*

(Shall we observe here that though 'heat' is a mass noun, Shakespeare has used it as a count noun?.)

Love can be renewed by forgetting old love.

You have expelled me from your mind and heart as one heat expels another and as one nail is by strength driven out by another.

Julie keeps her former lover in memories and fresh lover in heart.

Mind is for remembering former love, mouth is for flattering present love and heart is reserved for future love.

- *Proteus: Love, lend me wings to make my purpose swift,*

(Proteus is a young nobleman from Verona. He was in love with Julia till he saw Silvia. He tried to rape Silvia, but when he identified the person in disguise as Julia, he again fell in love with her, forgetting Silvia.)

Love, lend me wings to fly far away from the girl whom I am in love with.

Love, lend me wings so that I can fly with imagination.

Love lent him wings to make his purpose swift, but Anger lent his father energy to cut off his (son's) wings.

I am not a Proteus and there is no need for you to be in disguise of any girl.

Having got his wings clipped, Roger is praying for wings to make his purpose swift.

- *Julia: A thousand oaths, an ocean of his tears*

*And instances of infinite of love*
*Warrant me welcome to my Proteus.*
*Lucetta: All these are servants to deceitful men.*

Oaths and tears are the servants to deceitful men. (not to deceitful women?)

Innocent girls fall a prey to oaths, tears and instances of infinite love.

Without knowing that he is a Proteus, the girl is in love with him.

Thousand oaths and oceans of tears sentimentally and emotionally perish innocent girls.

He can melt any girl's heart with his thousand oaths and ever-flowing crocodile tears.

His oaths were borrowed from politicians, tears from crocodiles, but his love for her is his own.

- *Julia: His words are bonds, his oaths are oracles,*

*His love sincere, his thoughts immaculate,*
*His tears messengers sent from his heart,*
*His heart as far from fraud as heaven from earth.*

(immaculate- undefiled, clear, pure)

(Girl 1: Why do you love Peter?

Girl 2: His words are bonds, his oaths are oracles, his love is sincere, his thoughts are immaculate, his tears are messengers from his heart and his heart is as far from fraud as heaven from earth. )

Your words may be bonds, your oaths may be oracles, your love may be sincere, your thoughts may be immaculate, your tears may be messengers sent from your heart and your heart may be as far from fraud as heaven from earth, but I don't love you.

I ornamented my words as oracles, built my love with bricks of sincerity, squeezed my eyes to bring tears and walked from heaven to earth, but she simply rejected my love proposal.

The girl says that she cannot send her tears as messages through Whatsapp.

The boy is found ornamented in words, but naked in thoughts.

- ***Valentine: More than quick words do move a woman's mind.***

A woman's mind moves quicker than quick words.

Prem felt quickly hurt, when Roja quickly changed her love.

Her loves moves as quick as her words.

I can run faster than a horse, but cannot take a single step with a woman's mind?

Joe was removed from the post as his mind was moving with every girl's mind.

He removed her from her mind, as he could not move with her mind.

- ***Valentine: Flatter and praise, commend, extol their graces;***

*Though ne'er so black, say they have angels' faces.*
*That man that hath a tongue, I say, is no man,*
*If with his tongue he cannot win a woman.*

The power of a man's tongue is nothing before that of a woman's.

You are not able to win a woman with your tongue.

The girl impressed him with an angel's face, loved him with godly virtues, married him withpassionate promises, but now is killing him with a deadly and devilish tongue pouring words as venom.

He lost his tongue in his attempts to win her heart.

She can control anything, but not her tongue.

The man says, "A lady without a heart is better than a lady with a tongue".

- ***Duke: ..................................Love is like a child,***

*That longs for every thing.....................................*

(Boy: My love is like a child that longs for a child.

Girl: My love is like a prisoner that longs for freedom from you.
)

The girl says that her lover longs for everything, except for his love.

Her love for me longed for everything and so I have become nothing now.

Love begins blindly with everything, travels romantically through something and ends economically with nothing.

Love like a child longs for everything.

Her love longed for everything, and now there is a long gap between the lovers.

- *Valentine: What light is light, if Silvia be not seen?*

 *What joy is joy, if Silvia be not by?*
 ............................................................
 *Unless I look on Silvia in the day,*
 *There is no day for me to look upon;*

(What light is light, if your face be not seen

What joy is joy, if you be not by

What sky is sky, if you pass not as clouds in my mind and heart

Unless I look on you in the day

There is no day to look upon.)

My love for her has converted my sun into moon, my days into nights.

What pain is pain now, as I had all my pains in my younger days.

Unless I see my mother and father every day, the day is not the day for me.

- **Proteus: Time is the nurse and breeder of all good.**

Time is the best healer that heals all wounds.

When old parents are forsaken by their own children, time becomes their nurse.

He is too depressed and disappointed to be nursed even by time.

The boss squeezes the poor labourers round the clock and does not allow time to be their nurses.

Time is the nurse and breeder of all good.

The poor girl is too unlucky to be nursed even by time.

Even the clock shows time only to the rich.

The farmer says, "My clock never shows me the right time".

- *Launce: I am but a fool, ..............and yet I have the wit*

   *to think my master is a kind of a knave:..............*
   *...................................................................*
   *............................. a horse can do no more:*
   *Nay, a horse cannot fetch, but only carry;..............*

Sam was terminated from service as he had the wit to think his master was a kind of a knave.

Life has made me a horse used both to fetch and carry.

I am an unfortunate horse that is forced to fetch and fated to carry.

He is a fool, but he is intelligent enough to find out the true colour of his girl friend.

He is a knave, but has a heart.

Young children carry school bags as horses carry heavy luggage.

("If the ass is summoned to the wedding, it is to carry wood" is an Arabic proverb.)

Though he himself is a fool, he brings to light the foolish deeds of others.

- *Launce: ..............as black as ink.*

He writes about peace though his heart is as black as ink.

His words are as white as a paper, but his thoughts are as black as ink.

Let the darkness of the society disappear with the drops of your ink.

His fair and bright face with many pimple scars looks as black as ink.

Every word the writer uses is as black as ink.

He has in his pen ink enough to write boasting of himself, but not enough to condemn the social evils.

- *Speed: .............She hath more hair than wit, and more*

  *faults than hairs, and more wealth than faults.*

You have more hair than wit and more faults than hairs.

He has only hair, not wit, but his faults are more than his hair and his wealth is more than his faults.

Some politicians venture to commit more faults because of more wealth.

Her hair is as countless as her faults.

His hair has withered, but not his faults.

You can get wigs, but not wit.

- *Proteus: Write till your ink be dry,*

Great writers write till their ink gets dry.

Some students write, during exams, till their ink be dry, but fail miserably.

He won't stop writing even if his ink gets dry.

The student has written only his name and Reg No till his ink be dry.

(Once when a teacher was dictating notes in his class, a student was just looking at him. The teacher asked him why he did not take down the notes. The student replied that his ink was dry. The teacher got angry and gave him his pen, commenting that his (student's) ink was as dry as his brain. Then he continued dictating notes. He lost his temper when he saw, after some time, the student just looking at him without taking down the notes. He furiously said to him, "Are you mad? Still you do not bother to take down notes". The student replied humbly and politely that his (teacher's) pen also was dry. )

- *Proteus: ...............golden touch could soften steel and stones,*

A golden touch heals the mind faster than the body.

He tries to soften steel and stones, not knowing the warmth of a golden touch.

A golden touch means more than words.

What I need from you is not gold, but a golden touch.

His heart is too stony to be softened by a golden touch.

With a golden touch, she softened her husband's mind and made him buy a gold chain for her.

- *Proteus: We'll wait upon your grace.................................*

He is waiting upon her grace without knowing that she is a lady withoutheart.

He was waiting upon her grace for 3 decades and has now understood that she is graceless.

Do not wait upon anyone's grace, except God's.

He is knocking at the door of grace without knowing that it is made of iron.

After waiting upon the grace of the govt in vain for such a long time, the poor farmer committed suicide.

"Better to wait for death than to wait for my children's grace", said the old woman.

"Better to go to my grave than to seek his grace", said Roger.

- *Valentine: If crooked fortune had not thwarted me*

I would have come offwithflying colours, had crooked fortune not thwarted me.

If the king had not seen the queen in his life, he would not have felt crooked fortune thwarting him.

Crooked fortunes are in disguise and so I do not seek fortunes.

She says that she will seek her fortunes even if thwarted by misfortunes.

(Candidate 1: Your own uncle was in the interview panel!

Candidate 2: I would have been selected for the post, if crooked fortunes had not thwarted me. )

- *Speed: ...................................it's an honourable kind*

*of thievery.*

The candidate has copied the whole thesis, but claims that it is an honourable kind of thievery.

She said to her boy friend, "By stealing my heart, you say that it is an honourable kind of thievery".

(Reporter: Sir, why did you accept the bribe?

Politician: Mind your words. It is an honourable kind ofthievery.
)

Even thievery becomes honourable, if thieves have wealth and power.

(In a meeting- Our Hon'ble Minister is noted for his honourable kind of thievery.........)

- *Proteus: ............Silvia is too fair, too true, too holy,*

***To be corrupted with my worthless gifts.***

Our nation needs officers too fair, too true, too holy to be corrupted with worthless gifts.

(Dr A.P.J.Abdul Kalam recollects in his auto-biography 'Wings of Fire' an incident that happened when he was five years old. When his father was elected President of the Rameswaram Panchayat Board, an unknown person carrying a parcel came to his house and the innocent Kalam collected it from him as his father was not at home. His father, on returning home, saw the parcel and felt terribly upset. The parcel contained a gift- an 'angavasthram' (a towel people those days used to put round their necks as a mark of honour or prestige), sweets and fruits. He beat his son Kalam and advised him to never accept gifts. This advice deeply embedded in Kalam. His father also quoted from Manu Smriti that the divine light, by accepting gifts, gets extinguished in a person. )

Worthless gifts corrupt human minds.

Her mind is too holy to get plagued with false promises and worthless gifts.

You cannot corrupt my mind with worthless gifts.

The company has recruited worthless workers by getting from them worthless gifts.

- ***Proteus: ..........................I am but a shadow;***

In some cases, the real culprits escape and the shadows are put behind bars.

Shadows in many cases become scapegoats, don't they?

The officer is but a shadow in these cases.

She is too lonely to have her own shadow.

Benito is such a criminal that he disguises himself in many shadows.

There is no identity card for shadows.

- ***Silvia: As full of sorrow as the sea of sands,..........***

After marriage, her life has become asfull of sorrow as the sea of sands.

My mind is fuller with more sorrows than the sea of sands.

All sands can be taken away from seas, but not sorrows from my mind.

The sea full of water reminds me of the sorrows that my mind is full of.

Sands are visible in the absence of waves, but my sorrows are not so.

- ***Julia: A fox to be the shepherd of thy lambs.***

The rays of his lusty eyes are hotter than the rays of the angry sun. If you leave young and beautiful girls under his care, it is nothing short of leaving lambs under the careof afox.

He looks like a lamb, but he is a fox.

Tom is a lamb at home, but a fox everywhere.

Though he is a fox, this lamb seeks his shelter.

A fox cannot and should not be the shepherd of lambs.

- ***Proteus: ...........pearls are fair; and the old saying is,***

***Black men are pearls in beauteous ladies' eyes.***

(The authors remember having read in some book that God Himself likes black colour so much that the top of every man (black hair at the time of birth) is black in colour. The British people, besides their being proud of their culture, heritage and language, are proud of their bright skin colour, which resulted in the Black being ill-treated on many occasions. Once, an Indian and a British man happened to travel together in the same compartment of a train. In their conversation, the latter told the former that God loved the British people very much. When the Indian asked him to give him the reason for that, the British man said that all are white in England, unlike Indians of different colours, mostly dim. The Indian just smiled and said, "Dear Mr White! Have you seen donkeys? They are all of the same colour unlike horses, which are of different colours".

The English are also proud of their language. Responding to the 'oft-made' utterance that 'The sun never sets on the British Empire', Mr Shashi Tharoor said, "Perhaps, God does not trust the White people even in the dark". )

(Girl 1: Why do you wish to marry a black boy?

Girl 2: Black boys are pearls in beauteous girls' eyes. )

I don't mind being black, for I am a pearl in beauteous ladies' eyes.

(Lady 1: My life after marriage is an utter failure because of Shakespeare?

Lady 2: Shakespeare!!!

Lady 1: I married a black man as Shakespeare said, "Black boys are pearls in beauteous ladies' eyes. But my husband's mind and heart are as black as his skin. )

- *First Outlaw: ...............I must bring you to our captain's cave:*

*Fear not: he bears an honourable mind,*
*And will not use a woman lawlessly.*

You can meet our boss any time, for he bears an honourable mind and will not use anyone lawlessly.

He honours all with his honourable mind.

Better to stay in a den of ferocious beasts than to enter your captain's cave.

Though he is a lawyer, he uses everyone lawlessly.

He seeks legal points for his lawless acts.

Our captain is an honourable man bearing an honourable mind.

- ***Silvia: Had I been seized by a hungry lion,***

  ***I would have been a breakfast to the beast.***

John is so angry with her thathe would make her his breakfast, if he were a hungry lion.

Better to be a breakfast to a hungry beast than to be a feast to the lusty eyes.

Better to be seized by a hungry lion than to bear the hot and horse words of some human beings.

He might be unmindful of a nearing hungry lion, when his eyes are on her.

She feels being seized by a hungry lion, when she was called by her teacher for not completing her homework.

Going near him when he is angry is as harmful as going near a hungry lion.

If the team had not completed the project on time, the project manager would have made them his breakfast, lunch and dinner.

# CHAPTER FOUR

# A MIDSUMMER NIGHT'S DREAM

- **2Egeus: With duty and desire we follow you**

We follow our leader, not with desire but with duty.

He pretends to follow me with desire, but follows me with duty.

They follow him neither with dutynor with desire.

Youngsters, with duty and desire, must follow the footsteps of great leaders.

Many of them are following their political leader with duty today in order to fulfill their desires tomorrow.

- **Lysander: The course of true love never did run smooth.**

The course of my love runs but not smooth.

There is no course on love-making for one to attend for love can neither be taught nor learnt, but be felt and experienced.

The course of his love with her runs not smooth because neither her father nor her brother is smooth.

She says to him, "The course of our love will run smooth only if you complete your course".

The course of their love was so smooth that it ended up in smoke so smoothly.

- **Helena: My ear should catch your voice, my eye your eye,**

**My tongue could catch your tongue's sweet melody.**

Your ear caught my voice; I lost my voice, your eye my eye and I lost my sight and your tongue my tongue and I lost sweet melody of my life.

There are many who raise their voice for the voiceless, but brutally silencing the voices that are raised for reasons at home.

His cousin is too deaf to catch your ears and too blind to catch your eye.

Many of us have ears, but lend them not, eyes, but observe not, and tongues, but speak not.

Some of us do not ear more, do not eye any, but tongue gets us into trouble by excessive use.

John Milton could not see with his eyes, but he did with his heart and mind. Paradise Lost is a great treasure in the Paradise of Literature.

(It is said that God has blessed us with two eyes, two ears, but only one tongue. So let us hear more, observe more, but speak less. Tongue is a powerful weapon that can turn heaven into hell and hell into heaven. One who does not know how to control his/her tongue cannot control anything. Sweet words may come from well-poisoned tongue and bitter words from well-polished tongue. There are honey-tongued hypocrites. A hypocrite is more dangerous than an enemy. The mind of an enemy can be well-studied, but not that of a hypocrite. Sweet melody is a feast to ears; Nature to eyes, sweet/polite words to tongue and peace of mind to lead a happy life.
)

- **Hermia: I give him curses, yet he gives me love.**

The saint says that he cannot give blessings to one who always curses him.

He wants her to express her love for him at least through curses.

You can curse me, but love me. Curses are tolerated for the sake of love that may blossom one day or other.

Curses one day or others are sure to go in search of the inventor.

He loves her and so gets curses from her brother.

You curse me as you see my face, but you will love me when you see my heart.

You cannot expect love from a cursed heart, nor can you expect curse from a kind heart.

My love for her became strong through all her curses.

The pain of love is felt more by curses than by blessings.

• **Hermia: ...........he hath turn'd a heaven into a hell.**

Blind love for her has converted his heavenly life into a hell.

I love heaven but I am afraid of the evil forces on my way that might push me into hell.

His hell-like life has become a heaven after her entry into his life.

"My life becoming a heaven or hell is in her hands", says Tony.

Her tongue is so venomous that it can turn a heaven into a hell, blessings into curses.

"Better to be in hell with Lucifer than to be in heaven with you", says Black to his wife.

• **Helena: Love looks not with the eyes, but with the mind**

(Here the authors wish to make a mention of a historical love started with the eyes and remain even today as a monument for innumerable eyes as recorded by famous Tamil orator cum writer Valamburi John in one of his books titled "Kathalum Kamamum-Part-I" (Love and Lust). The incident narrated by Valamburi John in Tamil is translated into English as follows

340 years ago. Thimmappa Nayakkan was ruling over Mysore. His Darbar Hall was flooded with people in hundreds and fifties, and the very entry of Nandini, King's daughter made the Hall the center of attraction. People were there to see the dance of Nandini.

Her dance was a great feast to everyone's eyes and she received thundering claps from the audience as she brought before everyone's eyes a dancing peacock spreading its wide, beautiful and colorful wings. Nandini then was 23 years old. Being a paragon of beauty, she became the dream girl of every prince.

It was the day of Dasara (a festival) and the whole city of Mysore looked like a 'paradise on earth' and the day was marked with a number of events which included a photo exhibition. Princess Nandini visited the photo exhibition, without perhaps expecting that her heart would get lost there on seeing the photo of a handsome boy. Astonished at the amazing appearance of the boy, Nandini lost herself and was just staring at the photo for a very long time, totally unaware of what happened around her. She felt the young boy in the photo literally conversing with her heart. He was so handsome that even a skilled sculptor could not carve a statue of him to a 'T'. Princess Nandini looked at the photo with her eyes, with her mind and with her heart. Though the photo was not for sale, Nandini, being the princess, bought it as she could not leave there without her mind and heart in the form of a photo.

After reaching the palace, she quarantined herself with the photo of the boy and she almost started her life with the photo in her own world of imagination, forgetting food, waterand sleep. Daysbecame nights and nights became days. The beautiful peacock forgot its dance. All halls of the palace looked dark and dull as Nandini did not come out of her own room. She was keeping her eyes closed as she did not want even the image of the boy to leave her eyes. How can an affectionate father happily mingle with all when his belov'd daughter is a solitary reaper? It is an affectionate father that reads his daughter's mind. The daughter who was jumping joyfully here and there like a young deer with all her flesh and blood is now found as a skeleton as if she were suffering from some bone-melting disease. The beautiful parrot of the palace looked dull all the time. The cuckoo of the palace had lost its magnetic voice. What can be the reason for one's indifferent attitude at teen age other than the intoxicating love?

King Thimmappa Nayakkan sent his soldiers all over and to every nook and corner to bring the boy that his daughter was madly in love with. Milk could be taken even from the most ferocious and untrained female tiger, if it were the desire of a ruler. The soldiers with great difficulties found out that the young boy hiding himself in the photo was none but the prince ruling over Valliyoor, a place in Tirunelveli District now. Pandian was his name. The soldiers themselves lost their senses at the very sight of the handsome prince and decided that he would be the perfect match for their princess.

The news that the image had been found out in reality reached the palace and Thimma Nayakkan got simply delighted, and desired to perform his daughter's marriage with her dream boy.Hearing the most joyful news, Nandini felt her heart composing music of the first water. The palace that remained a Pandemonium due to the clouds of sorrows became a Paradise with the sun and the moon jointly beaming to remove the dark clouds. Princess Nandini's desire was expressed to Prince Pandian. Does love come by force? After three days, Pandian said that he was not willing to marry Princess Nandini. Three months passed on. King Thimma Nayakkan's soldiers rounded up Valliyoor in disguise. The hands of the lady who served Pandian food were well-oiled. Money makes everything. Some drug not harmful to one's life was mixed with the food and it took Prince Pandian to the unconscious stage during which he was being taken to Mysore by the soldiers. When they were crossing a place called Vaduhachimathil (a few kilo meters from Valliyoor and Eruvadi), Prince Pandian got back his senses and sensed what had happened. Nearly hundred heads would have rolled like kicked balls here and there, had he had a sword in his hands. Even the greatest warrior might feel paralyzed without weapon during sudden and unexpected attacks. Quite unexpectedly he pulled a sword from a soldier and stabbed himself to death, being unable to tolerate the act of a great warrior being used as a cog in the machine for the sake of an unknown princess' love.

The body of Pandian was kept in Vaduhachimathil (near Eruvadi now). The news of his death brought shock waves and the soldiers from Valliyoor rushed to Vaduhachimathil and arrested the soldiers of Mysore. Broken hearted Nadini with her father and others rushed to Vadhachimathil and they reached there in three days. The people of Valliyoor were taken away by the beauty of Princess Nandini and did feel that none but Nandini would be the perfect match for their prince. But the fate of the prince brought tears in the eyes of the people. The tears that flowed from innumerable eyes wet the land there, but could not extinguish the flames of the fire that were with its red tongue swallowing the body of their young Prince. None could have imagined that it would happen then. Princess Nandini unexpectedly jumped into the fire and immolated herself to win the heart of her dreamy boy at least after death. The handsome Prince and the beautiful Princess became ashes due to the uncontrollable hunger of fire, but it could do nothing with their souls that together disappeared into the sky to live with love. In memory of his belov'd daughter Nandini, and Prince Pandian that she was in love with, King Thimmanayyakkan erected a monument at Vaduhachimathil the very next year, which still reminds the visitors of the love of Princess Nandini with Prince Pandian. )

Princess Nandini looked at her lover with her eye, mind, heart till she was alive, but now with her soul.

His love for her looks not with eyes, but with the mind, but the mind is in disorder.

How can you see my love when you keep your eyes and mind closed?

He is so flirtatious that he cannot see any with love.

- **Quince: You may do it extempore for it is**

**Nothing but roaring.**

The speaker is roaring and the audience is snoring.

The speaker boasts of speaking extempore though it is nothing but roaring.

Though boring, the actor's speech is received by his mad fans with thundering claps.

He is just roaring on the stage as there is nothing either on his tongue or in his mind.

The speaker is continuously roaring to conceal his ignorance.

Better to sleep near a roaring lion than to sleep near snoring uncles.

The lady says to the police, "Sir, my husband is causing noise pollution at home by roaring throughout the days and snoring throughout the nights".

- **Titania: To give their bed joy and prosperity**

His love for his wife is exposed only on bed.

Nights make him a beloved husband, but days a benevolent dictator.

The couple gives their bed joy and prosperity only at nights. Days make them poles apart.

Only their bed knows the stories of the young couple's joy and prosperity.

He hates his wife so much that even their bed looks red in anger.

The poor farmer says, "After hours of toiling under the hot sun, it is my bed and pillow that I consider my only joy and prosperity".

- **Titania: The human mortals want their winter here;**

**No night is now with hymn or carol blest;**
**Therefore, the moon, the governess of floods,**
**Pale in her anger, washes all the air.**

(The human beings do not have their winter pleasures here. Their nights are not blessed with hymns and songs. Therefore, the moon, who rules the tides is pale with anger and fills the air with moister so that all thediseases caused by dampness are prevalent here. )

When shall my summers become winters? When shall my nights get filled with hymns or coral blest? When shall my dry mind get wet with warm love? When shall the blessings from the above pour on me?

It is your anger that makes your life pale and redirects all your favourable winds against you.

He is so bad that even the air he breathes needs to be purified.

Many poor tenants have become victims of floods and the moon has shown its powers as governess of floods.

His unreasonable and unwanted anger has ultimately made his face pale.

He is so poor that he can neither wait for his summer nor for his winter. As he has no hope of any spring in his life, he is waiting for his autumn.

- **Oberon: ....it should pierce a hundred thousand hearts**

(Here the authors are reminded of an oft-told story that describes motherly love. A boy fell in love with a girl, but she told him that she would marry him on the condition that he must kill his own mother and bring her her heart. The boy in total intoxication out of stupid and mad love for her accepted the condition and committed matricide without an iota of conscience. Taking his mother's heart at hand, he was going to see her girl friend to prove his love for her. But on his way he fell down as he did not notice a big stone lying in the middle of the road. His mother's heart that slipped from his hands continued to beat and said, "Oh my belov'd son! Take care of yourself". )

Your tears may pierce a hundred thousand hearts, but there are thousand people but not with even a single heart.

Many innocent girls have fallen victims to his piercing eyes, not knowing that he has no heart.

The boy said to the girl, "Many have pierced my heart many a time with reason or without reason and you for your part can do so if you are so willing.

My intention is not to pierce, but to pacify your heart.

His heart is so strong that it cannot be so easily pierced.

My heart can be pierced for the sake of our nation several times, but certainly not for any selfish reason even once.

Cardiologists can cure your heart, but cannot fill it with love and compassion.

• **Helena:..............my heart is as true as steel**

His heart was truer than steel and stronger than iron, but I don't know how he died of heart attack.

The cardiologist can cure your heart, but the bill he gives can attack one's heart.

How can you expect her heart to be as true as steel when her tongue is a bundle of lies?

She is so true in her heart that I wonder whether her heart were made of steel.

Though she has a heart as true as steel, it is not in the right place.

• **Lysander: Love takes the meaning in love's conference.**

(Love knows what is really meant when lovers talk. The meaning of love is felt, enjoyed and experienced when it is expressed in not only romantic but also beautiful words. Many of the Tamil songs written by outstanding poets like Kannadasan, Vali, Vairamuthu have their echoes in innumerable minds and hearts beyond ages, time and space as the lines are beautifully decorated with words of high level imagination and creativity. A few lines of the song of the Tamil movie 'Jeans' written by Poet Vairamuthu are given as an example here. The second stanza of the song expresses not only the hero's (lover's) strong love for the heroine, but also his rich desires that he imagines to fulfill and to fill the heroine's heart with warm love.

"Alahiya Nilavil oxygen nirappi

Angay vunakkoru veedu seivein

Vunnuyir kaakka ennuyirkondu vuyirukku vuyiraai vuraiyiduvein

Mehathai pidithu methaihal amaithu melliya poo vunai thoonga vaippein

Thookkathil maranthu veirkkintrapothu natchathiramkondu naan thudaippein

Paalvannapparavai kulippatharkkaha panithuliyellam seharippein

Thevathai kulitha thulihalai alli theertham enray naan kudippein". – Poet Vairamuthu in Tamil

The meanings of the above lines are translated into English as follows

Oh my sweet heart!

I shall fill the moon with oxygento make there a home for you

My soul shall become the sword to protect your soul

Collecting all clouds, I shall make a bed for you to sleep (as you are as soft as a flower)

I shall fan you with stars when you feel sultry in sleep

I shall collect the drops of white snow for you to bathe (You are a bird as white as milk or snow)

I shall collect the drops of the water that flows over you to drink as holy. (Theertham-holy water)

A few more lines of another song written by Poet Vairamuthu for the Tamil movie titled 'Indian' are given here. Kamal Hassan is the hero and Manisha Koirala is the heroine of this movie. The excessive possessiveness of the lovers for each other is beautifully revealed in the lines.

"Male: Vun peirai yaarum sollavum vidamaattein

Antha suhathaiyum tharamaattein

Vun koonthal pookkal

Vilavay vidamaattein-athai

Veyilil vidamaattein

Female: Pengal vaasam

Ennaithavira ini veesakkoodathu

Annai Therasa
Avaraithavira pirar pesakkoodathu
Male: Nee pohum theruvil
Aangalaividamaattein-sila
Pengalai vidamaattein
Nee sinthum sirippai kaatril vidamaattein-athai
Kavarvein tharamaattein
Female: Pudavai kadaiyil
Pennin silaiyai
Nee theendakkoodathu
Kathal kottai
Karppukkarasa nee thandakkodathu". (In Tamil)
Meanings of the above lines are given below
Male: None shalt be permitted to pronounce your name
The joy of doing so is mine.
I shall not let the flowers on your hair to have a fall
Nor shall it go dry by the scorching sun
Female: Thou shalt not have the smell of any (woman) save mine
Nor shalt Thou utter a word with any (woman) save Mother
Tesresa.
Male: No male shalt be permitted to enter the street you dwell in
Even some female too
The wind shalt not be allowed to take away your smiles that
scatter
Smiles of yours are meant only for me.
Female: Touch not even the female mannequin
In a garment that displays saris
Love is a fort, oh my belov'd lover
Cross not the borders. (a strong fort not for others to enter)
(My heart is a fort with entry restricted. It is only for you. )

• Lysander: ..............one heart we can make of it;

**Two bosoms interchained with an oath;**
**So then two bosoms and a single troth.**

(We can think of them as one heart. Our two bosoms are bound together with an oath of love. They are united by a single truth. )

The couple has been living with two bodies but with a single heart.

True love needs no oath, no promissory note, no warranty or guarantee.

Two bosoms were interchained with an oath, but the chain used for interchaining was not strong enough to knit them together for long.

A number of truths with a single lie make all the truths questionable.

It is the truth that serves as the bridge between two hearts.

A marriage is solemnized to unite two minds and two hearts by filling a number of stomachs with delicious food and a number of minds with joy and by extracting blessings from a number of hearts.

- **Helena: Deserve a sweet look from Demetrius' eye**

Peter says, "Lucy! don't I deserve at least a smile from you?

A sweet look from two beautiful eyes benumbs a young boy's all six senses.

A look from her eyes, a smile from her lips and a word from her mouth have paralyzed all his organs.

She teaches me many lessons with her silence and absorbs the maximum from me with a single look.

Her look is sweet, but not she.

- **Hermia: To pluck this crawling serpent from my breast**

The coward is so flirtatious that he will pluck the crawling serpents and scorpions from fleshy breasts.

Can one's character be judged just because he unintentionally plucks a crawling serpent from one's breast?.

It is not the breast that matters but the harming serpent that crawls on it.

Whenever she gets headache, she suffers unbearably as if her brain were being eaten by four or five scorpions.

She did not feel harmed by the crawling serpent on her breast, but by the deliberate touch of the evil hand that leisurely plucked it.

• **Flute: As true as truest horse that yet would never tire**

(as faithful as a faithful horse that would nevertire)

I am a truest horse that that tire not.

He got tired in the Olympic though he is a truest horse.

The truest horse runs not till it tires, but till it dies. (Do hard work.)

He walks like a horse but his wife moves like a snail.

A horse may or may not be true but must not be tired.

• **Titania: Thou art as wise as thou art beautiful**

( Hearing much of George Bernard Shaw's knowledge and wisdom, a beautiful girl fell in love with him, despite his appearance not being good. One day she made up her mind to propose her love to Shaw and she did so, saying that she wishes, by marrying him, to beget a baby who would be as beautiful as she and as wise as he. Shaw immediately asked her what to do if the result were contrary to her expectation. )

(Due to the wisdom of a man being much talked of in a town, a stranger met him to find out the reality or to test his wisdom. He caught hold of a bird, and standing in front of the wise man with the bird in his hands folded behind, he asked the wise man what he had in his hand. The wise man replied that it was a bird. He asked him what bird it was. The wise man replied that it was a parrot. Then he asked the wise man whether it was alive or dead. The wise man replied that its being alive or dead was in his hands. )

It is said that knowledge is acquired through learning, and wisdom through experience.

He is nice, but not wise.

He is neither nice nor wise.

Scholars used to express their wisdom through timely wits.

(Former Chief Minister Mr Anna Durai was noted for his wisdom, knowledge and in particular presence of mind. He was a Member of the Parliament in the year 1965. When he came out the premises of the Parliament once, a reporter with the intention of testing his special faculties much talked of everywhere, asked him to give one thousand words without the first alphabet 'A'. Anna immediately replied that he could write from 'one to nine hundred and ninety nine". He said that the number of words was still 999. Anna said, "Add 'stop' and it comes to 1000". )

Your beauty lies in your wisdom.

To be both wise and knowledgeable is really God's blessing and gift.

(Socrates says that the pursuit of knowledge is as essential as the air we breathe. Socrates was nominated one of the Seven Pillars of Wisdom. Socrates' nick name is the 'source'. Socrates says, "Know thyself".

One day Socrates met a young man on the streets of Athens. "Where can I find my bread?, asked Socrates to him. The young man responded. "Where can wine be found?", continued the philosopher. The young man replied. "Where can the good and the noble be found?", asked Socrates. There was no answer. Socrates said, "Follow me to the streets and learn". )


- **Titania: ......pluck the wings from painted butterflies**


He is so cruel that he will pluck the wings even from the painted butterflies.

Cruelty of children cannot be decided by their plucking wings from butterflies. (It is not the action, but the age that matters. )

Cruelty may begin from one's pluck of wings from butterflies.

Butterflies are not safe in the hands of playful children.

Many Juliets of today with smart phones lose their safety because of their Romeos.

Life cannot be re-set, as wings plucked from a butterfly cannot be re-fixed.

A suckle is not needed to pluck the wings from a butterfly.

- **Titania: looks like a watery eye**

The poor farmer's eyes were watery when he was told that his son was wasting his hard earned money like water.

The farmer's eyes are watery as there is not even a single drop of water for cultivation.

There are many painful stories behind his watery eyes.

His eyes are so watery that they challenge the rain in wetting the land as quickly as possible.

My mind is so flooded with worries and pains and if my eyes were fixed with the sky, there would be only rainy season.

- **Hernia: thou......hast given me cause to curse**

He is busy looking for causes to curse some Tom, Dick or Harry.

Cursing everyone once for no cause, the saint is now seeking blessings from the Most beneficent and the Most merciful.

There are causes and causes to curse the rapists and the brutal murderers.

The mother-in-law curses her daughter-in-law as she has no cause to curse her.

My mother neither curses any for any cause nor seeks any cause to curse any.

The poor people say, "We have every cause to curse our MLA and MP, but we are too tired to curse them hereafter". We have already supplied their ears with curses sufficiently.

- **Demetrius: Pierc'd through the heart with your stern cruelty**

By breaking our love, you have pierc'd through my heart with your stern cruelty.

Dr Abdul Kalam pierc'd through every Indian's heart with his patriotic spirit and strong love for the nation.

There are many who pierce through others' hearts with hot and harsh words.

The poor women stood still when her heart was pierced with stern cruelty for umpteenth time.

The counselor has pierced through the mind and heart of the counselee with his timely advice.

- **Demetrius: this zeal of bliss**

She considers her grandmother's kiss a zeal of bliss.

My dad's gift on my birthday is a great zeal of bliss.

Nothing on earth is a great zeal of bliss but mother's love.

The innocent people consider the very appearance of the MLA of their constituency a great zeal of bliss.

- **Helena: If you were men, as men you are in show**

**You would not use a gentle lady so**

You are a man in show but you cannot show any quality of a man.

Had he not misused the gentle lady so, he would have been considered gentle.

(Man 1: I saw a gentleman who was slapping his first wife in front of his third wife.

Man 2: Say I saw a man, not a gentleman. )

(A gentleman is one who does not hurt one's feelings.)

Would you use such harsh words, were you really gentle?

He is a man only in show.

Really he is what he really shows himself.

- **Helena: I am sure you hate me with your hearts**

How can I hate you with my heart when my heart is withyou?

What makes you hate me with your heart?

How could you expect with no heart to like you or hate you with heart?

As I cannot hate you with my mind, I do it with my heart.

My heart has become warm only after I hate you with my heart.

He hated everyone with his heart with or without cause and now he is without a heart.


• **Helena: I be not so in grace as you,**

**So hung upon with love, so fortunate,**
**But miserable most to love unlov'd?**
**This you should pity rather than despise.**


(I am not so favoured as you, not so smothered in love, not so fortunate, but miserable, loving but not being loved. You shouldpity me for this, rather than despise me. )

He is hanging upon love, but a sword of Damocles is hanging upon his head.

Even grace is not in favour of your gracious love with the gracious angel.

He is fortunate in everything but not in love.

His life of fortunes became that of miseries because of love.

His fortune will start with his failure in love with the girl.


• **Lysander: Although I hate her, I'll not harm her.**

**Hermia: What? Can you do me greater harm than hate?**

(Among lovers and couples, the anger of the male is severely punished with the silence of the female. However, 'Silence' is silenced whenever there is a quarrel between a mother-in-law and daughter-in-law. )

They loved each other so much that they, even after a break up, are unable either to hate or to harm each other under any circumstances.

She might have done me greater harm than hate.

She does not hate me, but harms me with her silence.

The man says to his friend, "What can be a greater harm for a husband than the silence of his wife?".

Hate me, harm me but love me.

She has married him unwillingly in order to willingly hate him and harm him.

- **Helena: When she's angry, she is keen and shrewd.**

**She was a vixen when she went to school.**

(When she is angry, she is bitter and shrewd. She was bad-tempered when she was at school. )

It is quite strange that she is calm and quiet when she is angry.

He becomes a vixen only when he goes to school.

He is keen but not shrewd and his wife is not keen, but shrewd.

Those who are keen and shrewd may not possibly be innocent.

Helena becomes a vixen whenever she sees her husband's face.

- **Bottom: Do not fret yourself too much in the action.**

(Do not take too much trouble over this. )

She frets herself in every action and now she faces reaction for her every action.

Problems get complicated only because you fret yourself too much in the action.

The beloved mother frets herself too much in every action for the sake of her children.

It is the unwanted tension that generally makes one fret oneself too much in every action.

The student frets himself too much in every action, except in examination.

- **Theseus: These couples shall eternally be knit.**

(During marriages, it has become quite common in these days that those who bless the couples consciously or unconsciously, mechanically or memorably, knowingly or unknowingly, willingly or unwillingly say that the couple must live like Tom and his wife, Dick and his wife or Harry and his wife. No one has the mind to say"I wish the couple lived like me and my wife". )

I wish the couple be eternally knit.

John and Jercy who got knit as lovers now have got knit as a couple.

The couple is knit in joys, not in sorrows.

It is the eternal love that makes the couple be eternally knit.

The couple is knit whenever there is no guest at home.

Garden of Eden is not required for the couple to be knit, but even a hut in a desert shall suffice.

- **Demetrius: These things seem small and undistinguishable**

**Like far- off mountains turned into clouds.**

The village boy had his own dreams and desires but fate and poverty have miserably made them all seem small and undistinguishable like far-mountains turned into clouds.

Politicians look big, gigantic and angelic and helpful neighbours at the time of election, but after election they seem small and undistinguishable (even invisible) like far-off mountains turned into clouds.

He is so mad that he can even think of clearing with his handkerchief the clouds that cover a mountain and breaking with a stick a mountain.

Drops of snow that cover the plants and flowers are as beautiful as the clouds that cover the mountains.

My ambitions may now seem small and undistinguishable like far-off mountains turned into clouds, but my hard work will remove the clouds and make the mountains look closer, brighter and visible.

- **Theseus: One sees more devils than vast hell can hold.**

The world is so filled with sins that hell must be more accommodating than heaven.

The husband says, "Those who live with devils at home will live with angels in heaven".

Devils outnumber angels and so must be the hell vaster than the heaven.

Better to be pleasant prisoners of a narrow heaven than to be perpetual sufferers of a vast hell.

The father says to his newly married daughter, "It is a woman who can convert a house into a heaven or a hell. Let me visit another heaven on earth".

Some live good by birth, some by nature, some by choice and many by the desire to enter heaven after death.

You can't find angels in hell, nor can you find devils in heaven. But you can find both angels and devils together on earth.

He must be either so innocent or so foolish that he seeks devils in heaven and angels in hell.

- **Theseus: The forms of things unknown, the poet's pen**

**Turns them to shapes**

Not anyone's pen can turn your poems and articles to shapes, but a poet's.

He is so imaginative that thoughts flow from his mind even before the first drop of ink flows from his pen.

Even the irregular forms of things known or unknown can be turned by the poet's pen into shapes.

It is a passionate poet that can pen artistically and creatively.

My article totally lost its shape after its being touched by your pen.

Even a shapeless poem would get a perfect shape, were it penned by Poet Bharati.

• **Robin: If you pardon, we will mend.**

(Is there any mistake that is unpardonable?. The question is either debatable or hypothetical to be answered. The taste of pudding is in eating and similarly the pain of pain is in experiencing. Only the affected can say whether a sin is pardonable or unpardonable. Chances to mend are deniable to some who make scars through unforgivable sins that remain for ever. It is said that justice delayed is justice denied. An incident that happened in Tamil Nadu during the spread of Corona shook the whole country. Keeping in mind the severity of Corona, the govt imposed the rule that all commercial shops and trade centres be closed 8 PM. At Sathankulam (a place that belongs to Tuticorin District, Tamil Nadu), one Mr Jeyaraj aged around 60 and his young son, whose marriage had been fixed, were taken by the police into custody on June 18, 2020 on the charge that their mobile shop had been kept open just a few minutes beyond the time fixed by the State Govt. It was allegedly said that the son in his attempt to save his father manhandled by the police had used some words which had aggravated or rather increased the heat of the already boiling minds of the police. Both the father and the son were beaten black and blue without even an iota of mercy. Third degree methods were employed. When the severely wounded victims were produced before the judicial magistrate, he remanded them to police custody on the production of a fitness certificate from a local doctor and the wounded victims were tortured to death under police custody. Their death brings to one's mind John Donne's heart-melting lines on death

"Death be not proud
Though some have
Called thee
Mighty and dreadful

For thou art no so".

"Penny wise; pound foolish" is a proverb in English. The felons escape, but fate plays with those who commit little errors. The incident shook not only the vicinity, but also the whole country and even people abroad. Tears may stop, wounds may heal but the scars remain. The boisterous and unruly attitude of the police, taking law into hands, was condemned by all at levels. Such incidents make the word 'pardonable' meaningless. Though an error is not a mistake till it is rectified, there are certain crimes, which in no way can be tolerated. However, punishment is not the solution for mistakes pardonable either generously or on humanitarian grounds. Chances are given so that the result might be hopefully consoling. One may mend one's attitude. Former Chief Justice, Govt of India Justice V.R.Krishna Iyer says, "Every saint had his past and every criminal hashis future".

Saints and criminals cannot be judged by their appearance. Former Chief Justice of India Mr Krishna Iyer says, "Our freedoms are in peril if our courts suffer pusillanimity or arrogance". The Sathankulam incident makes us add that our freedoms are in peril if the Government and the police Dept, besides our courts, suffer pusillanimity and arrogance. Justice Krishna Iyer adds that "Every soul has a sculptor within, if you know to carve it out. Inside every prisoner is a latent talent. No man is born a criminal". (52) He quotes Bernard Shaw saying that "The object of punishment is to improve and nobody is improved by injuries". (52)

Justice Krishna Iyer says, "If you treat a man like an animal, then you must expect him to act like one. For every action, there is a reaction. This is only human nature. And in order for an inmate to act like a human being you must trust him as such. Treating him like an animal will only get negative results from him. You can't spit in his face and expect him to smile and say thank you. Law is not a brooding omnipresence in the sky but a behavioural omnipotence on the earth". (69)

A criminal lawyer in order to be successful as a criminal lawyer must not be a criminal, but must know (study) criminals and crimes.

The police at Sathankulam police station may mend, but their treatment of the innocent victims is unpardonable.

He can never be pardoned as he has no mind to mend.

There are some who mend and get pardon every now and then.

# CHAPTER FIVE

# THE MERCHANT OF VENICE

- **Antonio: In sooth, I know not why I am so sad.**

  **It wearies me; you say it wearies you;**
  **But how I caught it, found it, or came by it,**

  **.................................................**
  **........... I have much ado to know myself.**

(In sooth – in fact)

Sadness may result in madness in case of extreme depression and frustration.

All know why she is mad, but no one knows why she is sad.

The old lady saddened and maddened all, and now time saddens and maddens her. (As you sow, so you reap. )

When you have much ado to know yourself, you make much ado to know about others.

Socrates says, "Know thyself".

Whatever wearies you wearies me.

Nothing wearies him and so he is found wearing the years. (To wear years-to look young)

In his attempt to hide his sadness, he was betrayed by his own face.

(The face is the index of the mind.)

My face cannot express the grief my heart is filled with.

Many of us journey joyfully, but our luggage is full of sadness.

I don't know why our team members are making much ado about nothing.

- **Gratiano: ........let my liver rather heat with wine**

**Than my heart cool with mortifying groans.**

Tom is so depressed that he wishes to consume wine that might collapse his liver, but not to have a heart that is filled with groans.

Many do not bother about their livers that are destroyed by liquor, but about their hearts that are burning with groans.

Despite doctor's advice, he is drowning himself into bottles and bottles of wine.

Better to have a non-functioning heart with joys than to have a functioning one with sorrows.

Let my liver rather heat with wine than my heart cool with pain.

(Drinking smoking are injurious to health. By smoking, one smokes away one's hard earned money and invites cancer. About drinking, Mr Krishna Iyer, former Chief Justice of the Supreme Court says, "At the first cup, man drinks wine, at the second cup, wine drinks wine and at the third cup, wine drinks man". )

- **Gratiano: .........................silence is only commendable**

**In a neat's tongue dried.**

(Friend 1: When did you feel that silence is commendable?

Friend 2: After marriage..............)

(Interviewer: Why don't you answer my questions?

Candidate: Silence is commendable. )

(Wife: I don't know why I married you. I have been asking you for a gold necklace for two years, but you never respond. Do you have a frog in yourthroat?

Husband: Silence is commendable. )

Better to patiently control anger than to harshly reveal it.

Better to harshly pour out anger than to silently suppress it.

She is so talkative that her tongue never gets dried.

("Rolling stone gathers no moss" is a proverb in English. In Tamil, similar proverbs are "Vurundodum kallil paasi padiyathu" and "Aavdaiyatha vaayil arisi nanaiyathu".)

Better to be silent than to hurt someone with harsh words.

Thiruvalluvar in the Chapter "Adakkamudaimai" (Possession of self-restraint) says,

"In flesh by fire inflamed, nature may thoroughly heal the sore;

In soul by tongue inflamed, the ulcer health never, more".

"Theeyinal chuttapun vullarum; aarathey

Naavinal chutta vadu". (In Tamil)


- **Bassanio:** .......................................sometimes from her eyes


**I did receive fair speechless messages:.................**

**Nor is the wide world ignorant of her worth;**


(Friend 1: I receive more messages from her eyes than from her mouth.

Friend 2: Don't worry. Aftermarriage, you cannot conveyanymessage either throughyoureyes or throughyour mouth.
)

The messages from her eyes are quite contradictory to the ones that I receive from her mouth.

Study her heart before you strain yourself on her eyes and lips.

Eyes speak more than lips in love.

Eyes are active in love and lips in lust.

Language is forgotten at the very sight of her talking eyes.

Even foolish lovers understand messages that they receive from beautiful eyes.

My heart moves along with her eyes.

Non-verbal communication is more communicative than verbal communication in love and lust.


• **Nerissa: ...................superfluity comes sooner by**

**white hairs, but competency lives longer.**

(superfluity- excessiveness of what is sufficient or required)
White hair may be the symbol of old age, but not of wisdom.
Competency lives by inspiration and incompetence by influence.
Competency becomes incompetent enough to raise its head, when incompetence is blessed by luck and time.
Competency may live longer, but it is proper recognition that makes the life of competency healthy and happy. When intelligence, wisdom, competency and hard work are left unnoticed and unrecognized, foolishness, incompetency and laziness sarcastically smile and mock at them.
Flattery overcomes competence and intelligence in many work places.


• **Portia: Good sentences, and well pronounced.**

**Nerissa: They would be better, if well followed.**

You frame sentences well, but with heart-breaking words.
He is a person to be listened to, but not to be followed.
He plucks words as flowers, but constructs sentences that prick readers like thorns.
He is a saint with well-pronounced sentences, but ill-practised deeds.
Easier to preach than to practise.
It is strange that sentences well-uttered sometimes are not well-written.

The sentences are so bad that they cannot be pronounced or followed.

- **Nerissa:** .............................holy men at

**their death have good inspirations;**

Many of us become holy, while nearing the gatesof death.

Holy men inspire, butdo they perspire?

Holiness lies not in words, but in deeds.

One cannot wait till death to get inspiration.

His heart is so stony that it cannot be inspired either by his own death or by the death of his near and dear ones.

It was only one's last bed that makes one's thoughts holy.

The lady in power is so arrogant that even her death bed cannot make her mature. .

She is holy in light, but a ghost in darkness.

(Birth is the messenger of Death.)

Ambitious people believe in 99 % perspiration and 1 % inspiration.

- **Portia:** ........................he is every man in no man;

He loves me so much that he, though he is no one among everyone and nothing among everything, will give me something even out of his nothing.

(Friend 1: I am the best.

Friend 2: Yes, among theworst.)

Hard work makes nobody somebody.

Be careful with her for she is an expert in making nothing everything and everything nothing.

He is nobody, but he projects himself as everybody, whenever he talks to somebody.

It is better for one to be none, not harming others, than to be someone harming everyone.

- **Portia: I think he bought his doublet in Italy, his round**

  **hose in France, his bonnet in Germany, and his behaviour everywhere.**

She bought her doublet in Italy, house in France, bonnet in Germany, and her husband is now a beggarin India.

The politician has his breakfast in Germany, lunch in France, dinner in England, but needs votes in India.

In one of the Tamil movies titled "Ninaithalay Inikkum", the following stanza in one of the songs is quite similar to Shakespeare's lines given above

"Kaalai Japanil coffee
Maalai New Yorkil cabaret
Iravil Thailandil jolly
Ithilay namakkenna veili?
Ingum engum nam vulaham
Vulaham namathu pocketilay
Vaalkkai parakkattum rocketilay
Iravu poluthu namathu pakkam
Vidiya vidiya kondaduvome". (In Tamil)
"Coffee in Japan in the morning
Cabaret in New York in the evening
Romance in Thailand at night
Where do we have boundaries?
The world belongs to us everywhere
The world is in our pocket (hands)
Let our life fly (in joy) by rocket
Life from dawn to dusk is ours
Let us celebrate it beyond dawn and dusk. (In English)

- **Portia: If I live to be as old as Sibylla, I will die as chaste**

  **as Diana,...........................................**

(In Roman mythology, Sibylla was a prophetess famous for her extreme old age (as much as the sand grains that she held in her hands) granted to her by Apollo and Diana, in Roman mythology, was the goddess of virginity.)

She wishes to live long as Sibylla, but not like Diana.

He was blessed with a wife, who could not live long as Sibylla, but live like Diana.

When you doubt your wife, I feel Diana, goddess of virginity being doubted.

Tony would be worse than a doubting Thomas, even if he married Diana, goddess of virginity.

His eyes are so jaundiced that even the goddess of virginity might create in his eyes clouds of doubts.

He is ready to marry any Diana, but he does not want any to look as old as Sibylla.

(Daughter-in-law: Doctor! is my mother-in-law alive, despite the fatal accident?

Doctor: She has been blessed by Sibylla. What can I do?)


- **Portia: ...................if he have the condition of a saint**

  **and the complexion of a devil, I had rather he**
  **should shrive me than wive me.**


shrive-to confess/ to receive

wive- to marry (a woman)

(Saint is one, who lacks worldly pleasures. Saints and Gurus are dispellers of darkness. )

I do not want to marry a man, who, with the complexion of a devil, has conditions of a saint.

Your complexion reminds me of a saint, but your deeds of a devil.

He is ready to wive her, as no one gets to be wived by him.

Varun is so mad after her girl friend that he would make any sacrifice in his life to make her his wife.

• **Shylock: I will buy with you, sell with you, talk with you, walk with you, .........................but I will not eat with you, drink with you,................................**

(Professor: How was my class lecture this morning? (in a market place)

Student: I will buy with you, sell with you, talk with you, walk with you, but I won't stay in your class.

Professor: !!!)

(Husband: You love me?

Wife: I will buy with you, sell with you, I will eat with you, I will drink with you, but I never speak lies. )

Husband: ??? )

My friend bought with me, sold with me, talked with me, walked with me, but disappeared in a fraction of seconds, on his seeing his girl friend.

One can buy with you, sell with you, talk with you, eat with you, drink with you, even suffer and suffocate with you, but won't accompany you to your grave.

Father says to his son, " Oh my son! I am getting old. How long can I walk with you, run for you, toil for you!".

(Young girl: Sir, my lover bought with me, sold with me, talked with me, walked with me, dined with me and drank with me, but now he lives with someone.

Police officer: You chatted with him in the park, dined with him in restaurants, had ice cream with him even in winter, insulted your parents with him, but now you have come to the police station without him. )

• **Antonio: ....................................I neither lend nor borrow**

**By taking nor by giving of excess,**
**Yet, to supply the ripe wants of my friend,**
**I'll break a custom.**

I have broken my policies just to supply the ripe wants of my innocent parents.

I won't break a custom even if pressurized to supply the ripe wants of my dear and near ones.

He neither lends money, nor borrows, but steals.

The old man has got exhausted by giving everything of excess.

Father said to his son, "I cannot toil under the sun from dawn to dusk just to supply all your ripe wants".

Many innocent parents strive hard and make sacrifices to supply the ripe wants of their children today and become 'Not wanted' tomorrow.

- **Shylock: ..............................you neither lend nor borrow**

**Upon advantage.**

He does everything uponsome advantage.

Sacrifices of parents are not based upon advantages.

Many of us lend and borrow, but upon no (or some) advantage.

He lends upon advantage, but borrows upon disadvantage.

Advantages at the time of borrowing may result in disadvantages at the time of returning.

- **Antonio: The devil can cite Scripture for his purpose.**

**An evil soul, producing holy witness,**
**Is like a villain with a smiling cheek;**
**A goodly apple rotten at the heart:**
**O what a goodly outside falsehood hath!**

(In Tamil, "Satan vedam vothuhirathu" is a proverb. In English, it is said, "The devil can cite Scripture for his purpose".)

Some saints indulge in devilish deeds in a saintly garment.

Vedic words are on his tongue, not in his heart.

Unholy souls are experts in producing holy documents and holy witnesses.

He has been using Scripture to safely cover his fraudulence.

You smile like a hero, but cheat like a villain.

"All are not saints that go to church" and "Appearance is deceptive" are oft-quoted proverbs in English. .

Among us, there are many villains, but with smiling faces.

Villains in saintly garments are more dangerous than villains with the strength of an evil giant.

- **Shylock: ........ sufferance is the badge of all our tribe;**

(sufferance – endurance, patience)

"Blessed are the meek for they shall inherit the earth" is a proverb in English.

Sufferance is the badge of those, who understand life.

Sufferance strengthens human relationship.

Sufferance must be the badge of the entire humanity to attain peace.

Sufferings give one more pain in the absence of sufferance.

Many of us suffer a lot with no sufferance.

- **Shylock: A pound of man's flesh, taken from a man**

  **Is not so estimable, profitable neither,**
  **As flesh of muttons, beefs, or goats.**

Human flesh is neither estimable nor profitable as flesh of muttons, beefsor goats.

"Beware of dogs or you will find your flesh in their teeth" is the sentence on the board hanging outside his relative's house.

The cruel man says, "I can be hospitable to my dog with the sacrifice of your flesh".

He looks as fleshy as a beef and so the girl, who is as osseous as a Skelton refuses to marry him.

He says that he eats flesh of muttons, beefs and goats to look fleshy.

Man jumps from heaven to earth out of arrogance, power and ego, though all know that human flesh is nether estimable nor profitable after death.

- **Bassanio: I like not fair terms and a villain's mind.**

  He is a villain, but with a mind filled with fair terms.
  He seems to be a hero, but with a villain's mind.
  His language contains fair words, but his mind contains foul thoughts.
  He speaks like a hero, but acts like a villain.
  The man with a villain's mind talks to all with a smile on his face.

- **Morocco: Mislike me not for my complexion,**

  My complexion makes you mislike me.
  He has two complexions, one on the screen and the other off the screen.
  Face may be the index of the mind, but not of the heart.
  He mislikes me, whether he likes me or not.
  The girl mislikes him not for his complexion, but for his being a bundle of contradictions.
  People mislike their not for his corruption, but for his complexion.
  (Nirad C. Chaudhury in his autobiography "Autobiography of An Unknown Indian says, "I have now to tell the story of another and a more serious misconception, which is entwined with the central problem of our relationship with Englishmen, or to be more exact, with all Europeans-the problem of colour. Their fair complexion

was a matter of great curiosity and still greater perplexity with us, and we wanted to know why they were fair and we were dark. One theory was that we had been darkened by the sun whereas they had been bleached by the cold, both of us travelling in opposite directions from a golden or rather brownish mean. It is believed by some of our demonologists that the ghosts of cold countries are grey in complexion, brown could become pink". (133)

Nirad Chaudhury adds that "Now, one day Primeval Lord told me in great confidence that all English babies were actually born dark as we were, but that immediately after birth they were thrown into a tub filled with wine and it was the wine which bleached their skin white". (134) )

- **Morocco: I would outstare the sternest eyes that look,**

    **Outbrave the heart most daring on the earth.**
    **Pluck the young sucking cubs from the she-bear,**
    **Yea, mock the lion when he roars for prey,**
    **To win thee,...................................**

The innocent girl says, "When the boy was in love with me, he said that he would pluck the youngsucking cubs from the she-bear and mock the lion that roars for prey to win my heart, but after marriage, he could not save meeven from a street dog that chased me".

Better to sleep near a roaring lion than to sleep near my snoring father.

(Girl: Tom, your friend Jone is in love with me. He says that he is a tiger. Is it true?

Tom: Yes, but without teeth

Girl: !!! )

(Woman 1: Is your husband so bold?

Woman 2: Yes, he is so bold that he would outstare the eyes that have lost sight, outbrave the heart that awaits the third attack, pluck the milk bottle from a crying baby and mock the lion in a well-locked cage that roars for prey.

Woman 1: ??? )

Bravery lies neither in plucking the young sucking cubs from the she-bear, nor in mocking the lion when he roars for prey, but in controlling anger.

The boy is so cruel and so ill-tempered that he would even kill the she-bear to pluck its young sucking cubs.

Peter like one mocking the lion when he is roaring for prey is severely criticizing his boss when his family is crying for food.

- **Launcelot: Certainly my conscience will serve me to run.**

  **.......................The fiend is at mine elbow.**
  **my conscience, hanging about the neck of my heart,**
  **.....................................................................**
  **I should be ruled by the fiend................................**
  **.........................................................theJew**
  **is the very devil incarnation; and, in my conscience,**
  **my conscience is but a kind of hard conscience,............**
  **my heels are at your commandment;........................**

Everything serveshim very well, except his conscience.

He is arguing with the officersof IT Dept, keeping his rivals at his elbow.

Varun says, "My conscience is so soft that it never pricks me".

It is strange that we are on some occasions ruledby our friends and loved by our fiends.

Yourheels may beat my commandment, but they are unwilling tomove.

( Lady 1: How is your mother-in-law?

Lady 2: the very devilincarnation)

- **Launcelot: ........................... I will try confusions with him.**

None can confuse him, because he confuses others.

Principal: Madam! What's the problem with your students?

Teacher: Sir! They often try confusions with me.

Principal: Whenever I ask you anything, you confuse me with some expression. )

He is expert in trying confusions with everyone, except with his wife.

Some of us read too many books and confuse themselves, consult too many doctors and collapse their health.

"Tom is an expert in trying confusions and so he can be asked to hold negotiations with the workers", says the Managing Director

- **Launcelot:........................it is a wise father that knows**

**his own child.**

A wise father interprets his son's silence.

His son is wiser enough to paralyze his father's wisdom, whenever the latter's wisdom is employed to find out the follies of the former.

He is wise in everything, but not in knowing his son.

He is so wise that he knows everyone's sons, except his.

Davis lost his wisdom in all his wise attempts to know his son.

Some fathers employ all their wisdom to know their sons and reveal all their foolishness in their attempts to satisfy the society.

- **Launcelot: .............let's have no more fooling about it, but**

**give me your blessing: I am Launcelot, your boy
that was, your son that is, your child that shall be.**

(Launcelot Gobbo, originally Shylock's servant is a young and quick-witted fellow. As he is badly-fed in the household, he switches his allegiance to Bassanio. He teases remorselessly about the Jewishness of Jessica, with whomhe is friendly with. )

(Father-in-law to his newly wedded son-in-law: Dear boy! She was my daughter yesterday, your wife today and mother to my grandchildren tomorrow.

Son-in-law: Your bungalow and car were yours yesterday, and yours today and mine tomorrow.

Father-in-law: !!!)

I wish to be a Launcelot and I don't mind being badly-fed or ill-fed or not fed at all.

The priest gives one blessings, but gets curses from everyone.

You are so dull headed that you cannot even think of becoming like Shylock's servant even you touch the sky.

With all signs of aversion on face, the old lady is giving all her blessings.

- **Launcelot:.........I am sure he had more hair of his tail**

  **than I have of my face when I last saw him.**

I have more hair on mychin than my horse has on his tail.

What can I do, if hair does not grow on my chin?. You want me to fix the tail of a horse on my face?

He has as much hair on his chin as a horse has on his tail.

The hair on his chin reminds me of a horse with more hair on his tail.

The saloonist says, "Better to shave a horse's tail than to shave your naughty son's head".

- **Gratiano: ...........lovers ever run before the clock.**

(Time for lovers seems to flow faster and the whole day seems shorter for lovers.)

(Boy: We lovers ever run before the clock.

Girl: Till marriage?)

The lovers run before and after the clock without knowing their time.

The clock never shows many of the lovers their time.

He has only bad time because he was blindly running before the clock in his blind love with the unworthy girl.

The lovers even run before the clock and their parents are searching for them round the clock.

• **Jessica: ..........love is blind, and lovers cannot see**

**The pretty follies that themselves commit;**
**For if they could, Cupid himself would blush**
**To see me thus transformed to a boy.**

(Cupid and Diana are the two deities. Cupid is said to be blind. )

Love is so blind that pretty follies seem to be wise deeds.

Love has made me a Cupid.

Love in many cases blinds lovers till marriage, but after marriage even the blind get vision.

She is so beautiful that his eyes cannot see any, but her.

Love is blind till the lovers awake or open their eyes with their minds.

Love becomes blind, as long as lovers face each other with hearts.

(Here is a poem in Tamil. )

"Kathalukku kangal illai enbathu poi

Vun kangalai paarthapirahuthan kathalikkavay thodanginein".
(In Tamil)

That love is blind (Love has no eyes.) is a lie.

I started loving only after seeing your eyes. (in English)

• **Jessica: .............must I hold a candle to my shames?**

How shameful the old arrogant is to hold a candle to everyone's shames!

I cannot hold a candle to my shames.

Better to hide his shames in darkness than to hold a candle to one's shames.

He is so intoxicated that he holds a candle to his shames.

Some of us cheat the world by holding a candle only over the virtues.

People vote for the politician, as he never holds a candle to his shames.

The officer is so corrupt, so dishonest, so filthy that he must hold a number of candles to all his shames.

- **Morocco: Who chooseth me shall gain what many men desire;**

  ...........................................................
  **Who chooseth me shall get as much as he deserves;**

  ...........................................................
  **'Who chooseth me must give and hazard all he hath'**
  **How shall I know if I do choose theright?**

She has chosen everything right on earth, except her husband.

He is not able to make his choices, as choices try confusions with him.

My desire is right, but my decision is wrong.

Many of us know the right choices but take wrong decisions.

His foolishness lies only in his considering all the wrong choices the right choices.

- **Morocco: A golden mind stoops not to shows of dross;**

  (dross −waste/ impure/ worthless)
  I have a golden mind that never stoops to shows of dross.
  (Greedy Girl: What is your qualification to love me?
  Boy: I have a golden mind.
  Greedy Girl: cannot be used to make a ring even for a new-born baby.
  Boy: !!!)

A golden mind is made of good thoughts in mind and love in heart.

- **Morocco: All that glisters is not gold**

All that glittersis not gold.
She is gold, but never glitters.
His son is so innocent that he considers anything and everything that glitters gold.
Praise refused to marry her, but she does not glitter though she is gold.

- **Nerissa: Hanging and wiving goes by destiny.**

He is hanging because of wiving.
(Friend I: I am getting married shortly.
Friend II: Hanging and wiving goes by destiny. My best wishes to you.
Friend I: !!!)
(Lawyer: The guilty must be hanged, your Honour!
Judge: He can be released, because he is getting married shortly.
Lawyer: Thank you, your Honour!)

- **Shylock: ...........................................................it will**

**feed my revenge. He hath disgraced me, and hindered
me half a million; laughed at my losses, mocked at
my gains, scorned my nation, thwarted my bargains,
cooled my friends, heated mine enemies; and what's
his reason? I am a Jew. Hath not a Jew eyes? Hath
not a Jew hands, organs, dimensions, senses,
affections, passions? fed with the same food, hurt
with the same weapons, subject to the same diseases,
healed by the same means, warmed and cooled by
the same winter and summer, as a Christian is? If**

**you prick us, do we not bleed? If you tickle us, do**
**we not laugh? If you poison us, do we not die? And**
**if you wrong us, shall we not revenge?If we are like**
**you in the rest,...........................................**

Forget and forgive. Never feed your revenge.

Revenge feeds revenge and those, who have a quest for revenge, miserably fail as victims of revenge.

Revengemay quench one's thirst, but it may plaguethe inventor.

I grace on every occasion, but he disgraces me on all occasions.

He has hindered me half a million.

Thanks a million

A human being neither cries at one's gains nor laughs at one's losses.

You cool my enemies and heat my friends for some cheap gains.

You heat the minds of my foes by warming their hearts.

(Teacher: Can you write like Shakespeare?

Student: If you teach us, do we not fail? And

if you send us out, do we not delight?

if you do not award more marks, shall we not revenge?

Teacher: ???)

He has fed his revenge so violently that his good health has got food-poisoned.

You can feed the poor in stead of feeding your revenge.

The old lady was feeding her revenge as long as she was in power, but she is hungry. (She is suffering now. )


- **Portia: Let fortune go to hell........................**


Misfortune is unfortunately too fortunate enough to be fortunately in heaven and fortune isunfortunately too unfortunate to unfortunately remain in hell.

Which has the upper hand-Hard work or Luck? Though it is debatable, luck might buy the debaters, even before hard work puts forth its arguments.

If fortune goes to hell, will misfortune not stay in heaven?
What are you going to gain out of your fortune? Let it go to hell.

- **Bassanio: How many cowards, whose hearts are all as false**

  **As stairs of sand, wear yet upon their chins**
  **The beards of Hercules and frowning Mars;**
  **Who, inward search'd, have liverswhite as milk;**

(Hercules-Hero of strength

Mars- God ofWar) (It is said that the month March originates from Mars. )

(really a great beard- a beard worthy of Hercules)

(When one feels scared, his/her face turns white, as liver becomes as white as milk.

Description of liver as being white as milk may be to describe a person getting frightened.)

He speaks as if he were the descendant of Hercules and Mars, but he is, in fact, a coward with his heart as false as stairs of sand.

He speaks like Mars while talking to others, but he just meows while talking to his wife.

When he heard the news, his face became so scared that his liver would have become as white as milk possibly visible to the x-ray eyes.

The world is deceived with ornament and let your ornament be impressive, whether your deeds are good orbad.

I am neither a Hercules to show my strength nor a Mars to bless warriors in a battlefield, but a person of literature to teach you about Hercules and Mars.

- **Portia: ................unlesson'd girl, unschool'd, unpractised.**

Among us are there many unlesson'd, unschool'd, unpractised, but wise.

The young girl is highly matured, though unlesson'd, unschool'd and unpractised.

Though unlesson'd and unschool'd, he has become the minister for education.

• **Bassanio: And there is such confusion in my powers.**

She abused and misused her powers as she herselfhad confusion in her intellectual andadministrative skills.

He continues to remain as a slave to his wife, as there is confusion in his powers.

There is no confusion in your powers, but in your potentials.

Has USA become most powerful by creating confusion in every country's powers?

The manager says that he wishes to continue in power though there is such confusion in his powers.

• **Lorenzo: ..................with all my heart;**

**I shall obey you in all fair commands.**

He is ready to obey you all in fair commands, but not with hisheart.

With all his heart, he will obey you, but not in fair commands.

Your commands are not fair and so I shall not obey you with all my heart.

He has no heart at all, then how can you expect him to obey his helpless parents, whether the commands are fair or foul?.

With all his debit and credit cards, he is ready to obey any Tom, Dick and Harry in all commands fair or foul.

• **Lorenzo: Fair thoughts and happy hours attend on you!**

Fair thoughts attend onme, but during unhappy hours.

Fair thoughts and happy hours attend on him, but he has many faces.

When will fair thoughts and happy hours attend on me?

His thoughts are foul, but his words are fair and he makes everyone unhappy with his happy hours.


- **Launcelot: .................................the sins of the father are**

  **to be laid upon the children; therefore, I promise**
  **you, I fear you. I was always plain with you,..........**

The sins of his father accepting bribes during his entire period of service have now miserably fallen on his innocentchildren.

Father was crucified for the sins of his sons.

I do not want my sins to be laid upon my children.

It is your fearless mind that makes you commit sins though they are laid upon your innocent children.

Be plain with me. –Be frank with me.


- **Jessica: ..................there is no mercy for me**

  **in heaven, ............................................**

In heaven there is mercy for those, who have mercy on earth.

His heart is so dry that there is no mercy in it.

I am merciful to all and I shall have mercy in heaven.

Is Merciful God in heaven where there is no mercy?

The sins of the people on earth has made heaven merciless, hasn't it?


- **Launcelot: ...................................they have all stomachs.**

  Many of us love our pet animals and birds, but we forget the fact that they havestomachs.

The boss said to him, "You are working for your stomach".

I think that of all your organs, only your stomach is active.

I cannot eat to fill your stomach.

The rich run just to reduce their belly size; the poor do to get something for the stomach.

(Boss: Your salary is Rs 2000 per month.

Coolie: Sir, I cannot ask my wife and children to remove their stomachs.)


• **Lorenzo:** ...........................................


**the whole wealth of thywit in an instant?**


In his attempts to instantly show the whole wealth of wit to his girl friend, he revealed his foolishness, and lost his love.

I cannot show the whole wealth of my wit in an instant.

The politician said, "I can show you all the whole wealth of my wit, but not my wealth".

(Interviewer: Can you show the whole of your wit in an instant?

Candidate: Oh, sure, if the whole salary of my whole life is given in an instant. )


• **Portia: The quality of mercy is not strain'd,**


**It droppeth as the gentle rain from heaven**
**Upon the place beneath: it is twice blessed;**
**It blesseth him that gives and him that takes:**
**'Tis mightiest in the mightiest:**


Not only the quality of mercy, but that of true love never gets strained.

Mercy is twice blessed; it blesses the giver and the receiver.

The love shown by parents is never strained.

Mercy gets strained when it is advertised.

The depressed girl says, "I have been looking at the sky since I lost my happiness, but there is not even a bit of mercy from the above".

The greedy man says, "In stead of mercy, it can be currency that must drop as the gentle rain from heaven".

"Currency blessth him that gives and him that takes", says the corrupt officer.

- **Shylock: There is no power in the tongue of man**

  **To alter me: I stay here on my bond.**

He had power in his tongue till he got married.

His wife has full powers in her tongue and so he is out of power.

The candidate's tongue was totally absent during the interview.

There is no power in your tongue now, but still you keep on talking.

It is the power in the tongue that has made our leader win the election.

He says that he stays here just on a bond.

The wife tells her husband that she cannot live with him on his bond.

He lost his interest in his job about 10 years ago, but his commitment to his bond continues for another 10 years.

You cannot love anyone on your bond.

- **Shylock: How much more elder art thou than thy looks!**

  (Tom: How much more elder art thou than thy looks!
  Brown: Thank you
  Tom: Why do you thankme?
  Brown: You didn't say that I look more **older** than I am.)
  (Teacher: A boy in Std X looks like you!
  Girl: Sir, he is my older brother.
  Teacher: Say he is your elder brother. )
  (Newly wedded wife to her husband
  Wife: How do I look?
  Husband: You look older than you are.

Wife: You blind stupid...................(Husband runs away.)

• **Bassanio: ...............I am married to a wife**

**Which is as dear to me as life itself;**

He loves his wife as he loves his life.

He lost his life, after his wife coming into his life.

Diana says, "Life is dear to me, but never my husband".

A social worker is dear to the society as he/she is to his/her life itself.

After marriage, he lost both his wife and life.

He says that his life is his wife, but he says that his life is meaningless.

• **Lorenzo:...................let the sounds of music**

**Creep in our ears:**

Let my grief find a relief by the sounds of music.

(Father: Why are you using ear phone and listening to songs all the time?

Son: Sounds of music creep in my ears).

Only sounds creep in my ears, where is music?

We forget our worries when the sounds of music creep in our ears and the gentle breeze embraces us.

I don't want the sounds of music to creep in my ears, as the voice of my belov'd fills my ears with words sweeter than the sounds of music.

• **Portia: He knows me as the blind manknows the cuckoo,**

**By the bad voice.**

The girl says to her boy friend, "You are too blind to see my beauty, too deaf to hear my voice, too ignorant to know my knowledge, too weak to know my strength, too heartless to win my heart, too unkind to know my kindness, but more cunning than a fox in possessing my dad's properties".

I know her as the blind man knows the cuckoo by the bad voice.

He is so strange that he knows the cuckoo by the bad voice and the crow by the sweet voice.

His assessment of others is so apt that he judges the cuckoo by its voice, horse by its speed, elephant by its strength, lion by its majesty, fox by its cunningness and honey bee by its hard work.

(Dr Johnson says, "We rank the best by the worst performance and the worst by the best performance. )

A priest in a wine shop or cabaret goes down in the estimation of others and a criminal in a place of worship goes high in the estimation of others.

# CHAPTER SIX

# THE MERRY WIVES OF WINDSOR

- **Evans: ............if we leave our pribbles and prabbles,.......**

(pribbles and prabbles- empty chatter and petty quarrels)
Do something worthwhile, leavingyour pribbles and prabbles.
His neighbours are wasting their precioustime on pribbles and prabbles.
Pribbles and prabbles are quite common in most of the houses.
You come to office every day, but you get your salary not for any work of yours, but for your leaving your pribbles and prabbles.
John retired from service last week, leaving in his work place pribbles and prabbles.

- **Shallow:.............................................................**

**thank you always with my heart,...................**

"Forget to do good and you mayfind salvation yet
But forget gratitudeand you're headed for destruction'snet".-Thiruvalluvar
You thank me, not with your heart, but with your lips.

You say that your words of gratitude are wet, but they affect me with unbearable heat.

How can you say that you thank me with your heart, when you do not have a heart?

When 'thanks' pours out from heart, words, however powerful and appropriate they may be, become weak.

You extract works from me with words from heart, but thank me with words from lips.

He thanks you with his heart, but he has his heart in the wrong place.

I donot want to be thanked by any heart that is dry. (from any person without mercy?)

She is so positive that she acknowledges thanks, whether it are from one's heart or lips.

- **Slender: I'll rather be unmannerly than troublesome.**

Better to be unmannerly than to be troublesome.

He is both unmannerly and troublesome.

There are some, who are troublesome only when they are unmannerly.

Joe being troublesome is more intolerable than his being unmannerly.

Some politicians are knowingly mannerly, but unknowingly troublesome.

- **Falstaff: .........................the appetite of her eye did**

**seem to scorch me up like a burning-glass.**

I love her me so much that the appetite of her eye did seem to scorch me up like a burning-glass.

The saint says, "I am unable to be a saint, when the appetite of her eye scorches me up like a burning-glass".

I can be a saint till I look at her eyes.

The appetite of her eye scorches me so much that it makes me experience the heat of fire.

The appetite of her eye scorches me so much that I am afraid that I might lose my eye-sight.

Had the appetite of Meena's eye not scorched up Arun like a burning glass, he would not have married her and his life also would not have broken like a glass.

* **Mistress Quickly:** ..........................................I'll

**ne'er put my finger in the fire,.............**

Knowing well that your fingers will get burnt, you put them in the fire.

When I put my fingers in the fire, I did not get them burnt, but when my eyes eyed her eyes, it caught fire and burnt myself into ashes. (I became nothing.)

It is foolish that one puts one's fingers in the fire in order to know the heat of the fire.

It is foolish to consume poison in order to know the duration of its harmful effects.

Your words are so harsh when you are hot that one could better put one's fingers in the fire than to receive your words by ears.

His mind freezes out of joyful chillness when someone puts fingers in the fire.

He is so out of his mind that he won't feel the heat even if his whole body were put in the fire.

* **Mistress Ford:** ...............................the wicked fire of

**lust have melted him.....................**

Though he is burning with the wicked fire of lust, he wishes to remaina bachelor.

His wings of love have now turned wicked fire of lust.

You get into trouble when your wicked fire of lust burns someone.

My wicked fire of lust can be put out only when I own my dream girl of beauty and live with her in full possession of love.

He looks saintly, but the wicked fire of lust is melting him.

In spring, the gentle breeze of love moulds him, but in summer, the wicked fire of lust melts him.

When she comes closer and closer to me, the wicked fire of lust uncontrollably melts me.

I love her so much that my heart, if I donot see her, fails to function even at the consumption of bemarinone.

When my eyes are filled with her beauty, I become so unconscious that I could undergo a heart surgery without the effects of anesthesia.

Pots and pots of chill water cannot put out his wicked fire of lust that is melting him all the time.

He is so lustful that even oceans cannot put out his wicked fire of lust.

Even though it is snowy, he is hot due to his wicked fire of lust.

"Malarinum mellithu kaamam; silar athan

Sevvi thalaippadu vaar"- Thiruvalluvar (in Tamil)

"Love's tender, as tender, as a slow-opening flower

Not many know-the less perhaps the better!-its secret hour". (in English)

Your lust is licensed and hence does not need any valley.

(licensed lust- lust after marriage recognized by the society?)

Lust is more tender than the petals of flowers, but it, in its fullest form in the total absence of love, is more painful than the pain due to the bite of the claws of a ferocious tiger.

In the Tamil movie titled "Deiva Thai", the burning feeling of lust out of unity between two bodies with a single mind is described by Kannadasan, an outstanding Tamil poet as follows

"Nenjodu nenjai sheirthaal

Theeyodu panjai sheirthaal" (In Tamil)

"Chest was kept close to breast
As sponge was kept close to fire". (In English)


• **Mistress Ford: ..................................It would**


**give eternal good to his jealousy.**


His jealousy has made his eyes yellow in colour.

Lucy is so strange that she is jealous of herself.

The psychiatrist says that her jaundice can be cured, but not her jealousy.

Tom is jealous of everyone around him, as it gives him eternal pleasure.

Healthy jealousy contributes a lot to one's elevations in life.

Thiruvalluvar says about envy or jealousy as follows

"Koduppathu alukkaruppaan sutram vudupathum

Vunbathum in(t)rik kedum"- Thiruvalluvar (in Tamil)

"If you're jealous, you're scripting your own ill-fate

You stand as your own enemy, stone in hand, at your own gate".
(In English)


• **Pistol: Take heed, have open eye, for thieves do foot by night.**


(Take heed-take care)

(Thief: Your Honour! Shall I, duringchill nights of snowy season, do foot by day?

Judge: ???)

(Judge: Did you do foot by night?

Thief: No, Your Majesty! I went by car as the street is full of dogs at night. )

He never has his eyes open, but judges everyone.

We keep our eyes open by day and thieves by night, don't we?.

He is a full-time professional thief that he does foot by day and night. Neither the sun nor the moon is visible to him, as even his visibility is loyal to his profession.

You have your eyes, but never open; you have your ears, but never hear.


- **Shallow:** ......................................**skip like**

  **rats.**


He skipped like a rat without knowing that many cats are behind him.

Whenever I ask him questions, he just skips like a rat.

I cannot just skip like rats when there are responsibilities on my head.

When his wife comes like a cat, he skips like a rat.

There is another expression in English; 'to run like baffled rats'. It means 'to run like rats in extreme fear'.

Seeing the police, the thieves ran like baffled rats.

Seeing his wife holding a cane in hands, White ran like baffled rats.


- **Mistress Quickly:** ...................**she leads a very frampold life with him,**


(frampold-bad-tempered, angry, disagreeable)

As she is not in his mind and heart, she leads a frampold life with him.

She has been leading a frampold life with him for the past 27 years.

Better to remain under the wings of mother than to live a frampold life with the life partner.

Though Mary lead a very frampold life with John David for more than 6 decades, she never made any complaint about him.

Fed up with a frampord life led with the rich fellow, the lady wishes to lead hereafter a happy and content life with some poor man but with a heart.

- **Falstaff: Money is a good soldier,.........**


Money is my good soldier, but it never allows me to become the captain.

Money has always been my soldier, but it has never helped me to be a winner in any battlefield.

Money is my good soldier, but I am a bad miser.

Money must be an honest soldier.

If money were a good soldier, I would have as many soldiers as possible.

The politician considered money his only soldier, but the soldier killed his peace of mind to ensure nation's economy.

- **Falstaff: Hang him, mechanical salt-butter rogue!**


He is a salt-butter rogue, but he wins everyone's heart easily as he has a lot of butter on his tongue.

His words are softer than butter, but the intended meanings behind every word of him causes wounds.

The manager says that he never likes to deal with mechanical salt-butter rogues.

(In English, even punctuation marks are important. It is said that wrong placement of a comma in a sentence written by a judge helped a person escape death. Read the following two sentences to understand the change of meaning just because of the wrong placement of just a single comma.)

Hang him, not release him.

Hang him not, release him.

- **Ford: .....................................My heart**

**is ready to crack with impatience.**

As she ignores me, my heart has become so dry that it might start to crack, as the earth dry gets cracks.

His heart, though not dry due to tears, has cracked with groans.

Fill your heart with patience, as there are cracks with impatience.

Rahul says, "None on earth can make cracks in my son's heart as it is made of iron".

Arul is sure that there cannot be any crack in his heart, as he has no heart.

The old man wets his heart with tears due to unbearable pains.

His heart will become dry, if he does not pour out his groans through tears.

Why do you heat her heart, when there are already cracks.

The depressed parents say, "All civil engineers and architects in this earth cannot set right the cracks in our hearts".

Before marriage, love, after marriage life made cracks in his heart.

There may be cracks in my heart, but I shall continue my journey for there is no crack in my mind.


- **Shallow:** ...................................................**He is a**


**curer of souls, and you a curer of bodies.**

Go to a saint to get your soul cured, but to a physician to get your body cured.

You can cure neither your soul nor your body, as you trust neither God nor physician.

I am so mentally and physically wounded that I can be cured neither by a curer of souls nor by a curer of bodies.

Keerthi is so mentally retarded though she is in the midst of curer of souls and bodies.

He is neither a curer of souls nor a curer of bodies, but the curable words that fluminously flow from his mouth make people visit him, seeking cure.

- **Page: ................you have yourself been a great**

  **fighter, though now a man of peace.**

Knowing the ill-effects of fights, he has now become a manof peace.

His face has two colours- red and white. (anger and peace)

He is a fighter in the street, but at home a man of peace, but his wife is a fighter at home, but a woman of peace in the street.

Even though Aslam claims himself to be a man of peace, he has himself been a great fighter.

- **Shallow: ...................................though I now be old**

  **and of the peace, if I see a sword out, my finger itches to make one. Though we are justices and doctors and churchmen, ....................we have some salt of our youth in us.**

Swords remind warriors of the battlefields**that** they had faced.

Although he is a retired teacher, if he sees board and chalk, his heart itches to teach.

Though he is pretty old, the salt of his youth makes him very active.

Peace cannot be attained through swords, but through words of love.

The colour of peace cannot be red, as peace has nothing to do with blood.

We may be justices, doctors and churchmen, but we have some salt of our youth in us.

- **Shallow: What, the sword and the word? Do you study**

**them both, Master Parson?**

(The words 'sword' and 'word' bring to one's mind two great men- Alexander the Great, whose sword was swift in wars and brought him victory and made him one of the greatest warriors of the world, and Diogenes, whose every word contained some philosophical thought and who won laurels as one of the greatest philosophers of the world. The dialogues between Alexander the Great and the Greek philosopher Diogenes are considered witty, indicating intellectual and philosophical thoughts of high standard. Diogenes, one of the founders of Cynic philosophy was a philosopher of intellectual controversies. Not only great philosophers, but Alexander the Great himself could not escape his comments. Once Alexander the Great said to Diogenes, "People in hundreds and fifties meet you, seeking your advice and wisdom, but they do not meet me, despite my being considered Great". Diogenes replied to him, "I am sharpening my brain and you are sharpening your swords. (word and sword). "If I were not Alexander the Great, I would like to be Diogenes", said AlexandertoDiogenes. Diogenes replied, "If I were not Diogenes, I would like to be Diogenes himself". Diogenes' words and deeds were quite strange. There is no doubt that pen is mightier thanthe sword. )

When words get ignited by mind and tongue, the sword is sharpened by hands.

Poisoned tongue causes wounds in the mind and sharpened sword causes wounds in the body.

Master of swords wins in the battlefield; man of words wins in the world.

Wounds by words are more hurting than wounds by swords.


- **Falstaff: What made me love thee? Let that persuade**

  **thee there's something extraordinary in thee.**

  ...............................................................

  **.........I cannot. But I love thee, none but thee; and thou deserves it.**

What should not have made you love me has made you love me.

It is quite strange that she loves him for his vices and hates him for his virtues.

As he is below ordinary, anything a little ordinary in her seems to be extraordinary to him.

(Boy: I cannot. But I love thee, none but thee; though you deserve not.

Girl: I cannot. But I cheat thee, none but thee; though you deserve most.

Boy: ???)

He loves thee, none but thee, but.....but...wishes to marry not thee, but thy friend.

There is nothing extraordinary in me, except my love for thee.

There is something extraordinary in her for which I love her most.

- **Mistress Quickly: A kind heart he hath. A woman would run through fire**

  **and water for such a kind heart.**

I need a kind heart that I would run through fire and water.

She loved him so much that she ran through fire and water to win his heart and won it, but after marriage, he set her on fire and collected her ashes as if he were asked to collect diamond stones thrown on him from the above.

Kindness is in your words, not in your heart.

An affectionate mother would run through fire and water, journey over rivers and through woods to save her children.

- **Falstaff: ....................my belly's as cold as if I had swallowed**

  **Snowballs**

On seeing him after quite a long period, his mother felt her belly getting cold as if she had swallowedsnowballs.

My belly is so burning that I cannot cool it even by swallowing snowballs.

I am so infuriated that I cannot swallow snowballs to cool myself.

So cool and calm Arivu is that anyone might get the doubt that he might swallow some snowballs every day.

I cannot order snowballs online to keep myself cool.

• **Falstaff: .............................to build upon a foolish woman's**

**promise.**

Many young boys invite their own ruin by building upon foolish and selfish girls' promises.

He has lost himself by building upon a foolish girl's promises.

People build upon the incredible and grandiloquent promises of the politicians and pull the wool over their own eyes. (to pull the wool over someone's eyes- to deceive someone)

He is ill-treating his aged parents, building himself upon his wife's words.

Building upon the foolish promises of lusty lovers, many innocent girls have foolishly lost themselves.

• **Ford: ...................................................If I**

**have horns to make one mad, let the proverb go with
me- I'll be horn-mad.**

I wish I had horns to make her mad, as she maddened me with herlove.

I am horn-mad, but you are born-mad.

I would lose my horns if one were made mad of it.

He wishes to have horns at least to make someone mad.

Everyone finds fault with his horns for his own or her own madness.

- **Mistress Page: Wives may be merry, and yet honest too.**

Karim is sad, because his wife is so much dishonest as she is so much merry.

His wife is honest in words, not in heart.

The girl says, "I shall be merry, but my being honest lies in my husband's honesty".

He has become a saint, as his wife is neither merry nor honest.

By testing his wife's honesty in most dishonest ways, my friend has made his honest wife totally dishonest.

- **Ford: My intelligence is true. My jealousy is reasonable.**

The old lady's intelligence is false, but her jealousy is true.

His intelligence is verbally true, but has not been reasonably tested even once.

Unreasonable jealousy betrays one's yellow eyes.

Being jealous of one's intelligence is healthy and reasonable.

My true intelligence is not sufficient enough for me to deal with unreasonable jealousy.

- **Falstaff: they would melt me out of my fat drop by drop,.............**

(Boy 1: Why did you break your love with her?

Boy 2: Her father melted me out of my fat drop by drop. I felt breaking her love immediately instead of getting my whole body immersed in the drops of blood.

Boy 1: Thank God! You told me this on time.

Boy 2: ???)

Our teacher will melt me out of my fat drop by drop, if I do not submit my assignment on time?

I love her so deeply that I won't break it, even if I am melted by electric shock.

- **Falstaff: .....................................O powerful love, that in some**

  **respects makes a beast a man, in some other a man a beast.**

Love is so powerful that it makes a beast a man and a man a beast.

Love has caged his senses so much that he has become a wild beast.

I do not know whether I could marry him or not, because he speaks like a man, but behaves like a beast.

The man became a beast, as his love was mercilessly rejected by her.

Because of her mad love with the worthless, unreliable and cunning girl, the boy behaves even with his affectionate parents worse than a wild beast.

- **Mistress Quickly: Lust is but a bloody fire,**

  **Kindled with unchaste desire,**

Lust is such a bloody fire that it even burns love.

Chaste desires result in love and those unchaste in lust.

(Judge: Don't you know that lust is a bloody fire?

Girl: My Lord! I was kindled with unchaste desire.

Judge: That bloody fire has now burnt your desire to live with him.)

Bloody fire of lust, when fanned by flames further, makes a man a beast.

Unchaste desire stems from love that is not true, doesn't it?

The bloody fire of lust makes him use romantic language, but he has pulled the wool over innumerable eyes.

# CHAPTER SEVEN

# MUCH ADO ABOUT NOTHING

- **Messenger: But few of any sort, andnone of name**

The chairman says, "There are 2800 employees working with me but with none of name".

Better to be a person of at least my name than to be one of no name.

The researcher says, "I cannot but laugh when I receive comments from nameless persons".

There are many guides in this area of research, but none of them is of any name.

The parents have advised Roger to be a person of name and fame.

He has lost everything, including his name.

Reaching the top is difficult and maintaining the top is a challenge.

Thiruvalluvar's views about renown are as follows

"Von(t)ra vulahathu vuyarntha puhal allaal

Pon(t)rathu nirpathon(t)ru yil". (in Tamil)

"Recognition, praise, renown-these in the world stand high

Without those three backing your life you'd have lived to but die!". (In English)

- **Messenger:.................He hath borne himself beyond the promise of his age, doing in the figure of a lamb the feats of a lion: he hath betterbettered expectation than you must expect of me to tell you how.**

(He has shown more valour than it can be expected of him at this age. He appears to be a lamb, but he is valiant like a lion. In fact, I am not able to tell you about his deeds, as he has surpassed all our expectations. )

Aspirants achieve beyond the promise of their age.

He is a lamb in appearance, but a lion in deeds.

He will convert all our expectations of him till now into great expectations in the days to come.

The young boy might become a politician because he is giving all promises beyond his age.

He is a lamb at home, but a lion in the street. (His wife never comes out. )

- **Beatrice:........... he hath an excellent stomach.**

(to have an excellent stomach- to have an excellent appetite)

Even an excellent stomach will get upset if food is taken from this hotel.

Only your stomach is excellent.

One cannot go to the battlefield with an excellent stomach.

( Lazy Son: Why am I not at all successful in life, dad?

Dad: You always try to prove the strength of your stomach, not of brain.

Lazy Son: I shall continue my chat with you after finishing my dinner?

Dad: ???)

(The veteran Tamil actor Kamal Hassan during a Tamil Programme namely Bigg Boss humourously made a mention of people having pet animals and birds. We remember to name the pet animals and birds, but forget the fact that animals and birds too have excellent stomachs. In Tamil, actor Kamal Hassan said, "Peyar vaikka marappathillai. Aanal so'ru vaikka maranthuviduhirome". It means that we remember to name them, but forget to feed them. )

Can anyone only with an excellent stomach come up in life?

Food is just to quench one's hunger, not to fill one's stomach.

Water is just to quench one's thirst, not to get wasted. (Let us save rain water for the sake of future generation.)

(Prophet Muhammad (Peace be upon him) was willingly living in abject penury and preached that fasting makes one realize the immensity of hunger. He said, "The stomach for the sake of good health could be filled as follows

one part with food

one part with water

one part to be left empty)


- **Messenger:A lord to a lord, a man to a man; stuffed with all honourable**

**virtues.**

I am stuffed with all honourable virtues, but surrounded by dishonourable vices.

He is a lord to a lord, a man to a man, but not at all a man at home.

Even though he is not stuffed with honourable virtues, it is eerie that he is very honourable while dealing with others.

He is a lord to a lord, a leader to leaders, a good father to his children, an adviser to the wrong doers, an elixir to the needy, but a beast to his wife.


- **Beatrice: ........... I had rather hear mydog bark at a crow than a man**

**swear he loves me.**

(Boy: Darling! I love you.

Girl: I had rather hear my dog bark at a crow than you swear you love me. )

(In Tamil is is said, "Sooriyanai paarthu naai kuraikkirathu", which means that "The dog barks at the sun". The dog may go on barking, but the sun silently (violently during summer) continues its work. Great aspirants need not bother about the obstacles or negative or adverse comments made on them by others. Being sensitive to criticisms or adverse comments is one of the great obstacles to one's progress. Crows just fly from trees to trees, but the dogs might damage their throats by barking at them continuously. )

(Wife: I am going on barking like a dog, but you do not care to respond.

Husband: This crow unable to fly is staying at home. )

This dog has already barked at many a crow, and is barking at you now. Beware of him.

(This guy has already cheated many girls, and you now. Beware of him. )

Mary finds more delight in hearing some street dog bark than in listening to her husband's songs.

The dog lost its throat out of its continuous bark at the crow.

Let him bark like a dog; I will just fly like a crow.

- **Don John:............. I am not of many words, but I thank you.**

"Man of words is the man of the world", says Ben Jonson.

(Now I request Mr Bean to propose a vote of thanks...

Mr Bean: I am not of many words, but I thank you. )

I am a manof words, butyoudo not deserveto be thanked.

Better to be a personof no wordsthan to be aperson of harshwords.

He does not care to thank any, though he is a man of manywords.

Though I had words in mind, I lost them on the stage due to stage fear.

Words may express thanks, but gratitude is felt and experienced by hearts.

She is a woman of many words, but no word of hers is of any value or meaning.

"When words abound that soothe, why use those that swipe
With ripe berries around, why pick those unripe?".
–Thiruvalluvar (Chapter 10-Right speech)

"Iniya vulavaaha innatha kooral
Kaniyiruppak kaaikavar(nt)hatru"- Thirukkural in Tamil

- **Benedick: ...........she's too low for a high praise, toobrown for a fair**

  **praise, and too little for a great praise.**

(She is so low that she cannot be praised high, so dark in complexion that she cannot be considered fair and so small in size that she cannot be praisedgreatly.)

She was too careless to be trusted with responsibilities, too talkative to be shared with matters of confidentiality, too immature to be expected with mature dealings and so was removed from the post over night.

She is either too low for a high praise or too little for a great praise and therefore she is not fit for me.

Though the fellow is too low for a high praise, he is just praised to the skies.

- **Benedick: Would you buy her, that you inquireafter her?**

  **Claudio:Can the world buy such a jewel?**

Father and Mother-can one buy such jewels?

I considered her a jewel and bought her, but now I have sold myself.

Her face reminds me of gold, but her heart of iron.

He just inquires after her, but has no idea to buy her.

The world can buy such a jewel, but I wish to stay away from the world.

Jewels! Beware of those, who inquire after you.

Fortunately I inquired after her, or unfortunately I would have bought her.

He bought that jewel despite his parents' advice, but now the jewel has enslaved the whole family.


- **Claudio: In mine eye she is the sweetest lady that I ever looked on**


In mine eye, she is the sweetestlady, but in the eyes of ophthalmologists, I am ill-eyed.

In mine eye, my mother is the sweetest lady that I ever looked on.

In your eye, everyone is the sweetest, but you are a sugar patient.

( It is said that beauty lies in the eyes of the beholder. Plato also said this. According to a study by the neurologists of University College London, an area of the brain behind eyes lights up. This area is known for pleasure, value and judgment. An artful beauty is found when the experiences that are stored in the part of the brain co-relates with the art being viewed.

Researchers at the University of California have found out that some area in brain both in men and women gets activated when they are in appreciation of beauty. Let us cultivate the habit of appreciating art and beauty.)

(Boy: In mine eyes, you are the sweetest lady I ever looked on, Rosy.

Rosy: Hello! You have eyes! I am Mary, Rosy's aunt.

Boy: ???????)

- **Don Pedro : .........................look pale with love**


He looks pale not due to ill-health, but due to love.

Love looks fresh and fleshy, but it makes many look pale.

Love and look pale.

(Dad: It is the age for you to love, but not the age for you to look pale.

Son: It is my love that makes me look pale.

Dad: Continue your love..........

Son: What do you mean? Are you happy that I look pale?

Dad: Of course not, but I am happy that I look younger than you when you look pale.

Son: !!!)

Disappointments and frustrations in love miserably drown lovers into the deep ocean of depthless pain, making them look pale.

(Father: Sir, my son looks pale. He says that he is suffering from rheumatic fever.

Doctor: I shall check up and let you know.

Doctor (after check up): Sir, your son is not suffering from rheumatic fever, but romantic fever.

(Father looks pale now. )


- **Don Pedro: And tire the hearer with a book of words.**


The speaker is a book of words, but no page contains any information or meaning.

(Speaker: Ladies and Gentlemen! It is my pleasure to tirelessly tire you all with a book of words till you get tired.

Audience:???)

I hired the speaker just to tire the audience, but not to torture the audience.

There are hearers, but without ears.

The writer is happy to tire his readers with his books.

- **Don Pedro:What need the bridge much broader than the flood?**

(A bridge much broader than the flood is not required.)
There are walls much broader than the roofs and there are bridges much broader than the floods, but there are many human minds not broader than those of the kids.

His tongue is broader than his whole body. (He is so talkative?)
Her heart is bigger than her house. (She is so warm?.)
(Man 1: Why are you afraid of your wife?
Man 2: Her hands are broader than her tongue.)
A dedicated and passionate teacher makes his/her class room broader than this world with his/her connotative teaching.

- **Don John: I had rather be a canker in a hedge thana rose**

 **in hisgrace.......**

(I had rather be a dog-rose (without value) in a hedge than be a cultivated rose in its beauty. It better suits my whim to be hated by all than to shape mybehaviour in order towin the love of others.)
I had rather be a beggar in every street than a lover in her single heart.
Better to be a thorn in a valley than to be a rose in his grace.
She innocently believes that she is the only rose in his grace, but he is so gracious to have as many roses as possible in his grace.
He is a thorn, but there are many innocent roses in his grace.
She is a rose in appearance, but a thorn in characteristics.
The girl wishes to be a rose in some known hero's grace than to be some unknown villain's hedge.
(Here the authors are reminded of the poem titled "Muthir Kanni" (an aged virgin girl yearning for a life partner for a pretty long period). The poem is as follows (in Tamil).
Muthir Kanni
Thenralay! ennaimattum vittuvittu veesu

Nilavay! Paalil vooriya vun kirana(n)gal en veettu vaasalil vilaveindam

Pookkarihalay! Intha theruvil en veettai kalithuvidun(n)gal

En kanakkil muppthiyeilu kodaihalay mudinthana

En kanavuhalilmattum kuthiraihalin kulambadihal

Aanal entha raja kumaranum en veettu vaaslail irangavay illai

Parakka ninaithu vaan paartha en ilamai

In(t)ru puthaiya ninaithu boomi paarkkirathu

Kanneeril karainthathu kan mai mattuma?

Ilamaiyum ilamaiyum

Kannathil viluntha melliya pallangalil

En kanavuhalin samaathihal

Kanna kathuppil oru velli kambi kathodu peisuhirathu

Muthalil nirkka povathu ethu?

Maathavilakka? Vun moocha?

Engirukkiraai en Sha Jehan?

Irantha pinnay Taj Mahal veindam

Irukkumpothey oru kudisai kodu

Engirukkiraai en Ramanay?

Intha Sita(i)

Manavaasam kaanunmunnay vanavaasam kondalay

Veindaam Sha Jehanum Veindam Ramanum Vendam

Neeyavathu Ravana Neeyavathu Pushbaha vimaanama keittein?

Oru kalla thoniyilaavathu"- Poet Vairamuthu

The above poem is given in English as follows

Oh Breeze! Just brush me over some time

Oh Moon! With your white gleam do not lighten my door

Oh! Flower vendors! Kindly go past my house

In my calculation, I have seen 37 summers

In my dream come the horses galloping

But no prince arrived at my door!

My youth that looked upon the sky to fly above now looks at the ground to be buried.

Tears not only took away my eye liners, but also my youth

The dimple in my cheeks speaks the burial ground of my dreams

A silver stand speaks into my ears
Which is the first to stop-my menses? Or my breath?
Where are you, my Sha Jehan?
I want not a Taj Mahal after my death, but at least a hut now.
Where are you, my Rama?
This Sita has seen the dry land even before she could wed
No, I want neither Sha Jehan, nor Rama
Raavana! At least you..... you........
I ask not for the Pushbahavimaana
But     in     stealth     will     you     love     me?
(http://vairamuthu.wordpress.com)

- **Don John:though I cannot be said to be a flattering honest man, it must not be denied but I am a plain-dealing villain, I am trusted with a muzzle and enfranchis'd with a clog; therefore I have decreed not to sing in my cage. If I had my mouth, I wouldbite; if I had my liberty, I would do my liking: in the meantime, let me be that I am, and seeknot to alter me.**

(Even though I cannot earn a name as an honest man, I cannot deny that that I am a plain-dealing villain. I am trusted that I am like a dog muzzled or like a horse hobbled. So I have made up my mind not to be happy in my captivity (cage). I would bite one, if my mouth were free and I would do as I wish, were I given liberty. In the meantime, let me be what Iam and do not tryto change me. )

He is a plain-dealing villain, but he has never dealt with any villain.

Tom is physically very strong and mentally very weak and he can be trusted with his muzzle, not with mind.

Samuel has his mouth, but is unable to bite, he has his liberty, but he is unable to do his liking, for he is married now.

The candidate successfully proved the strength of his muzzle in the interview and so miserably failed.

He is so shirty that he has his muzzle in his tongue.

Birds can sing gleefully on trees, not in cages.

Better to live happily in the natural growth of a tree with broken branches than to be caged in a cage made of sandal wood.

In his attempts to become somebody, he became nobody.


- **Beatrice :.............................He that hath a beard is more than a youth; and he that hath no beard is less than a man; and he that is more than a youth is not for me; and he that is less than a man, I am not for him; ......................................................**


(He with a beard is more than a youth and one without a beardis less than a man. He who ismore than a youth is not for me and he who is lessthan a man, I am not for him. )

(Daughter: Dad! I would like get myself married to someone with a beard or someone without a beard.

Dad: Do not confuse me for God's sake.

Daughter: He that hath a beard is more than a youth and he that hath no beard is less than man. So I wish to marry someone who is more than a youth or someone who is less than a man.

Dad: It is better that you remain unmarried.

Daughter: !!!)

He looks like a lion in beard, but like kitten without beard.

When he is more educated than I, I am not fit for him. When he is less educated than I, he is not fit for me. So who fits me aptly is one who is as qualified /educated as I am.

(The concern of the adults is that the youth are not useless, but use less. The youth are not careless, but care less.)


- **Beatrice:................wooing, wedding, and repenting, is as a**


**Scotch jig, a measure, and a cinque-pace; the first suit is hot and hasty, like a Scotch jig, and full as fantastical; the wedding,**
**mannerly modest, as a measure, full of state and ancient try and**

**then comesrepentance, and with his bad legs, fallsinto**
**Thecinque-pace faster, and faster, till he sink into his grave.**

(Woo (verb)- to woo means to try to persuade someone tomarry oneself)

Jig- A light, brisk musical movement)

Cinque-pace- a lovely dance

(Bachelor: Hello! I am wooing now. What next?

Married man: Marrying..........

Bachelor: What next?

Married man: Repenting........

Bachelor:!!!)

(Wooing, wedding and repenting are like a Scotch jig, a measure and a quick dance, the first suit is hotlike a Scotch jig and the wedding is mannerlyand modest and married man, when his bad legs fall into repentance, moves towards the grave. )

(Parents: All ouradvice not to marry him fell on your deaf ears, but now you say thathe istoo cruel to live with..............

Distressed Daughter: I was blind while wooing and blinder while wedding, but now I have got my eyes while repenting.)

More than wooing and wedding, it is repenting that teaches blind lovers many lessons.

Wooing and wedding filled my heart with joy, but now repenting with sorrows.

For blind lovers, the sky glitters with stars till wooing, the sky gets dark with clouds while marrying and repenting shows them the effects of lightening and thunder and makes the sky invisible.

(Friend 1: It seems that you are busy wooing these days.

Friend 2: only wooing till wedding

Friend 1: When wedding?

Friend: When I become mature enough to bear repenting. )

- **Beatrice:** .............................the commendation is not in his wit,

**but in his villainy; for he both please men and angers them.**

His villainy is commendable, not his wits.

(Wife: I am unable to assess whether you are a hero or a villain. You both please me and anger me.

Husband: Whenever you make food fit for the gods, I am your hero.

Wife: I don't mind your being either a hero or a villain, for neither your villainy nor your heroism is commendable. )

Though he is a wicked villain, he has a commendable wit.

He is a peculiar villain that he angrily pleases and pleasantly angers others.

- **Claudio: Friendship is constant in all other things**

  **Save in the office and affairs of love:**
  **Therefore all hearts in love use their own tongues;**
  **Let every eye negotiate for itself**
  **And trust no agent; for Beauty is awitch**
  **Against whose charms faith melteth into blood.**

('save' here means 'except.)

Love is between two hearts, and none is required in the middle.

Friendship is constant in all other things, except in the office and affairs of love.

Love in every heart speaks its own language. Let every heart and every eye negotiate for itself. In matters of love, no agent/ representative/ broker/ middleperson/ mediator can be trusted.

(Beauty is a witch with its charm melting the faithfulness of even friends into passion.)

How can I expect her heart to use its own language, when she has no heart at all?

How can I expect her eyes to negotiate, when her eyes do not have any sympathy on me?

Words become powerless when magnetic eyes are negotiating.

Her beauty is a witch that it melts my flesh into bones.

Beautiful angels become witches in the absence of love, don't they?

Witches look like angels to lusty eyes.


• **Benedick:.................................................................I**


**stood like a man at a mark, with a whole army shooting at me, She speaks poniards, and every word stabs:**


(poniard-dagger)

(I stood like a man fixed as a target with a whole army shooting at me. She speaks like daggers with every word stabbing me. )

While her speaking, her every word stabs me more sharply than a dagger.

Her every word stabs, but I bear because I am her husband.

When my boss was shouting at me with all harsh and horrible words beyond dictionaries, I felt like a whole army shooting at me, but I was standing like a pillar, as the sight of my poor daughters yearning for their bread to quench their hunger was in my mind's eye.

Her words may stab you, but won't harm you.

(Tom: Every word of your wife stabs you, but you observe silence.

Peter: Silence is the perfectest herald of joy.)

Every word of hers stabs me so much that she might have sharpened her tongue with some sharpening machine.


• **Claudio:Silence is the perfectest herald of joy:**


(best messenger of joy)

For some, silence is the perfectest herald of sorrow.

Do not consider his silence the perefectest herald of joy, as it may be of sorrow beyond words.

(Interviewer: I am asking you questions, but you do not open your mouth!

Candidate: Silence is the perfectest herald of joy. )

(Friend 1: I must tell my wife that silence is the perfectest herald of joy.

Friend 2: I too need that joy in my house.

Friend 1: !!!)


• **Claudio: ...........................Time goes on crutchestill**

**love have all his rites.**

(Time appears to go slow like a lame man walking with crutches until the marriage rites are performed. )

Time goes on crutches till love, it makes cracks in life after love.

True love needs no rites, but it needs the right path of life.

Most of us feel that time goes on crutches just before marriage, but it gets wings after marriage.

Time goes on crutches till lovers become old.


• **Don John: Any bar, any cross,any impediment will be**

**medicinable to me:**

(I consider any obstacle that stops this marriage a medicine tome. )

He is so confident that he converts any bar, any cross and any impediment into a medicine.

Great aspirants convert any bar, any cross and any impediment into medicines to cure their deficiencies.

(Girl: What happened? Your face and whole body are full of wounds!

Boy: I thought there won't be, in our love journey, any bar, any cross, any impediment. But alas! Your dad and goonda-like brothers have made me take medicines along with injuries.)

In the fields of education and research, bars, crosses and impediments teach one many valuable lessons.

Bars, crosses and impediments must be converted into opportunities.

When I take every step forward, some bar, some cross, some impediment throws me back.

There is no life without any bar, cross or impediment, is there?

- **Benedick: ........the world must be peopled.**

(Here the word 'people' is used as averb. )

(The world must be populated.)

If every house is peopled, the world ultimately is peopled.

The company has only been peopled, but there has been no productive work at all.

The leader of the less populated country tried his level best to get his country peopled, but finally his own house got peopled.

- **Don Pedro:....................He hath a heart as sound as a bell, and his**

**tongue is the clapper; for what his heart thinks his tongue speaks.**

(He has a sound heart like a bell and his tongue is likethe clapper (striker of thebell) andhis tongue speaks what (whatever?) his heartthinks. )

I think she hath a heart as sound as a bell, because whenever I enter her heart, it rings rhythmically.

The tongue cannot speak whatever the heart thinks, can it?.

He lost his tongue as he spoke whatever his heart thought.

He hath a heart as sound as a bell at the very sight of his girl friend.

Her heart thinks something, but her tongue speaks something else.

Some lovers acquire proficiency in any language easily, but find it difficult to understand what their girl friends have in their hearts.

Here the authors are reminded of the following Sanskrit proverb

"Avarshnam athi varshanamsha

(Sh)threnaamsha sitham

Purush'sha baagyam

Theivo na janaathi

Kutho manushya". (In Sanskrit)

The above lines are translated into English as follows

Even the Angels (divine or from the Above) cannot predict scarcity out of no rain or extremity of rain, the thoughts in the inner minds of a woman and the day that favours a man.

- **Don Pedro:.........................here's no true drop of**

  **blood in him, to be truly touched with love.**

(He must be a traitor, if he is in love.)

He is a renowned blood donor, but not even a single drop of his blood is touched with love.

(Boy: I will donate my blood for you.

Girl: But the cells of love in my blood will get lost.)

("Blood is thicker than water" is a proverb in English.)

Only his blood is positive. (Can we mean that he is negative?)

Every drop of my blood is truly touched with love, but no blood test reveals that.

There is not even an iota of love in his blood, which now is badly in need of dialysis.

- **Don Pedro: There is no appearance of fancy inhim**

(outward appearance)

I like you because there is no appearance of fancy in you.

His appearance is good, but of fancy.

That appearance of fancy helps many frauds come up in life is really unfortunate.

I wish to marry a person with no appearance of fancy.

She has her own appearance on the screen, behind the screen, on the stage and off the stage.

* **Dogberry :** ...............................................tobe a well-favoured

**man is the gift of fortune, but to write and read comes by nature.**

(To be a man with good features is the gift of fortune, but to write and read is the gift of nature.)

He has not been gifted with the gift of writing effectively and meaningfully, but with the gift of whatever he writes being read by a number of readers.

Man considers himself the gift of fortune, among all creatures, but all creatures except man are not able to express their views.

I do not know whether I am a well-favoured man or ill-favoured man, but I must be a man.

* **Borachio:** ...............................................**when rich villains have**

**need of poor ones, poor ones may make what price they will.**

(When rich villains need the services of the poor, the poor ones may demand whatever price they want.)

Money makes everything and it makes a hero a villain and a villain a hero.

Money is in my hand and how I spend it is in my mind.

When money is available with villains, it increases villainy deeds.

It is time for you to make what price you will, as rich villains are in need of your services.

He is a rich villain, but poor hero.

It is money that makes any dance to anybody's tune.

- **Claudio: You seem to me as Dian in her orb.**

  **As chaste as is the bud ere it be blown;**
  **But you are more intemperate in your blood**
  **Than Venus, or those pamper'd animals**
  **That rage in savage sensuality.**

(You seem to be as chaste as the moon in her orbit and as pure as the bud before it gets blossomed. But you are more lustfulin your blood than even Venus or thosepampered animals that rage in savage sensuality. )

Her very appearance makes him more intemperatethan Venus.

He is as Dian in his orb and as chaste as the bud before it is blown, but becomes more intemperate than Venus whenever he is swayed by the extreme heat of the sun.

Are you an animal to rage in savage sensuality?

My mind is as chaste as the bud, but my tongue is as polluted as mud filled with filth.

(Judge: Even if your blood is dialyzed, it is of no use.

Rapist: Why, your Honour?

Judge: Venus lives in every drop of your blood. It is advisable for you meet a psychiatrist.)

I could feel the presence of Venus in every drop of his blood, whenever his eyes are focused/ fixed on any beautiful girl.

- **Don John: ...............There is no chastity enough in language...**

(vulgar language)

Once Tamilaruvi Maniyan, a great writer in Tamil said, " Dress your words when you use them. Naked words might hurt others".

Chastity is in the use of language is the indication of chastity in culture.

Though he is a waste, his language is chaste.

It is not knowledge of grammar that makes one's language chaste, but culture.

He has enough knowledge of languages, but he has scarcity of chastity.

He is not able to impress anyone with his costly dresses, because his words are naked.

Though he is too poor to buy some dress, people respect him, for every word of his is well-dressed.

Chastity in thoughts results in chastity in language.

Chaste language reflects one's culture.

- **Beatrice: ................O God! That I were a man, I would eat**

  **his heart in the market-place.**

(Angry man: I will eat his heart in the market place.

Friend: Not at all possible

Angry man: Why?

Friend: He has no heart at all. )

The police are so angry with the accused that they, if caught, would eat his heart in front of the police station.

The innocent girl says, "If I think of eating his heart in anger, can I get back my heart as it was?. It is all my fate".

The new rowdy plans to become No 1 rowdy by eating every rowdy's heart in the market place.

Tutu was man a man with a single good heart, but now by eating someone's heart in the market place, he has become a beast.

The Romeo of our street needs more hearts to win more hearts.

- **Beatrice: ...............................manhood is melted into**

  **curtesies, valour into compliment, and men are only turned**
  **into**

  **tongue, and trim ones too: he is now as valiant as Hercules,**
  **that only tells a lie and swears it, I cannot be a man with**

**wishing, therefore I will die a woman with grieving.**

(Manhood is melted into curtesies, valour into compliment and men are turned into talkers with their tongues being smooth too; he is now as valiant as Hercules telling a lie and swearing it. As I cannot be a man, I will die a womanwith grief. )

Hercules, according to Greek mythology, is a Roman hero noted for his strength and valour which his father Zeus also was noted for. Hercules is famous not only for his strength and valour, but also for his numerous far-ranging adventures.

(Dad: I consider Ron a suitable match for you, as he is as strong as Hercules.

Daughter: Am I going to prove my strength in my married life, dad?

Dad: He would protect you in danger.

Daughter: What would be my fate, if your Hercules became Koalemos or Hades or Aporia?

Let me marry a person like Cupid (Eros), as one needs love in life.

Dad: Though it is difficult, I shall try my best, my daughter. )

(Koalemos is the god of stupidity, Hades, the god of the dead and Aporia the god of want, difficulty and powerlessness. Cupid otherwise called Eros is the god of love. )

(Friend 1: What do you think of me?

Friend 2: You are a Hercules everywhere, except while talking with your wife. )

Some politicians go out with Herculeses as they are afraid of nearing the common people.

(Friend 1:Better to die a woman with groans than to live a man with wishes.

Friend 2: Better to die a husband grieving than to live with a wife wishing. )

- **Leonato: ...............My brother hath a daughter**

**Almost the copy of my child that's dead**

"As is the king so are the subjects" is a proverb in English.

As is the father so is his daughter.

Vineeth is the chip of the old block. – He has the characteristics of his father.

His pain of having lost his beloved mother is getting relieved, on seeing his beloved daughter, almost the copy of his mother.

He is almost the copy of his father not only in words, but also in deeds.

- **Benedick:Thy wit is as quick as the greyhound's mouth;**

  **it catches.**
  **Margaret: And yours as blunt as the fencer's foils, which**
  **Hit, but hurt not.**

(Your wit is as quick as the greyhound's mouth. It hits as quickly as the greyhound catches its victim.

And yours is as blunt as the fencer's blunt sword, which hits but does not hurt.)

A greyhound might miss its prey, but I never my quick wit.

Your wit is as blunt as the fencer's foils. It hits, but not hurts.

His wit is as quick as the greyhound's mouth, but his sister's is quicker than a greyhound's mouth.

- **Benedick: ..................I was not born under a rhyming planet,**
  **nor I**

  **cannot woo in festival terms.**

Any girl that talks with him falls easily intohis verbal trap and I think that he might have been born under a rhyming planet.

Bharati's poems are so beautiful that he might have been born under a rhyming planet.

As he cannot woo her in festival terms, he has kept his currency pockets open.

He uses words as if he were born under a rhyming planet.

Peter says to his girl friend, "Please believe what I say and accept my love. To further convince you, I was neither born under a rhyming planet, nor blessed with the special skills of wooing in festival terms".

Were I born under a rhyming planet, I would fill her heart with innumerable rhymes.

Only while wooing, he speaks rhymes as if he were born under a rhyming planet.

His rhyming planet has not attracted even a single star so far.

He is neither born under a rhyming planet, nor woos in festival terms, but wins hearts easily.

- **Benedick: .............to be the trumpet of his own virtues,**

Some of us delight in trumpeting own virtues.

Some of us trumpet own virtues in order to hide vices.

Some politicians have made it their habit to deliver rodomontade speeches.

When one trumpets one's virtues too much, too much of his/her vices come to light.

He has trumpeted his own virtues till his trumpet got damaged.

When he trumpets his own virtues, his own brother trumpets his vices.

(Here the authors wish to share with the readers how Mr Kamarajar, former Chief Minister of Tamil Nadu honestly acknowledged his defeat in his own constituency. During some state election, he was nominated as a candidate in his own constituency, Virthunagar, Tamil Nadu against the DMK candidate Mr P.Seenivasan, but quite surprisingly Mr Kamaraj lost the election. Among politicians, who, after being defeated in election by a margin of more than two lakhs and even more, take pride in saying that they had lost by a very narrow margin, it was Mr

Kamaraj, who honestly said, "People have defeated me and I have lost the seat", in spite of the fact that his opponent had won just with a margin of only 1285 votes more than him. Kamarajar never trumpeted his virtues and so people trumpet his real virtues even after his death. Great leaders live even after their deaths. His simplicity made all recognize him as Gandhiji of the South India. )

- **Claudio:...........Death,...................**

**Gives her fame which never dies.**
**So the life that died with shame**
**Lives in death with glorious fame**

(We have heard of birth with glorious fame and life with gloriousfame. But death with glorious fame makes one live after death. J.B.S.Haldane in his "What I Require From Life" highlights his requirements in life. J.B.S.Haldane says, "Of all men whose deaths are recorded, I consider that Socrates' was the most enviable. He died for his convictions when he could easily have survived by betraying them. He died at the age of seventy, still in full possession of his faculties, but having completed all the work which he could reasonably hope to do. And he died laughing. His last words were a joke". )

Birth is the messenger of death.

"When death comes to the seeker of knowledge whilst he is in that state (of seeking knowledge), he dies as a martyr". (al-Targhib wa-al-Taehib V.1.,p.97,No:16)

"When a man dies, his good deeds come to an end, except three; ongoing charity, beneficial knowledge and a righteous son, who prays for him". (Sahib Muslim, 3084)

(One of the Tamil actors and directors K.Baagyaraj while answering a reader's question in his magazine 'Baagya' about fear of death answered as follows

Do not fear Death. It won't come to you as long as you live. When it comes to you, you won't be alive. So do not fear Death.)

Even Karl Marx, the great materialist, was broken when his beloved wife passed away. (241)

To leave a gashing wound

"Lives of great men all remind us

We can make our lives sublime,

And, departing, leave behind us

Footprints on the sands of time". -Longfellow (245)

"Out, out brief candle!

Life's but a walking shadow, a poor player,

That struts and frets his hour upon the stage,

And there is heard no more; it is a tale

Told by an idiot, full of sound and fury

Signifying nothing". - Shakespeare in Macbeth

"I know that the day will come when my sight of this earth shall be lost, and life will take its leaves in silence, drawing the last curtain over my eyes". Gitanjali (76)

# CHAPTER EIGHT

# AS YOU LIKE IT

- **Orlando: ...................................................there begins my**

  **sadness..................................................................**
  **.................speaks goldenly of his profit..............**
  **..............to mutiny against this servitude**

(goldenly- in terms of highest praise)

To mutiny- to rebel

Servitude- slavery

It is sad that he is sad, but it is sadder that he makes others saddest.

(Doctor: When did your husband's sadness begin?

Lady: After his taking the food that I prepared, sir.

Doctor: Ok.. it must be food poison. )

Sadness may begin, trouble, but should not stay back.

It is sadness that makes one know the value of happiness.

None can predict when life brings one joy or sorrow.

He speaks goldenly of his wife.

Nivetha speaks goldenly of her husband whenever she goes with him to jewellery shops.

The officers mutinied against the new policies of the Govt.

He won't mutiny against this servitude, because he considers life more peaceful in chains than in crowns.

- **Oliver: Know you where you are, sir?**

You must know where you are standing now.
Destination is invisible to the ambitious.
She speaks very rudely, as she does not know where she is.
Some of the young students know neither where they are nor where they go.
The arrogant lady knows where every one is, but never cares to know where she is.

- **Orlando: ....................I would not take this hand from thy**

**throat till this other had pulled out thy tongue for**
**saying so;**

The politician said to the reporters, "Why are you pulling out my tongue for my answers to your questions?".
The police did not take their hands from the throat of the accused till they had got the truths about the murder case.
The teacher was pulled out from the job, as she pulled out the tongues of students for not answering her questions.
The girl said to the boy, "You want me to pull out my tongue for not talking to you?".
Even if her tongue were pulled, she would borrow tongue from someone in order to shout at her mother-in-law.

- **Oliver: ....................................you old dog;**

**Adam: Is "Old dog" my reward? Most true, I have lost my**
**teeth in your service.**

(Underdog- Someone at a disadvantage
Go to the dogs- go astray, go downhill)
A dog in the manger- Someone who neither enjoys anything nor lets others enjoy anything.

Am I a dog to be kept at your gate?

I do not mind being an old or even a street dog, but I do not want to lose my teeth in your service.

Balu says to his arrogant son, "This old dog did not lose its teeth by biting tasty bones, but in your service".

An uncared and unattended old father says to his rich son, "I supported you on all occasions, as long as I was an active dog. I was never a biting dog, but only an active dog barking, wagging tail in all directions for getting you your bread and barking at every office for getting you a job. Now I have become for you not only an old dog, but also an unwanted dog. I have lost my teeth, my eyes, my health out of my fatherly love".

• **Charles: ..........never two ladies loved as they do.**

Do two men love as they do?

Mother-in-law and daughter-in-law are proud of being poles apart.

The two ladies love each other when they go out, but awfully fight at home.

They are ladies outside, but at home they become cats and dogs.

Life with two wives has made him a saint.

• **Charles: .......................................there they**

**live like the old Robin Hood of England;**

(To lead a merry life in the woods like Robin Hood did in England in the olden days)

I am not the Robin Hood of England to live happily here.

I led my life like the old Robin Hood of England before marriage, but Robin Hood is only in name after marriage. (Old Robin Hood of England left me after my marriage.)

He had dreams of living like the Robin Hood of England after marriage, but I think Robin Hood could not bless him.

She is experiencing all sorts of tortures at the hands of her drunken husband, but she talks to her parents as if she were living with the old Robin Hood of England.

- **Oliver: .... .he will practise against thee**

  **by poison, entrap thee by some treacherous**
  **device, and never leave thee till he hath ta'en**
  **means or other;**

(Parents: Why do you demand such a huge amount for seeking alliance for our daughter?

Marriage broker: You want my free service?

Parents: Yes, of course

Marriage broker: You don't mind, if any boy I bring practises against your daughter by poison, entrap her by some treacherous device and never leaves her till he takes her life by some indirect means or other?

Parents: Please have our Debit and Credit cards at your own disposal.)

Many politicians entrap people with incredible promises.

There are many Romeos and Juliets entrapping each other with sweet lies uttered in sweeter language in sweetest words.

He need not get poison anywhere, but he has a tongue that is more poisonous than poison.

He has entrapped his girl friend with his honey-tongue.

- **Oliver: .....................................he's gentle, never**

  **schooled and yet learned full of noble device, of**
  **all sorts enchantingly beloved and indeed so much**
  **in the heart of the world and especially of my**
  **own people who best know him,.................**

Mr Kamarajar former Chief Minister of Tamil Nadu, though not schooled, was an appreciable administrator. He is still in the hearts of all those who best know him.

Those who think of the world will be thought of by the world.

It is really a pity that my own people do not know me.

Everyone knows him, except his girl friend.

Those who know her best will avoid her best.

She looks like an angel, but she is a ghost.

- **Rosalind: ....................Fortune reigns in gifts of the world,**

**not in the lineaments of Nature.**

(lineament- a distinctive feature that characterizes something)

Fortune does not reign in him, but he reigns in fortunes, though he is intellectually an absolute zero.

Ho wishes to own fortune that reign in gifts of the world, not in the lineaments of Nature.

"This is a poor man's house where fortune never reigns in gifts of the world", says the man.

Both Fortune and Nature forsake the poor on many occasions.

He has become lazy under the roof of Fortune and Nature

- **Celia: ...........................................always the**

**dullness of the fool is the whetstone of the wits.**

(whetstone- stimulant, tool, benchmark)

In politics, the weakness of people is the strength of politicians.

The so-called wits consider the physical weakness of others 'dullness of fools'.

You are the only so called wise man in our village and so very conveniently you have converted all our foolish dullness into wisdom.

"Be a fool, so that I can be wish" is his only policy.

Dullness, innocence and weakness of people are converted into votes at the time of elections. We can shout out of joy that "Democracy is a success" for our safe survival.

- **Celia:** .............................................**in the great heap of your**

**knowledge?**

He tells her that he had lost senses in the great heap of her beauty.

He gave his consent to marry her at the very sight of the great heap of the wealth of her father.

I love you neither because of the great heap of your wealth nor because of the great heap of the political power of your father, but because of the great heap of love that I have for you.

I had on him the great heap of confidence, but he has cheated me in all the possible ways.

Is it the great heap of your knowledge that has made you insult your own parents and teachers?

There is absolutely no any good virtue in his great heap of knowledge.

- **Touchstone:** ...................................**fools may not speak wisely**

**what wise men do foolishly.**

A wise man's day is worth a fool's life- An Arabian proverb

What is the difference between 'wisdom' and 'knowledge'?

A knowledgeable person may or may not be wise and a wise person may or may not be knowledgeable.

Knowledge- the fact of knowing about something; general understanding or familiarity with a subject, place, situation etc,

Wisdom- the ability to make a decision based on the combination of knowledge, experience and intuitive understanding.

We generally rank the best by the worst performance and the best by the worst performance.

"Everyone considers himself or herself the best and so the world is full of the worst". –Dr Johnson

(When two rich business magnets were once talking about their own servants in a casual conversation, one of them said that his servant was the most foolish and received similar comment from the other on his servant. They wanted to prove who the more foolish was between the two servants. The first business magnet called his servant, gave him Rs 10 and asked him to buy him a car. He obliged and left. After his leaving, the business magnet said to his friend, "See! I told you that my servant was most foolish. He is going to buy me a car for Rs 10". The second magnet called his servant and said to him, "Go to my house and find out whether I am there or not". He obliged and left. After his leaving, the second business magnet said to his friend, "See! I told you about the utter foolishness of my servant". Meanwhile, these two servants met at the market place and made comments on the foolishness of their bosses. The first servant said, "My boss is a fool. He wants to me to buy him a car for Rs 10. How can I buy it today?. He does not know that Sunday is a holiday". (He thought only of the day being a holiday, not of the amount being too small for anyone to buy a car.). The other servant said, "Your boss is better than my boss. My boss has a mobile phone. He could have called his wife on phone and asked her about his availability at home".)

(Once someone approached a wise man of his town and asked him who the wisest in the world was and got the reply "Socrates". He travelled a long and met Socrates and asked him whether he was the wisest in the world. Socrates said, "You are wrong. I am a fool". He got confused, came back to the wise man of his town and said to him, "You say that Socrates is the wisest in the world, but he says that he is a fool". The wise man said, "That was why I said that Socrates was the wisest".)

Knowledge and wisdom should not make one proud or arrogant.

It is bad that fools are not permitted to make wise remarks on the foolish deeds of the wise.

These words and deeds, though foolish, are valued high, as they are from the alleged wise mouth.

He is a fool, but speaks wisely.

He is wise, but speaks foolishly.

Better to be a fool than to be a snake in the grass.


- **Celia:** ............................................................**the little**


**wit that fools have was silenced, the little foolery
that wise men have makes a great show.**


Wit, though great, if of a fool, goes waste in the street, but a little wit, though not great, if from a wise, is preserved as a treasure.

There are many, though neither wise, nor foolish, who enjoy all privileges by means of JUST luck.

Fools suppress the little wisdom they have and the little folly the wise have becomes noticeable.

Fools succeed in making a great show of their deeds and the wise miserably fail to do so.

The wise never learn the art of making shows.

No one knows how to measure wisdom and foolery.

A wise man's little foolery is more tomtomed than a fool's Himalayan blunder.


- **Rosalind: With his mouth full of news.**


There is a great demand for this servant maid, as her mouth is full of news.

His mouth is full of news, all unreliable, but enjoyable.

(Housewife: I need a servant maid.

Husband: What do you expect of her?

Housewife: Nothing, but just a mouth full of news. )

I wonder whether her mouth was made for news.

Your mouth is full of news of which nothing is important.

- **Orlando: ..........................punish me not with hard thoughts,**

  **...........................let your fair eyes and
  gentle wishes go with me to my trial;**

Beat me with rods, but not with words.
   "Theeyinaar chutta pun vullarum-aarathey
   Naavinaar chutta vadu"-Kural (Tamil)
   "In flesh of fire inflamed, nature may thoroughly heal the sore,
   In soul by tongue inflamed, the ulcer health never more". –Kural
in English (Translated by G.U.Pope)
   Your face betrays your hard thoughts.
   He is hard in appearance, but not in thoughts and words.
   She, though experienced and aged, is soft neither in thoughts,
nor in words.
   Let your fair eyes and gentle wishes come with me.
   May I on me have your fair eyes and gentle wishes?
   Your fair eyes are only on your family, not on the society.
   He is gentle only in appearance, but not in his thoughts and
wishes.

- **Orlando: ..............must I from the smoke into the smother,**

   (From the frying pan to the fire)
   (To pass from bad to worse, from the edge of the fire into fire
itself.)
   I shall no more with the smother, as I have enough of my smoke.
   He jumps from the smoke into the smother.
   One does not jump from the smoke into the smother for smooth
survival.
   It is his teen age that leads him from the smoke into the smother.

- **Celia: ..........thy words are too precious to be cast away**

   **upon curs;**

Your words are far too valuable to be wasted on dogs.

My precious words might have been cast away upon curs rather than upon these living curses.

You are wasting your advice on curs.

These curs do not deserve to have your precious words.

Why should you waste your most precious words upon these worthless curs?

- **Rosalind: Treason is not inherited,..............**

Treason is not hereditary by liege.

He was imprisoned on charges of high treason.

I do not know whom he inherited high treason from.

Parents must be role models so that children would inherit all good qualities from them.

- **Rosalind: Beauty provoketh thieves sooner than gold.**

(Once there was a debate over the number of words used to express the same idea in Tamil and English. An expert in English said, "Beauty provoketh thieves sooner than gold. There are only six words". The expert in Tamil responded saying, "Ponninum kalvanai pozhivu theendum. There are only four words.)

Each language has its own beauty. Languages can be beautifully, but not venomously.

Is there any lady provoked neither by beauty nor by gold?

What provokes one more?-Beauty? Or Gold?

Nature provokes poets sooner than gold or currency.

Power provokes politicians (not statesmen and leaders) than anything else on earth.

- **First Lord: ...................................velvet friends,**

...................................misery doth part

**The flux of company.**

(Velvet friends- prosperous friends / soft-footed companions)

All his velvet friends forsook him, when the Court found him guilty.

Trouble has a remarkable power of driving friends away.

Friendship only with velvet friends has changed his total life style.

It is misery and misfortune that make one know the value of friendship.

All my friends who were born with silver spoons in mouths left me when misfortunes embraced me, but you were with me, though you were too poor to buy even a spoon for your bread.

Misery parts the flux of company.

The govt officer said, "I will admit my son in a school where he can get only velvet friends".

- **Duke Seniro: .............................he is full of matter**

He is full of matter, not of any manner.

You are full of matter that means and matters nothing.

What is the use of your being full of matter, when you do not love your father and mother?.

Tough Somu seems illiterate, he is full of matter.

Suman is full of matter, but if he opens his mouth and says something, there is absolutely no matter at all.

- **Adam: Their graces serve them but as enemies?**

He is gracious to all, but grace has no grace on him.

I have been gracious since my childhood, but grace has served me as my enemy.

I need none's grace, but God's.

He is not gracious, but grace serves him as a friend.

Her knowledge serves her but destructively.

- **Adam: .............................this house is but a butchery**

   **Abhor it, fear it, do not enter it.**

My house is neither a godown nor a butchery for you to get away.

The daughter-in-law says, "My house is like a temple, but my mother-in-law's house is a butchery. I shall abhor it and fear it, but I am destined to enter it".

The mother-in-law sincerely thanked her daughter-in-law for her having successfully converted her house into a butchery. The daughter-in-law replied that it was her duty and pleasure too.

It is a woman who makes her house a temple or a butchery.

Peter says that he would become a butcher if he enters this house.

"My husband's company with bottles has converted my house into a butchery", says the poor woman.

- **Adam: Though I look old, yet I am strong and lusty**

   **For in my youth I never did apply**
   **Hot and rebellious liquors in my blood,**
   **Nor did not with unbashful forehead woo**
   **..............................................................................**
   **I'll do the service of a younger man**
   **In all your business and necessities.**

Gohul is old, but lusty and his son is young, but not lusty.

bashful- not liking to be noticed

They said to the old lady, "How do you carry your unbashful face after ill-treating all your colleagues?".

He is very young, but he has hot and rebellious liquor in his blood.

I am at your disposal in all your business and necessities.

They are young couple, but they remind us of Adam and Eve when they share their sins.

All Adams and Eves do not wish to share their sins.

The professor says, "I trusted the serpent and so I have lost my Eve".

"In my house, my Eve is more poisonous than a serpent", says John

- **Touchstone: .........................................as all is**

**mortal in nature so is all nature in love mortal in folly**

Even the immortal is viewed mortal by lovers.

"All if fair in love and war" is a proverb.

He has sacrificed his wisdom to win her love.

The father says, "My son's sixth son was in coma as long as he was in love with the unworthy girl".

- **Celia: .........................................I like this place,**

**And willingly could waste my time in it.**

I like to purchase a lot in the busy streets of Paris and willingly could spend my time in it.

I like even a desert and willingly spend my time there, but If left with my lover.

There are some who willingly waste time by gossiping and unwillingly spend time by working.

When the son and the daughters of the present days are willingly wasting their time on mobile phones, the parents of the past days are unwillingly wasting their time, watching them and yearning to talk to them willingly.

- **Orlando: .........................................thou shalt not die for**

**Lack of a dinner,.........................**

(Officer: Finish all your works and go for lunch.

Attender: Sir, I have too many butterflies in my stomach.

Officer: You will not die for lack of a lunch.

Attender: Sorry sir, I will finish all works now.

Officer: Carry on, I will have my lunch and come. )

"As long as you are hungry, you cannot do anything worthwhile"-Swami Vivekananda


- **Duke Senior: I think he be transformed into a beast,**

  **For I can nowhere find him like a man.**

I think the old arrogant lady must have inherited her vices from some creature worse than a wild beast, because I can nowhere find a cruel administrator like her.

The girl's love with a boy of some other caste has transformed her father into a beast.

(No beast expects any man to become a man.)

(Is there any beast that has any extra belly?

Is there any beast that delights in the misfortunes of others?

Is there any beast that hurts the feelings of others?

Is there any beast that fights with others in the name of caste, colour and religion?

Is there any beast that is mad after power, position and wealth?

Is there any beast that drives away aged beasts?

Is there any beast that loves and forsakes?

Is there any beast that complains of failures and disappointments?

Is there any beast that commits suicide?

Is there any beast that has more than five senses?)


- **Duke Senior: ...............................Your gentleness shall force**

  **More than your force move us to gentleness.**

(You will find mildness a stronger compelling force than this show of compulsion in moving us to kindness.)

Your kindness forces me to attend your daughter's marriage, but my situation prevents me from doing so.

My mind is willing to attend the programme, but my body?

It is your gentleness that has made even the ungentle around you gentle.

One cannot be beaten to move towards gentleness.


- **Jaques: All the world's a stage,**

  And all the men and women merely players,
  They have their exits and entrances
  And one man in his time plays many parts,
  His acts being seven ages. At first, the infant,
  Mewling and puking in the nurse's arms:
  And then, the whining school boy with his satche!
  And shining morning face, creeping like snail
  Unwillingly to school. And then the lover,
  Sighing like furnace, with a woeful ballad
  Made to his mistress' eye-brow. Then a soldier,
  Full of strange oaths and bearded like the pard
  Jealous in honour sudden and quick in quarrel
  Seeking the bubble reputation
  Even in the cannon's mouth! And then, the justice,
  In fair round belly with good capon lined,
  With eyes severe, and beard of formal cut
  Full of wise saws, and modern in instances,
  And so he plays his part. The sixth age shifts.
  Into the lean and slippered pantaloon,
  With spectacles on nose, and pouch on side,
  His youthful hose, well saved, a world too wide
  For his shrunk shank; and his big manly voice,
  Turning again toward childish treble, pipes

**And whistles in his sound. Last scene of all.**
**That ends this strange eventful history,**
**Is second childishness, and mere oblivion**
**Sans teeth, sans eyes, sans taste, sans everything**


(Wife: You show me too much love and affection, you love me so much, my dear?

Husband: Life is a stage and I am an excellent actor.)

We fail miserably to understand others, is it because many around us are just acting?

Life for everyone has its exits and entrances.

Everyone enters life as an innocent and ignorant baby, leads life as person of omnipotence, omnipresence and omniscience, but becomes a saint at the time of exit.

Many play many parts in life, but a few remember their entrances, and are aware of their exits.

(Tom: Hi! Peter, why is your grandmother always angry with your grandfather?

Peter: He has become very old, but still he loves to mewl and puke in the nurse's arms.)

(Note: The seven stages of human life are beautifully describes by William Shakespeare here.)

Death is the last page of one's life history, isn't it?

Birth is the Messenger of Death.

Old age makes one childlike and so parents must be treated like children and loved like children.

('sans' means 'without') without teeth, without eyes, without taste, without everything)

There can be, at old age in particular, parents sans teeth, sans teeth, sans taste, sans everything, but not sans care and concern, that too by own children, can't it?

(Police officer: Why complaint against your own husband?

Wife: I can live without teeth, without eyes, without taste, without everything, but I cannot live with a husband who is always in a state of intoxication.)

- **Duke Senior: ............................., to question you about your fortunes.**

Why do you question me about my fortunes now, when my misfortunes once drowned **you in** fortunes?

One seeks one's fortunes by asking the fortunate questions about their fortunes.

By asking you questions about someone's fortunes, one cannot convert one's misfortunes into fortunes.

She says to him, "Only after your questioning me about my fortunes, all misfortunes became my uninvited guests".

Your questions about my fortune raise in my mind questions about your fortunes.

- **Corin: ...........................he that hath learned no wit by nature,**

**nor art, may complain of good breeding, or comes**
**of a very dull kindred.**

(A man without common sense, either natural or acquired, has either been very badly educated, or is commonly slow and stupid by nature.)

He has no wit even by nature.

He uses his natural wit unnaturally.

His wit is both natural and acquired.

His wit, though not natural, is acquired.

His wit, though not acquired, is natural.

He has made use of his natural wit only till his retirement.

He is slow by nature, but not a stupid.

- **Celia: O wonderful, wonderful, and most wonderful**

**wonderful and yet again wonderful, and after**
**that out of all whooping.**

(Very remarkable, most astoundingly remarkable, and even more remarkable than that, for my powers of expression entirely fail.)

(Girl friend: Am I good looking?

Boy friend: You.......your beauty....... wonderful, wonderful, and most wonderful

Wonderful and yet again wonderful, and after that out of my whooping.)

My tongue verbally fails to aptly describe your beauty.

I wish my eyes had the power of speaking, so that it describes whatever it swallows from your eyes as marks of beauty.

Can I borrow a rhymed tongue from someone to describe her beauty?

Only my power of expression fails, but, indeed, not my love.

- **Rosalind: ....................................Time travels in divers paces,**

    **with divers persons. I'll tell you who Time**
    **ambles withal who Times trote withal, who Time**
    **gallops withal, and who he stands still withal.**

(Time has a variety of spaces, and suits each to the individual with whom he travels. He gently jogs along like an ambling horse with some, and with others he breaks into a sharp trot, and yet again, with others he travels with the speed of a racehorse, and with a few he does not move at all. )

"Time and tide wait for none" is a proverb.

Is sleep the enemy of time?

Is laziness the enemy of time?

I wish to recruit for my companies the candidates with whom time gently jogs along like an ambling horse, not those with whom time does not move at all.

He says to her, "It is quite strange that time gently jogs along like an ambling horse, whenever I am on chat with you, but it does not move at all, whenever my professor is lecturing".

- **Rosalind: ......are you so much in love as your rhymes speak?**

  **Orlando: Neither rhyme not reason can express how much.**

His love for her girl friend is strong only in his rhymes.

She fell into his love of rhymes without knowing that he is a rowdy.

In love, many times rhymes block the sixth sense.

She is behind all my rhymes.

The boy says, "I have given her my every reason in rhymes and I hope she would accept my love with no reason".

I do not want your rhymes or reasons, but your love.

Before marriage, rhymes and reasons bring two hearts together, but after marriage, truths break them.

Rhymes are sweeter to hear as long as love remains in hearts.

His love for her began with rhymes, but broke with reasons.

I cannot purchase rhymes or reasons from any one to express my love for you, as I am not academically and poetically so blessed. I can just say that I love you.

- **Touchstone: .........................the truest poetry is the most feigning,**

  **and lovers are given to poetry; and what they swear**
  **in poetry, may be said, as lovers, they do feign.**

(Here we are reminded of Andrew Marvell's "To His Coy Mistress", aren't we?

Here are a few lines from the poem;

"My vegetable love should grow

Vaster than empires.................

..........................................................

And the last age should show your heart.

..............................................................

Time's winged chariot hurrying near;

..................................................
Thy beauty shall no more be found;
.............................then worms shall try
That long-preserved virginity.
And your quaint honour turn to dust,
And into ashes all my lust;..................)".
Poetry fosters lovers.

Love is mostly carried through poetry, isn't it? Lovers are given (handed over) to poetry.

(It is really mortifying when poetry is not comprehended.)

I can propose my love in prose, not in poetry. Development of my poetic skills lies either in your depth of love for me or in my death without your love for me.

Not his appearance, but his poetry made her fall into his trap.

Prose becomes poetry while in deep love, doesn't it?

It is said that prose in tears is poetry.

- **Touchstone: honesty coupled to beauty is to have honey a**

  **sauce to sugar**

(Virtue combined with beauty is as overpowering as honey and sugar.)

(Boy: You are beautiful, but not honest in love.

Girl: You are handsome, but not honest in vows.

Boy: You mean to say that both of us are not honest?

Girl: ...........yes

Boy: Shakespeare says that honesty coupled to beauty is to have a sauce to sugar.

Girl: Does honey need sugar? Is it not nauseating?)

- **Celia: "Was" is not "is"; besides, the oath of a lover is**

  **no stronger than the word of a tapster; they are**
  **both the confirmer of false reckonings.**

(Boy: My love for you **IS** true.

Girl: Will this **IS** become **WAS** after marriage?

(Boy: My English teacher has told me that I am wrong in the use of past tense.

Girl: You may be wrong in using past tense, but I hope not in the past.)

The girl says to the boy, "I just ignore your dark past. Trusting my future, I hand over to you my present".

Tapster is someone whose business is to tap or draw ale or other liquor.

Believe me. He is strong in his oaths, not in his love for you.

He delights in breaking both his oaths and love.

- **Celia: ……………………………He writes brave verses,**

   **speaks brave words swears brave oaths and breaks them bravely,……………………………………**

His love is not as brave as his verses.

He is brave in words, not in deeds.

The politician, while swearing in, bravely swore brave oaths, but bravely broke all oaths and the Judge bravely sent him to prison under the custody of a brave police officer.

He swears oaths bravely and publicly, but breaks them silently.

Bravery is not in words, but in deeds.

- **Silvius: Say that you love me not, but say not so**

   **In bitterness.**

If you do not love me, tell me, but not in bitter words.

Do you think that love perishes by bitter words?

I proposed my love in kind words, but my proposal was rejected in bitter words.

Love sweetly proposed by his heart was bitterly disposed by her tongue.

He says to her girl friend, "Say that you love me, but say not that you will marry me".

• **Silvius: You meet in some fresh cheek thepower of fancy**

   **Then shall you know the wounds invisible**
   **That love's keen arrows make.**

(When some bright face causes you to know the pain of love-sickness, you learn by experience the pain and agony caused by the imperceptible wounds made by the sharp arrows of love. )

The wounds caused by failure in love are more wounding than the wounds made by the sharp-pointed swords.

He looks fresh every time he proposes his love to every girl he comes across, but hides his wounds that every time he receives when every time his proposal is rejected.

My love is visible, but my wounds..............

My profound love for you has received nothing but wounds beyond heal.

He was honoured on the Valentine's Day for having received maximum wounds in maximum failures in love.

Wounds may vanish, but love?

• **Rosalind: .......... I am falser than vows made in wine.**

   (At the first cup, man drinks wine;

   At the second cup, wine drinks man

   And at the third cup, wine drinks man- Krishna Iyer, former Supreme Court Judge)

   (In Tamil, "Kudiharan pechu vidinja pochi" is a proverb about a drunkard's vows)

   A drunkard's vows in intoxication vanish in darkness.

   Vows made in wine cannot be taken for granted.

Do not trust his words of honey, for his words are falser than vows made in wine.

He speaks something when his tongue is in glass, but speaks something else when it is out of glass.

Whenever wine is in, wit is out.

- **Phebe: I love him not, nor hate him not; and yet**

  **I have more causes to hate him thanto love him:**
  **................................omittance is no quittance.**

Can you give me just one reason to hate me, if you do not have any reason to love me?

I neither love him, nor hate him, but just look at him, as I may either love him orhate him tomorrow.

Ijust quit, but not omit your heart.

I have more causes to love you than to hate you.

I have reasons neither to love you nor to hate you, but I have to marry you.

- **Jaques: I have neither the scholar's melancholy, which is**

  **emulation, nor the musician's, which is fantastical,**
  **nor the courtier's which is proud, nor the**
  **soldier's which is ambitious, nor the lawyer's, which**
  **is politic, nor the lady's, which is nice nor the**
  **lover's which is all these............. But it is a melancholy**
  **of mine own,**

(My melancholy is not that of a student, which is due to his longing to be the first scholar of the day, nor that of a musician, whose genius renders him fanciful and irritable. It is not the reserved hauteur of the courtier, neither is it the morose gloom of the dissatisfied, ambitious soldier. It does not resemble the professional gravity of the astute lawyer, which makes such an impression on his clients, nor the whimsical sadness of the lady; neither is it akin to the extreme depression of the lover which has much in common with all the rest. It is a melancholy quite peculiar to myself. )

My neighbour is a combination of a scholar's melancholy, a musician's fantasy, a courtier's pride, a soldier's bravery and a child's innocence.

Be brave when you are a soldier, be innocent when you are a child, be focused when you are a learner, be a learner when you are a teacher, be honest when you are a judge and be loving when are a mother and be caring when you are a father.

The boy says, "I am a great lover because I am a great liar".

There can be someone with only virtues, someone with only vices or someone with both virtues and vices.

- **Rosalind:** .................................................**I had rather**

   **have a fool to make me merry, than experience to
   make me sad;**

Better to be cheered by the foolish talk of a clown than to be saddened by wise experiences.

Sometimes we get wise experiences in the company of fools.

The boy says, "I would prefer to listen to foolish stories to listen to wise counsel".

He was quite normal as long as he was in the company of fools, but the entry of a single wise man in his life has made him abnormal and more confused than he was ever before.

- **Rosalind:** .............................**speak first, and when you**

   **were gravelled for lack of matter, you might take
   occasion to kiss. Very good orators, when they
   are out, they will spit, and for lovers, lacking
   (God warn us) matter, the cleanliest shift is to
   kiss.**

(Talk to her first and kiss her next because kissing would do well for filling up pauses, when there is nothing more to say.)

Jose just kisses her and says that he is gravelled for lack of matter.

Her oratory skills are obstructed by his awkward kisses.

I doubt his oratory skills when he is kissing her.

The orator is so romantic that he locks his oratory skills at nights.

Lovers lacking matter exchange their hearts through eyes.

• **Rosalind:** ................................. **The poor world is almost**

**six thousand years old, and in all this time there
was not any man died in his own person, videlicet,
in a love-cause. ...............................men
have died from time to time, and worms have eaten
them, but not for love.**

(videlicet-namely)

(The earth has existed nearly 6000 years, but no single man has died simply for the sake of love.)

The boy verballygives up his soul for her many times, but not virtually even once.

Worms can eat us, but not our love.

The girl says to her boy friend, "Better to be eaten by worms than to be swallowed by your eyes which are so lusty".

Vennila said to Joe, "You say that you have died from time to time to win my love. Hereafter, you must die, but just once".

• **Rosalind:** ................................................ **certainly a woman's**

**thoughts; runs before actions.**

(Husband: you just run fast in your thoughts, but I have to run in actions

Wife: you are my proud husband. I shall think more, make you run more so that you will run, run and run and maintain your health.

Husband (to himself): One day I must run with someone. )

My wife thinks and I run. (My wife cannot be blamed, if I have slip while running.)

Whenever his wife starts thinking, he starts running.

Actions without thoughts may go astray.

"Look before you leap" is a proverb.

- **Rosalind: men are April when they woo, December when**

  **they wed! Maids are May when they are maids**
  **but the sky changes when they are wives!**

(Men are as kind as April while in love, but cold and harsh in December when they get married. Girls are sunny and charming as May before wedding, but there are changes in their attitudes and storms come on after it. )

(Girl friend: Marry me in April, not in December.

Boy friend: I shall be with you only in May.)

(Wife (on phone): When will you come to India?

Husband (abroad): In May. I am reading Shakespeare's "As You Like It". )

(Boy: Why do you avoid me?

Girl: This is December.

Boy: so what?

Girl: I am Shakespeare's fan. )

(Life is a jungle, as long as you are single.

When you become double, you invite trouble). (Read somewhere)

The boys says to her, "If we can woo only in April, I wish every year had only Aprils with not even a single December".

"whereas you are concerned only about April, I am concerned only about December", says Diana to John.

(Life is a cage; birds in wish to fly away and birds outside wish to get in. (Read somewhere)

- **Touchstone: ...............".The fool doth think he is wise, but the**

  **wise man knows himself to be a fool".**

(Father: You do not know any proverb in English. You are a fool.

Son: I know only one proverb in English

Father: Tell me, fool

Son: As is the father, so is the son.

Father: !!!)

Wisdom beams in the presence of Humility, doesn't it?

He knows that he is a fool, but he becomes wise whenever he thinks he is wise.

It is a pity that fools test the wisdom of the wise.

The professor says, "I am not too foolish to consider me wise, nor too wise to consider me a fool".

In his strenuous attempts to publicize his wisdom, Samuel has displayed his utter foolishness.

- **Rosalind: I thought thy heart had been wounded with the**

  **claws of a lion.**

  **Orlando: Wounded it is, but with the eyes of a lady.**

I prefer my heart to be wounded with the claws of a hungry lion and the kick of an angry elephant, but not withthe eyes of my girl friend.

The sadist has wounded boys in hundreds, but her heart has not sheltered even one so far.

(Daughter: Dad! He says that my eyes wound him a lot.

Father: Go on looking at him. )

I become speechless whenever she speaks to me through her eyes.

The boy says, "Better to become blind than to be wounded with the eyes of my girl friend".

He lived even after being wounded with the claws of a lion, but died within seconds, on his being wounded with the eyes of the girl that he saw.

The face is the index of the mind; what about the eyes of a lady?

• **Orlando:** ................................. **But, oh how bitter a**

    **thing it is, to look into happiness through another**
    **man's eyes!**

Can I borrow your eyes to look into happiness, as it is invisible when seen through my eyes?.

That he has been looking into happiness only through the eyes of others is painful

When shall happiness be looked into my own eyes?

Peter looked into happiness through everyone's eyes and made everyone blind.

The poor man says, "Even with a clear vision unable I am to look into my happiness".

• **Audrey: I do desire it with all my heart, and I hope it is**

    **no dishonest desire to desire to be a woman of**
    **the world.**

"Man of words is the man of the world"-Ben Jonson We can say that man of desires cannot be a saint.

One must desire to be a human being with all one's heart for the sake of human relationship.

Man knows how to fly like a bird in the sky, swim like a fish in water, but does not know how to walk like a man.

The secretary says to the politician, "I am honestly talking to a dishonest man. When you honestly desire to become a dishonest politician, why should I not dishonestly desire to become a honest politician".

I do not want even my dreams to be dishonest.

The candidate says to the interviewer, "I may climb up dishonestly, but I will sit on the top honestly".


- **Duke Senior: By my faith, he is very swift and sententious!**


Swift-quick

Sententious- full of meaning- prompt

He is swift, but not sententious.

He is swift and sententious only for gains and not for losses.

By his faith, his girl friend is very swift and sententious but he is not faithful to his own faith.

The father says, "There is neither logic nor reason, but only by faith my foolish and innocent son says that his girl friend is very swift and sententious".

The new principal is sententious, but not swift.


- **Jaques: ..................................................... He's as goodat**


**Anything, and yet a fool!**

Keep him with you. He may be a fool, but he has his heart in the right place.

He is good at everything, except at the placement of his heart.

I am good at everything and so I just remain neither remembered nor recognized.

He is intellectually nobody, but verbally everybody.

He projects his nothing as everything and enjoys his life, but I am everything, but am projected as nothing. My wit gets wasted in the streets.

"Jack of all trades is a master of none" is a proverb in English.

- **Rosalind: To you I give myself, for I am yours.**

Thou art mine; I am thine; we are one.

At the very first sight, she gave herself to her boy friend and at the second sight she lost her life.

You may be mine, but I cannot give myself to you.

(Boy: To you I give myself.

Girl: My dad has advised me not to get anything from a stranger.

)

(Tom: I am yours. You?

Lily: Peter's.

Tom: !!!)

(Girl: I gave you myself.

Boy: I lost myself. )

- **Duke Senior: .................................................good wine needs no**

**bush, 'tis true that a good play needs no epilogue; yet**
**to good wine they use good bushes; and good plays**
**prove the better by the help of good epilogues!**

A good play needs no epilogue and our Chief Guest needs no introduction.

Your play needs an epilogue to find out whether it is good.

Good wine needs no bush, but he needs some liquor in the name 'wine', whether it needs bush or not.

Good plays need good epilogues, as good wine needs good bushes.

The power of bush in the wine has pushed him to the state of intoxication.

# CHAPTER NINE

# TWELFTH NIGHT

- **Orsino (Duke of Illyria): If music be the food of love, play on;**

**Give me excess of it,...........................**
**O, it came o'er my ear like the sweet sound**

Advantages of listening to music are as follows
   Happiness is increased.
   Stress and tension are relieved.
   Sleep embraces one.
   Depression is reduced or relieved.
   Mood is elevated while driving. (Music is the best companion to drivers)
   Learning and memory are strengthened.
   Performance in running is improved.
   Any work is facilitated.
   Music helps one eat less.
   (If music is the food of love, play on your musical instruments and give me an excess of music. Let it come over my earlike the sweet sound.)
   Music can be the food of love, but it cannot be put on plates. Music can fill your ears, but not your stomach.
   Give the depressed and disappointed music in excess for it is a great reliever of stress.

Even if my girl friend smiles, it become verbal and musical, and it comes over my ear like the sweet sound.

The musician says that the ears not filled with music are not ears at all.

(Patient: I am so much depressed that I might even finish my life.

Doctor: Take music in excess along with the tablets, and your depression will expire. )

For every mother, the cry of her baby is musical, coming over her ear like the sweet sound.


- **Captain: .....................Arion on the dolphin's back,**

**I saw him hold acquaintance with the waves**
**So long as I could see.**


(Arion is an ancient Greek musician. Attracted by the melody of his lute, a dolphin safely carried him on its back, when he was floating on the waves, but without any fear.)

Your music is so sweet that anyone would be reminded of Arion, who was carried by a dolphin attracted by his lute.

Michael becomes an Arion whenever he takes lute in his hand.

Samuel plays music as if he were an Arion, but his music is so horrible that all dolphins might drown him into the deep ocean.

His music is so sweet that the waves forgot waving when he was playing his lute.

Even though his music is as sweet as that of Arion, he is too unlucky to be carried by any dolphin.

All dolphins are found missing when he is playing his lute.

The sound of waves is so musical that even the dead dolphins that are carried by the waves might get life back.

How beautifully, without any musical instrument, the waves and the waterfalls make rhythmic sounds!

Your music during the wedding ceremony was so sweet that it would have held even Alode, Apollo, the Charites, Hymenaeus,

Melete and the Muses in rapt attention.

- **Captain: ....................she hath abjur'd the company**

  **And sight of men.**

(She has given up the company and sight of men. )
My friend is so shy that he abjures the company and sight of women.

Gopi abjures the company and sight of women whenever his wife is near.

Even though he is above 80, he takes pride in saying that he abjures the company and sight of young girls.

Vimala is such a disciplined girl that she abjures the company and sight of all men, except her father and brother.

The girl, despite a lot of advice, did not abjure the company and sight of unknown boys, and now happiness has abjured her company and sight.

- **Viola: I will believe thou hast a mind that suits**

  **With this thy fair and outward character.**
  **........................I'll pay thee bounteously,....**

(I believe that you have a good nature that goes well with your character. I shall pay you generously. )
I don't like to propose my love to her because her mind never suits with her fair and outward character.

Suresh is ready to work in any company that pays him bounteously.

Those who harm others will have to pay for it bounteously one day or other.

With your fair and outward character, you can impress anyone.

The husband says, "I have a mind that suits everyone save my wife".

I paid her bounteously but miserably failed to read her inner mind.

- **Maria: ..........................he would quickly have the gift of a**

  **grave.**

(gift of grave-death)

The invisible enemy Corona gave its innumerable victims the gift of a grave.

The old lady so abused and so misused all her powers while in office that all pray that she would quickly have the gift of a grave.

The gift of grave is a blessing for those, who serve the humanity till they die.

If she accepts my love, she will be the gift of my life; else I would like to have the gift of a grave.

Many of us get aware of the gift of the grave only in the evening of our life.

Even though he has many nails hit on his coffin, he has absolutely no sign of getting the gift of the grave.

- **Sir Toby: I'll drink as long as there is a passage in my throat.......**

  **.................he's a coward and a coystril..................**

(coystril-a mean fellow, knave) (as long as there is an opening in the throat)

He wishes to drink as long as the passage in his throat is completely blocked.

Tom is such a mad drunkard that he would drink even by borrowing a passage from someone's throat.

Many delight in the company of bottles during parties.

Even a saint becomes a coystril at the consumption of liquor.

The doctor says, "How can the patient take medicine when the passage in his throat has been completely eaten away by the power of the drinks he had?.

The drunkard says, "I don't mind being called a coward or coystril provided the passage in my throat is wetted by drinks".

- **Duke: ..................................................Diana's lip**

**In not more smooth and rubious, thy small pipe
Is as the maiden's organ, shrill and sound,
And all is semblative a woman's part.**

(Diana-the goddess of hunting and chastity. )
Rubious-red as ruby
Semblative-resembling
(Even Diana's lips are not so smoothand rubious. You have a clear throat that resembles that of a young girl. In all respects, you resemble a woman. )

I am in love with the girl because her lips are as smooth as rubious as those of Diana.

Though he looks gigantic, his voice is as the maiden's organ, shrill and sound, resembling that of a woman.

Only her lips are smooth and soft, but neither her tongue nor her heart.

Her smooth and rubious lips like those of Diana made me a great poet.

Her smooth and rubious lips are unwritten poems.

Why should I think of a heroic couplet, when I see her upper and lower lips?

(Nirad C.Chaudhuri in his Autobiography of an Unknown India (Part II) beautifully describes the girl he fell in love with as follows

"................The other girl, though not fair by Bengali standards, was very handsome in the face and beautiful in her figure. Nonetheless, it was not simply these but the vibrancy of her body and face, of every line in them, which overwhelmed me. The curves of her eyes, eyebrows, cheeks, lips, and chin were like little bows drawn taut and ready to let fly arrows any moment. If she moved her face from side to side or raised it with a slight jerk to look at the sky, it seemed to flash beams in all directions.

And her body was of a piece with her face. It had just that swelling in its curves which made its lines rhythmic and prevented any impression of staticity which even a slightly greater slenderness or embonpoint would have produced. When she walked her body vibrated within a very narrow range of frequency, and that seemed to create ripples in the air around her. I am sure that there is a critical limit to the flatness and the amplitude in the curves of a woman's body which alone is capable of producing such an effect. What I saw in her body was like the vibrato in playing the violin or soft-pedalling on the piano.

I fell head over heels in love with that vision. I am now convinced that a man's love for a woman is basically a matter of form, and therefore in its essence very abstract..........I worshipped her with my eyes, without ever giving the impression of staring or even watching. And only once or twice did I see her fixing her eyes on me as if she was conscious of my absorption in her. .........But her apparition haunted me for something like a year, and I remained in love with her. ...............All this foolish dreaming was my emotional food at the age of thirty!". (237-238)


- **Clown: .................................."Better a witty**

  **fool than a foolish wit".**

(It is better to be foolish but witty than to be witty but foolish.)
   She seems to be witty, but utter foolish.
   It is his foolish wit that projects him witty.
   He judges his wit on foolish parameters.
   There is no witty parameter to measure the foolishness of the so called witty.

All his foolish attempts to project himself witty finally revealed his utter foolishness.

Witty or foolish, one must be a human being.


- **Olivia: ....................you're a dry fool;**


(You are a dull fool.)

The company of dry fools has made him a dry fool.

We call others fools, concealing our own foolishness.

It is in the company of dry fools, one of my friends has become a dry fool.

Varun, though a dry fool, very cleverly makes others dry fools.

Knowing well that Tom is a dry fool, Lucy is in love with him. I think life will become dry, if they get married.


- **Malvolio: ................................infirmity, that decays the wise,**


**doth ever make the better fool.**


(Physical weakness due to old age weakens a wise man, but it always adds to the foolishness of a fool.)

The fool says that he has wisely converted his weaknesses into strengths.

Infirmities offer fools opportunities either to prove their foolishness or to project themselves as wise.

Every election weakens the minds of the people and strengthens the minds of the politicians' makes people unwise enough to think and politicians wise enough to act.

White says that his wisdom is so firm that it can never get dilapidated till he gets the gift of the grave.

He was a fool yesterday, a better fool today and the best fool tomorrow.


- **Malvolio: ....................an ordinary fool that has no more brain**

**Than a stone.**

(a fool that has no more intelligence than a stone)

He is an ordinary fool and his girl friend is an extraordinary fool.

He prefers to stand just like a statue (stone) either to conceal or to reveal his foolishness.

She is an ordinary fool that has no more brain than a stone.

There are some whose foolishness doesnot come to light till they speak with thier minds and hearts.

She would administrate better with a stone than with her brain.

The officer shouted at the lazy employee saying, "Better to use some stone that could be used as a paper weight rather than to use your brain that could be thrown to the dustbin as a waste paper".

- **Olivia: O, you are sick of self-love, Malvolio, and**

  **taste with a distempered appetite.**

(You are very much in love with yourself and you judge everything with a diseased mind.)

The manager of our company loves none, but himself.

The leader, being sick of self-love, loves all.

She tastes everything with a distempered appetite.

How could the judgement pronounced by a distempered tongue be fair?

How could you know the taste of the dish with your distempered appetite?.

Being so sick of her first love, Diana now looks at every soul with a distempered appetite.

He is so sick of her love that he doesn't mind being tasted with a distempered appetite.

Whatever food his wife makes, he tastes it with a distempered appetite.

His attitude is so strange that she cannot help feeling sick of his love. (She is fed up with him. )

- **Olivia: ....................................he's in the third degree of**

  **drink, he's drowned;...........................................**

Even in the fresh mornings, some are in the thirddegree of drink.

He is drowned in the very first degree of drink itself.

Some are men in the first degree of drink, become drunkards in the second degree and philosophers in the third degree. Beyond a level, they become so intoxicated that they cannot be identified as to who they are.

Some are found fairly dressed till they are in the second or third degree of drink.

Tiju is steady even in the third degree of drink.

He composes beautiful poems when he drowns in the third degree of drink.

Many drunkards drown themselves into bottles and their families into poverty.

The accused spoke the truth in the third degree of drink.

- **Viola: Most radiant, exquisite, and unmatch-**

  **able beauty,-........................................................**

The girl that I am in love with is radiant, exquisite, and unmatchable beauty.

Her beauty is matchable, but not with anyone on earth.

Beauty radiates when she smiles, and poems pour in when she speaks.

She is of unmatchable beauty, but her husband is not a match for her either in appearance or in character.

The marriage broker has a list of girls most radiant, exquisite, and unmatchable beauty, but he is unmatchable in uttering lies.

- **Viola: ...................................Tell me your mind:**

He tells me everything except his mind.

A leader is one who reads not only books, but also the minds of the people.

I can read any book written in Greek and Latin, but not her mind.

Unless you tell me your mind, how can I help you?

Lucy told everyone known or unknown to her her mind and she is suffering from severe headache.

The boy says, "One thing what I read of her mind is that she is most of the time out of mind".

He says, "Before I told her mind, she had given me her heart. Now she has been admitted to a hospital due to cardiac arrest".

A passionate lover knows well that a girl's mind is too deep to be measured and read whereas a clever lover knows that to measure and read a girl's mind is to go mad. .

- **Olivia: I thank you for your pains:**

I have pleasures at present because of my pains in the past.

Pains become pleasures when rewarded and recognized timely and appropriately.

Your pains for which I owe a lot cannot be just repaid with the single word 'thanks'.

Should your maximum pains be repaid with my minimum word 'thanks'?

What is most painful is that all my pains even after years just remain unacknowledged.

- **Sebastian: ...........................................My stars shine darkly**

   **over me; the malignancy of my fate might perhaps**
   **distemper yours;...............................................**

(Fortune is unkindto me. Perhaps, my bad luck maypoison your luck also. )

My star loses its light and shines darkly whenever I try to come up in life.

His heart is dim, but his star shines brightly over him.

Star of bad luck in most cases dims and diminishes the light of the star of diligence and intelligence.

It is his star that shines brightly even when he is in pitch darkness.

I do not want the malignancy of my fate to distemper even my enemies.

Oh my star! Shed your light at least on my grave.

So unfortunate the poor girl is that she is suspicious of the lucky star she was born under.

"Even the glittering stars shine darkly when we look at the sky", say the poor farmers.

- **Sebastian:** ..................................................**mine**

**eyes will tell tales of me.**

( My tears will express my grief. )

Her eyes boost me to write poems and short stories.

Her eyes tell tales of her love for me. She knows that my bosom is full of kindness.

I can become the best short story writer, if I swallow her eyes with mine.

The boy says, "Alas! I fell a prey to the tales her eyes told me!".

How can I listen to the tales of your eyes, when my eyes get lost at the very sight of your eyes?

I have no words to express my grief; mine eyes will tell tales of me.

(Interviewer: Why are you just looking at me without answering my questions?

Candidate: .......mine eyes will tell answers of me.

Interviewer: !!!)

- **Viola:** ....................................the pregnant enemy

(pregnant enemy- the ever-ready enemy, the devil full of tricks)

His pregnant enemy has made many innocent girls pregnant.

No one wants to have any acquaintance with him as he is a pregnant enemy.

In politics, one comes across pregnant friends and pregnant foes.

It is his unwanted use of tongue that projects him as a pregnant enemy.

Everyone considers him a pregnant enemy, except his pregnant wife.

(in the family way-pregnant in a family way- in a familiar way)

- **Sir Toby:** ..................................................... am I not

**of her blood?**

("Blood is thicker than water" is a proverb in English)

He has become a permanent and pregnant enemy of mine, though he is of my blood.

For some politicians, blood becomes thick only for thoseof their own blood.

Why differences? Why fight? Why ill-feelings? Everyone's blood is red, whether it is A negative or B positive.

Though not of my blood, there are many who are ready to shed blood for me.

Some are sucking our blood just because they are of our own blood.

The candidates of own blood are selected in the interview conducted this morning.

He wishes to find alliance of own blood for his daughter.

- **Duke:** ...............women are as roses, whose fair flower,

**Being once display'd fall that very hour.**

(Women are like roses. Their youth and beauty, having once blossomed, quickly decline like the beauty ofa flower. )

When wives are roses, husbands are thorns; when husbands are roses, wives are thorns.

He says that his rose will never have a fall.

He has many roses in his mind and heart, but he has consented to marry a rose of his parents' choice.

Though Jack is married, he tries to pluck out roses from the nearby gardens.

Women are as roses, whose fair flower being married by cruel husbands would fall that very hour.

Many girls are like beautiful buds under the care of their parents; when they become flowers, their marriages are performed; and after marriage they have their petals ruthlessly plucked by their cruel life partners.

- **Clown: Come away, come away, death,**

  **And in sad cypress let me be laid;**
  **Fly away, fly away, breath;**
  **I am slain by a fair cruel maid.**
  **My shroud of white, stuck all with yew,**
  **O, prepare it!**
  **My part of death, no one so true**
  **Did share it.**
  **Not a flower, not a flower sweet,**
  **On my black coffin let there be strown;**
  **Not a friend, not a friend greet**
  **My poor corpse, where my bones shall be thrown:**
  **A thousand thousand sighs to save,**
  **Lay me, O, where**
  **Sad true lover never find my grave,**
  **To weep there!**

(Come here, death. Let my body be put in a coffin made of the wood of a cypress tree which is a symbol of morning. Death, depart. I have been killed by a lovely but cruel maiden. Prepare a white-coloured shroud for me and cover it with the leaves of a yew tree. No faithful lover has ever died this kind of death. Let no sweet flower be thrown on my black coffin. Let no friends greet mypoor corpse, when my bones are buried in the earth. Let there be no sighs heaved over my dead body. Let my deadbody be buried in a grave which no sad, true lover can find in order to weep over it. )

The old parents are so sick of the activities of their only son that they are willingly awaiting their death by inviting diseases through constant worries.

Sleeping on the velvet cloth, the arrogant rich man humiliates the have-nots without knowing that just a coffin is his last bed.

He considered her an ever fragrant flower, but he would have never expected that even his coffin would not get even a single flower thrown by her.

Those who die of blind love expect at least their graves to get wet with a few drops of tears of the loved.

His suffocation is not due to Corona, but due to his mad love for a heartless girl.

It is the lover's grave that makes the loved realize that love is blind.

The girl says to the boy, "I shall be weeping till you find your grave".

The boy says, "I must go either to your heart or to my grave".

• **Duke: ...............................no woman's heart**

**So big, to hold so much; they lack retention.
Alas, their love may be call'd appetite,-
No motion of the liver, but the palate;-
That suffer surfeit, cloyment, and revolt;
But mine is all as hungry as the sea,**

**And can digest as much;.........................**

(The hearts of women do not have the capacity to keep love in them. Women's love may be described as a kind of hunger that is easily satisfied. Their love is not an impulse of the liver, the true seat of passion, but it pertains to the taste. But my love is as hungry as the sea with as much capacity as the sea. Make no comparison between the love that any woman can feel for me and the love that I feel towards Olivia. )

Rosy says, "My heart is so big that it can accommodate any number of hearts".

Many Romeos are roaming about in streets in search of their Juliets with great appetite for love.

Love takes many forms till it goes to the next stage. At some stage, it may lose all its forms when loves becomes infirm.

Vijay's love is as hungry as the aggressive sea and many girls have disappeared in its waves.

Though unable to get digested with his previous love with many a girl, the Romeo of our street is fresh for refreshing his love with someone.

- **Viola: We men may say more, swear more: but indeed,**

  **Our shows are more than will; for still we prove**
  **Much in our vows, but little in our love.**

(We men may express our love in more words and we may take more oaths. But in fact, our declarations of love are greater than our will to prove them by our actions, because we always assert much in our pledges of love but prove little in our deeds. )

He is not reliable whether he vows and loves.

Many of our Juliets do not know that their Romeos are not true either in vow or in love.

His love was only in his vows till he had his love.

Many romantic boys show their love only in vows and their love in vows remain till their eyes get intoxicated by the clouds of beauty.

Julie says that she doubts all those who speak more and swear more.

She says that her lover is rich in vow, not in love.

All lovers become politicians or even excel them in giving promises.

Even a man of promise becomes a man of promises when it comes to love.

Lovely promises, lame excuses, concocted lies, elaborate tissues of circumstantial falsehood, perjury and forgery are, in many cases, the weapons for Romeos to make Juliets fall into their traps.

• **Fabian:** ........................let me be boiled to death with melancholy.

(Let me be killed with the intensity of my regret. )

Your face is the indication of your getting boiled to death with melancholy.

The boy says to the girl, "You have hurt, insulted and humiliated me many times and you have even started questioning my manliness. Let me be boiled to death at least with manliness, if not with melancholy.

The disappointed lover's heart is so full of grief that even his grave would boil with melancholy.

There are many boiling with melancholy from birth to death.

Oh God! will you not extinguish my boiling heart by showering on me your wet and warm blessings?

The man said, "Let the ladies who tortured me due to intoxication of power get boiled to death with melancholy".

• **Sir Toby: .........we will fool him black and blue: -**

(We will make a through fool of him. ) –thoroughly or completely

What wisdom would you get in fooling everyone black and blue?

Your very thought of fooling all black and blue itself is foolish.

Her mind is full of clever plans to fool all around her black and blue.

The police beat the criminal black and blue. (The police beat the criminal severely.)

John had his face blackened in his attempts to fool all black and blue.

- **Malvolio: "Besides, you waste the treasure of your**

  **time with a foolish knight,"---**

It is unfortunate that the young students waste the treasure of their time with smart phones.

The time the lovers spend or waste is really a treasure of love.

He has become a fool by wasting his treasure of his time by arguing with the educated fools.

("I wasted time, now doth time waste me"-Richard II)

Sometimes we are made to feel that it is better for one to spend a little time with the uneducated than to waste the treasure of time with the so called educated.

I consider the time that I spend with my aged parents and enthusiastic children a treasure.

A dedicated teacher considers the time that he spends with his/ her students usefully a great treasure.

- **Malvolio: .....................................; but be not afraid of great-**

  **ness: some are born great, some achieve greatness,**
  **and some have greatness thrust upon 'em.**

It is unfortunate that many come up in life by having greatness thrust upon them and it is most unfortunate that they overtake those who thrust greatness upon them.

He was neither born great, nor achieved greatness.

Some of us without a little bit of shyness just boast of greatness just thrust upon them.

Greatness of greatness is felt when it is achieved by fair means.

Greatness thrust upon by foul means is more recognized than greatness self-achieved by fair means.

He was not born great, but achieved greatness.

"Trust me; my greatness was not thrust upon me", said the speaker.

There are some who are born poor, but try to achieve greatness (financially) by marrying daughters of the rich.

He lost his greatness, when it was, with excess and extreme weight, thrust upon him.

- **Olivia: If one should be a prey, how much the better**

**To fall before the lion than the wolf!**

(If one must be a victim, how much better it would be to submit to the master than to yield to the servant!)

Better to fall a prey before a lion than before a wolf.

If I were to fall a prey, I would to a lion, never to a wolf.

Though he was born majestically, he miserably fell a prey to wolves in his life.

Tom has volunteered himself to fall a prey, whether it is to a lion or a wolf.

When a majestic lion falls a prey, the cunning wolves have their time.

She is more cunning than a fox that she might make anyone fall a prey to her tricks.

- **Olivia: Love sought is good, but given unsought is better.**

(Boy: Love sought is good, but given unsought is better.

Girl: My love for you is sought, but mine for your younger brother is unsought.

Boy:!!!)

He is in search of love, whether it is sought or unsought.

Love unsought is stronger than the love sought.

Neither the love sought nor the love unsought made me experience an iota of love at all.

Love cannot be sought through advertisements or by force.

The love that I got unsought by luck is better than the love that I sought by pains.

- **Sir Toby: ..............................................taunt him with the**

  **licence of ink:**

(Attack him with sarcastic remarks. )

He felt hurt as he was taunted even by his friends with the licence of ink.

Your licence of ink can never make any scar in my mind.

I don't mind being taunted by any with the licence of ink.

As I taunted the corrupt officer with the licence of ink, he refused to give me my driving licence.

My mind has become so dry that it can't be taunted with the licence of ink.

It is with the licence of ink he taunts everyone he comes across.

- **Sebastian: I can no other answer make, but thanks,**

  **And thanks, and ever thanks;**

His thanks and thanks and ever thanks come from his lips, not from his heart.

My heart is filled with thanks and thanks and ever thanks, but my tongues expresses it just once.

I cannot repay you, but and so I thank you.

(Friend I: thanks, and thanks, and ever thanks for guarantying my loan.

Friend 2: I will thank, and thank and ever thank, if you clear the loan at the earliest. )

He thanked me so repeatedly that I needed twenty bags to contain and carry his thanks.

She cheats everyone either with her tears or with her thanks.

More than joy and pleasure, it is the sense of gratitude that is felt more by the heart and the mind.

- **Olivia: ...........youth is bought more oft than begg'd or borrow'd.**

(A young man's good will can more often be bought with hospitality and gifts than with appeals and entreaties. )

No one can buy the ideological, spiritual and patriotic youth.

The politician says, "There is no need for me either to beg or borrow as long as my bank passbook in many names is under the heavy weight of currency".

Those who make their old parents beg or borrow are unfit to claim themselves to be humans.

All my appeals and entreaties fell on his deaf ears and finally gifts and money helped me get things done.

- **Olivia: ............., this is very midsummer madness.**

(completely mad)

Even though he lives in a country where there is no summer, he has midsummer madness.

This is the very beginning of summer, but he has got midsummer madness.

The midsummer madness of his will affect the one who tries to cure it.

I have tablet for your disease, but not for your midsummer madness.

This is the very midsummer madness that makes her behave so arrogantly and so atrociously.

Her midsummer madness was revealed through her maladministration.

- **Fabian: If this were played upon a stage now, I**

   **could condemn it as an improbable fiction.**

(If such behaviour were shown on the stage of a theatre as part of a drama, I would condemn it as something unbelievable. )

If whatever he speaks behind the screen were screened publicly, his face would overflowwith public saliva.

Improbable fictions are unethically converted into historical facts.

His fiction is so full of improbabilities that it cannot be staged even for entertainment.

If the life of many of us were staged, the stage would be flooded with tears.

If the wicked lady tried to play upon her innocence on her face, I would slap her.

Whatever she says in her favour is nothing but an improbable fiction.

- **Fabian: .................................that keeps you from the**

   **Blow of the law.**

(Dr Abmbedkar is called the Father ofIndian Constitution. )

Here is an extract from former Chief justice Mr V.R.Krishna Iyer's book titled "Sublime footprint". It is said that there is no excuse for ignorance of law. Learners, especially the younger generation must know something about law.

"The Indian Constitution is the supreme law of the land. We call the dominant figures who shaped the Constitution as the founding fathers. While towering personalities like Jawaharlal Nehru, Sardar Patel, Rajendra Prasad, Rajagopalachari, Alladi Krishanaswamy Ayyar and a galaxy of jurists, statesmen and leaders of various sections of people moulded the founding deed, Dr Ambedkar was the Chairman of the Drafting Committee-the Mahar Manu of Nav Bharat. The collective labours of the Assembly resulted in that remarkable product, the Constitution. The enactment was complete on 26 November 1949 and came into force on 26th January 1950. The Democratic Republic of India thus sprang into existence on 26th January 1950 and we observe that day every year as Republic Day". (80)

Dr Ambedkar says, "........we must abandon the bloody methods of civil disobedience, non-cooperation and satyagraha. When there was no way left for constitutional methods for achieving economic and social objectives, there was a great deal of justification for unconstitutional methods. But when constitutional methods are open, there can be no justification for these unconstitutional methods. These methods are nothing but the Grammar of Anarchy and the sooner they are abandoned, the better for us". (81) (November 25, 1949)

"All are equal before law" is the quintessence of Indian Constitution.

(That will keep you safe from any legal consequences. )

(Here the authors are reminded of former Chief Justice of India Mr V.R.Krishna Iyer's views on law.

"The law barks at all but bites only the poor, the powerless, the illiterate, the ignorant".

Quoting Dickens saying that "Law may be an ass", Mr Krishna Iyer asks "can it also be a fox?".

Mr Krishna Iyer also adds that "Reform, not revenge, is the central idea of criminal justice". He beautifully says, "Every Saint has a past and every sinner a future". (201). He says, "Victimology is a developing branch of criminology". (204)

(In English, "The law-maker should not be a law-breaker" is a proverb. In Tamil, the equivalent proverb is "Veiliye payirai meikkalama?". "The mills of God grind slow but sure" is a proverb in English and the equivalent proverb in Tamil is "Arasan anru kolvaan; Theivam ninru kollum".)

A true citizen always stands by law.

It is said that Judgement delayed is judgement denied.

The corrupt should not escape the severe blows of the law.

How long can you keep yourself from the blow of the law?

You can keep yourself from the blow of the law, but not from the blow of your conscience.

- **Viola: Out of my lean and low ability**

  **I'll lend you something;**

(I will lend you a little money out of my own meagre and limited resources. )

My father and mother are so generous that they will lend the poor out of their lean and low ability.

He lent others everything that credited to his own lean and low ability.

He is lean and low now for he did not lend even a single pie as long as he was wallowing in wealth.

To lend something out of your lean and low ability requires just your mind and heart.

If everyone lends some out of his/her lean and low ability, there would be none economically lean and low.

- **Viola: I hate ingratitude more in a man**

  **Than lying, vainness, babbling, drunkenness,**
  **Or any taint of vice whose strong corruption**

**Inhabits our frail blood.**

(vainness-futility)

(I hate a man more for his being ungrateful than for his falsehoods, his vanity, hisnonsensical talk, and his drunkenness. I hate ingratitude more than the infection of any vicewhich corrupts human beings deeplyand which dwells in our weakminds andhearts. )

The MP of his constituency is gratefully noted for his ingratitude.

I can forgive him for lying, babbling, drinking and all other vices, but not his ingratitude.

It is a curse on the part of those who being plagued with ingratitude ignore their parents and leave them unwanted, uncared and unattended.

The strong candidate has again been fielded to contest the election this time on the basis of a strong record of strong corruption charges not strongly recorded in the court of law.

* **Sir Toby:** ...............................................................more

  **a coward than a hare: his dishonesty appears in**
  **leaving his friend here in necessity........................**

(He is more cowardly than a hare is. His dishonesty appears in his deserting his friend in need. )

His dishonesty appeared when he left his friends in honest necessity.

The girl says that she is willing to marry someone who is more cowardly than a hare.

He is honest in words and dishonest in deeds.

She is such a coward that even a hare would mock at his cowardice.

He never left his friends in necessity, but was left by them all in necessity.

- **Sir Toby: my young soldier, put up your iron: you are well**

  **fleshed; come on.**

(Put your dagger back in its case. You have tasted blood enough.)

Though the well fleshed solider has put up his iron, he has not yet put up his anger and cruelty.

The soldier is so patriotic that he wills to sacrifice his flesh and blood for his nation.

Had the soldiers put up their iron getting fleshed, the borders would have been flooded with blood and covered with flesh, due to unexpected attack from the neighbouring country.

I shall never put up my iron till I am well fleshed.

As long as there is flesh for flesh and blood for blood, there won't be any flesh or blood anywhere.

- **Clown: ....................................I am one of those gentle**

  **ones that will use the devil himself with courtesy:**

Our new boss is such a nice person that he treats even the devils with courtesy.

Though Tom is not gentle, he treats even devils with dignity and courtesy.

Knowing that he is so a gentle boy that he treats even the devils with courtesy, all the three witches of our street are in love with him.

His too much gentleness converts even devils into angels.

She does not mind treating devils themselves with courtesy provided her own devilish activities are safely screened.

- **Malvolio: ...............this house is as dark as ignorance,**

  **though ignorance were as dark as hell;.........**

(Where is Heaven? Where is Hell? Is Heaven a place filled with joy and prosperity even with the hot sun warming the dwellers with a warm heat and even with tsunami embracing them as a gentle wind? Is Hell a place of darkness? Is the Hell reserved for sinners to get punished in the cruellest manner possible for the sins committed in the previous birth? All views of Heaven and Hell are based on religious beliefs. Fed up with God's partial treatment after creation of the first man Adam, Satan thrown out of Heaven preferred to "reign in Hell than serve in Heaven". It also has become quite common among people to curse someone out of wrath or depression with the sentence "You go to Hell" and find some solace or to bless someone (after death) of out love, affection and emotion with the sentence "May God bless you with the place in Heaven!".

Former Chief Justice of India Justice V.R.Krishna Iyer was reminded of when he lost the Presidentialelection due to the politicalparty remaining neutral, contributing to his defeat. He was nominated by the Opposite parties against Mr R.venkataraman nominated and supported by the ruling party headed by Mr Rajiv Gandhi. After losing the Presidential election, Justice Krishna Iyer expressed his thanks to the members who voted for and against him for the sake of courtesy and culture. A few lines of his letter read as follows

"The Presidential polls are over; the process of swearing in of the new Rashtrapati brings the chapter of contest to a close. On this occasion, I owe love and thanks to all those who have voted for me, and even those who have abstained or marked against me. My profound gratitude goes to those legislators, those in a sore minority, who have reposed confidence in me, despite powerful adverse winds. .......................On the contrary, the eloquence of silence on the part of those who opposed me is a significant victory for the validity of my presidential ideology. I have great personal regard for the leader of the abstentionists but feel sad when I read poet Dante who once said: The hottest places in hell are reserved for those who, in a time of great moral crisis, maintain their neutrality". (195-196)

The poor girl is happy only in words, but her mind is as dark as hell.

The stupid and superstitious boy divorced his beautiful and innocent wife just because his house became as dark as hell, as soon as she entered.

Listening to music is really a great relief to the mind as dark as hell.

A mini library must be there in the house as dark as ignorance.

She is depressed because her house is as dark as ignorance and her mind is as dark as hell.

- **Clown: I am for all waters.**

(I can play any role.)

(The eminent lawyer Mr Ram Jethmalani during his lecture at Sastra University (School of Law), Tamil Nadu, said, "When you throw one politician into water, it will be pollution. When you throw all politicians into water, it will be a solution. ) (Source-Ram Jethmalani's speech at Sastra University- You tube)

(Interviewer: Could you be in charge of Research and Development?

Candidate: I am for all waters, sir

Interviewer: I hope water will not get polluted. )

He is for all waters, but consumption of liquor is the impediment to his progress in life.

He is such a drunkard that he is not for all waters, but for quarters.

It is really painful that potential candidates meant for all waters do not get promotion, when many not for a single cup of water enjoy all privileges.

Shivaji Ganesan was such an outstanding actor that all directors did consider him an actor for all waters.

The global market is in need of potential candidates who are for all waters.

- **Malvolio: ......................................I will live to be thank-**

  **ful to thee for 't'.**

(I will be thankful to you as long as I live.)

(Politician (before election): I will live to be thankful to thee for 't'.

People: How long will you make us live? )

He has helped me a lot and I must be thankful to him for 't'.

She offered me just a cup of tea, but she expects me to live to be thankful to her for 't'.

We must live to be thankful to the doctors, nurses and scavengers for 't' for their divine services during COVID-19.

- **Malvolio: They have propertied me; keep me**

  **in darkness, send ministers to me...**

(to have propertied- to have treated like a tool) ( ministers-priests)

Having been propertied by the party leader all these years, he has resigned his post.

Teachers, who keep their students in darkness, are not dedicated.

The ministers sent even from heaven cannot counsel him.

He got all the properties from his father-in-law, but he has propertied his wife and kept her in darkness all these years.

Even if I am kept in darkness, my mind will be shedding light.

I am not your property to get myself propertied by you.

He is so brilliant that he would shed light even if he were kept in darkness.

- **Clown: ..........................the better for my foes, and the**

**worse for my friends.**

(I am feeling better because of my enemies and I am feeling the worse because of myfriends.**)**

Pain is felt to the extreme when it is gifted by friend and pleasure is experienced to the extreme when it is gifted by foes.

Roger is so just that he has left the better for his deserving foes and the worse for his just dreamy friends.

The angry face of a foe is better than the villainy smile of a friend.

Better to be his foe to get the better than to be his friend to get the worse.

Better or worse, friends or foes, I leave the right to those worthy.

* **Duke: I'll sacrifice the lamb that I do love,**

  **To spite a raven's heart within a dove.**

(I will sacrifice the gentle boy whom I love in order to punish this woman who looks like a dove, but has the heartof a cruel raven.)

She is a raven within a dove and the innocent lamb sacrificed for her with the title 'husband' has now become another raven within a dove.

She is a raven in appearance, but a dove in character.

I will sacrifice the lamb that I love to avenge the raven within a dove.

I felt the first nail hit on my coffin when I got a notice from the bank asking to clear the loan cunningly borrowed by my friend and sympathetically guaranteed by me.

He is in love with a raven though his wife is a dove.

* **Sir Andrew: ...........we took him for a coward, but he's the**

  **very devil incardinate.**

(incardinate-embodiment)

He is a coward on the screen and a devil behind the screen.

The staff took the new manager for an angel, but she's the very devil incardinate.

The marriage broker showed him the photo of a coward before marriage, but in reality she is the very devil incardinate.

Innocent people take some for saints, but they blindly trust them till they have their experiences with the very devils incardinate.

We took him for a devil incardinate, but he is a real saint.

(Do not judge a book by its cover; do not judge anyone by one's appearance. There are snakes in the grass and there are roses among thorns. )


- **Duke: One face, one voice, one habit, and two**

  **persons, .............................................**

(They have the same face, the same voice, the same clothes, but they have tow separate bodies. It seems to be an optical deception produced by Nature, something that seems to be so, but is not. )

Does proxy in class mean "one face, one person, one habit and two voices?

The couple looks so well matched that they seem to have one face with resemblance to a 'T', have the same voice as if they had a single throat, have the same habit as if they imitate each other like an ape, but they are two persons.

Before marriage, they had one face, one mind, one voice and one heart. After marriage, they have two faces but without beam, two minds but without romance, two voices but without words and two hearts without love.

He is so mad after popularity that he wants every piece of mirror found even on the road side to reflect his face and the throat of every ass in any corner of the street to echo his voice.

Some of us have more faces but one face with visibility.

The husband and the wife say that they have one face, one mind, one voice and one heart, but they live in two houses.
(Son: Dad, I have your face, your voice, your habit..........
Dad: my ATM and credit cards too............)

# CHAPTER TEN

# ALL'S WELL THAT ENDS WELL

- **Countess: ..........................Love all, trust a few,**

**Do wrong to none: be able for thine enemy**
**Rather in power than use, and keep thy friend**
**Under thy own life's key:**

(How can I trust one, who loves none, trusts none, but does wrong to everyone on earth?

A successful leader is one, who loves all, trusts a few, but does wrong to none.

One cannot be forced to love someone, nor can one be forced to trust someone, but one can be taught not to harm any on earth.

Do wrong to none, whether you love all or trust all.

Love and trust for fellow human beings, if true, will not let you do wrong to any.

You may be my thick friend, but you are too innocent, too ignorant or too immature to be kept under my life's key.

Do not think of keeping your children under your life's key. Remember that they have eyes to see the world, ears to hear the world and wings to fly across the world.

I loved all, trusted all and did wrong to none, but now there is none to love me, none to trust me, but I have many to wrong me. Is this the way of the world?

I love all, though not loved by any, trust a few, though not trusted by any, and I harm none, though harmed by all.

- **Helena: Yet these fixed evils sit so fit in him,**

These evils sit so fit in him that I wonder whether he is fit for these evils or these evils are fit for him.

Vinoth speaks as if he were a saint when he has all fixed evils sitting so fit in him.

The peon says, "Does my boss think that these are my fixed evils?".

When all evils, to my pleasures, are fit to sit in me, I am unfit to speak of human values.

He said to his son, "Let bygones be bygones, but you need not stop your journey, feeling upset over the the evils sitting once so comfortably in you".

I think that he has ordered online a comfortable chair for all evils to sit comfortably in him, but he does not know that he cannot sit in any human heart.

- **Helena: ..................., you were born under a charitable star.**

Tom extends his helping hands to the needy and proves his birth under a charitable star.

One need not be born under a charitable star to help others, but one needs the charitable mind to help others.

Only the star that he is born under is charitable, nothing else.

Even though he was not born under star of any kind, he has become a star in the film industry.

One may be born under star of luck, but no star is in our hands. Hitch your wagon to a star and believe in hard work.

Kunal is uncharitable, though he was born under a charitable star.

- **Helena: .....................fear proposes the safety;**

(The word 'fear' is used both as a verb and as a noun.

(I fear none, but God. Fear in God prevents one from committing sins.)

"Men fear death as children fear darkness."-Bacon

"To conquer fear is the beginning of wisdom"- Bertrand Russell

"The only thing we have to fear is fear itself"- Franklin D. Roosevelt

(Fear is sometimes the outcome of extreme carefulness.

Your fear has kept you safe.)

"Fear I have not, fear I have not

Even if all the world opposes me.

Fear I have not, fear I have not,

Even if they judge me as the worst.

And tell things bad about me,

Fear I have not, fear I have not,

Even if I am fated to live by begging.

Fear I have not, fear I have not,

Even if I lose all my wealth due to desires.

Fear I have not, fear I have not,

Even if well endowed ladies with bra,

Throw their eyes at me.

Fear I have not, fear I have not,

Even if dear friends of mine,

Make me eat poisonous things.

Fear I have not, fear I have not,

Even if hoards of army,

With green uniform comes.

Fear I have not, fear I have not,

Even if the entire sky breaks,

And falls on my head,

Fear I have not, fear I have not"- Bharathi, an outstanding Tamil poet

While explaining the difference between 'Privacy' and 'Secrecy' to his daughter Mrs Indira Gandhi, Pandit Jawaharlal Nehru says as follows

"Privacy helps one work on establishment of individuality and it offers one freedom to think and act, whereas there are chances for errors to occur when there is room for secrecy or for hiding anything. Secrecy is the outcome of fear. We know what will happen when something is done out of fear".

- **Parolles: ....................................When thou hast**

  **leisure, say thy prayers; when thou hast none, remember thy friends;...................................................**

When you remember God in prosperity, God will remember you in poverty.

Am I a friend to be remembered when you have none to remember?

I am not a friend just to be leisurely remembered, but a friend to be affectionately recognized.

Many students say their prayers when they have exams and exam results.

Not places of worship, but exam halls remind students of God.

Man has leisure to eat, drink, sing, dance, play, sit, chat, write, read, but has no leisure to pray. The Created are not thankful to the Creator.

- **Helena: Our remedies oft in ourselves lie,**

  **Which we ascribe to heaven:.................................**
  **.................................- my project may deceive me,**
  **But my intents are fix'd and will not leave me.**

(Remedy is worse than the disease.

Slow learners need suitable remedial measures.

Your remedies lie in your own hands.

Music is the best remedy to the minds in darkness, depression and disappointment.

We ascribe (attribute) our fate and failure to heaven, don't we?.

Your agony has no remedy till it vanishes from your mind.

My hard work has deceived me, but not my confidence.

(There is a difference between 'confidence' and 'pride'. Read the following two sentences

I can perform well in any interview. (confidence)

I ONLY can perform well in any interview. (pride)

My intention never gets deviation, as it is fixed.


- **King: Youth, thou bear'st thy father's face;**

 **Frank nature, rather curious than in haste,**
 **Hath well composed thee. Thy father's moral parts**
 **Mayst thou inherit too! Welcome to Paris.**

(As is the father, so is the son.

As is the king, so are the subjects. )

Your face reminds me of your father, but not your words and deeds.

You are bearing your father's FACE ONLY. (not characteristics)

Smith is the bearer of his father's face/ heart/ mind.

I have inherited all these qualities from my parents.

Though he is very frank in his nature, he should not have been so frank, when he proposed his love to the girl. The girl also should not have so frankly reacted to his love proposal.


- **Bertram: His good remembrance, sir,**

 **Lies richer in your thoughts than on his tomb;**

(Good people live even on their tombs. )

The love of father and mother lies richer in everyone's memory than anything else.

None on earth has been guaranteed to live happily and peacefully from womb to tomb.

The industrial workers feel living on their tombs under heavy work pressure.

The forsaken parents say, "We are living now just to leave for ever and to live happily at least on our tombs".

The writer is not alive, but he is living in good remembrance.

- **Clown: ............................Service is no heritage:.....**

(Service to humanity is service to God.)
To save one's life during calamities is really a Yeoman's service.
"Better to reign in Hell than serve in Heaven"- John Milton
Service is no heritage, but culture.
Service of any kind is of no worth, unless one does any service with a willing mind to serve.

- **Countess: You ne'er oppress'd me with a mother's groan,**

   **Yet I express to you a mother's care:**
   **God's mercy,................................**

God is known for Mercy, father for care and concern, mother for love and affection and teacher for knowledge and wisdom.

You feel so depressed and so dejected out of isolation, still you need a god without mercy, a friend without concern and even a life without life. This will aggravate your mental burden. Let your grief find some relief.

I am blessed with such a good teacher that I feel the presence of of my mother in all her classes.

When a house is filled with mother's love and father's care, it becomes a home.

If one knows mother's groan at the time of delivering a baby, he/she will consider any groan absolutely nothing. )


• **Helena: I know I love in vain, strive against hope;**

    **Yet in this captious and intenible sieve**
**I still pour in the waters of my love**
**And lack not to lose still; thus Indian-like,**
**Religious in mine error, I adore**
**The sun, that looks upon his worshipper,**
**But knows of him no more.**


Though I know that I love her in vain, I feel like one delighting in wine.

I shall strive against hope, as long as I am hopeful of my hope.

I am hopeful of my mind that is made up of hope.

Lose anything, but not hope. Loss of hope results in loss of ambition.

Ambition without efforts is like a bird without wings.

Can I use the sieve to take away my mind and heart from her?

John is **religious** in his duties. (sincere)

Can you expect haters of heat to adore the sun, nor can you expect one suffering from nyctophobia to adore the moon? ('Nyctophobia' means 'fear of darkness'.)

There are many who know of others so more, but of themselves know no more.)


• **Lafeu: ........................... have seen a medicine**

    **That's able to breathe life into a stone,...............**


The doctor is so trustworthy that his patients believe that his any medicine can breathe life into even stones.

The doctor has converted his patients into stones by showing them the bills.

The patient got frozen like a stone out of fear, when the doctor stood before him like a butcher with a knife at the time of operation.

The artist has carved the statue so realistically that the viewers wonder whether he had had breathed life to stone that was cut for the statue.

The teacher breathes life to every lesson he/she teaches.

- **Helena: My duty then shall pay me for my pains:**

   **I will no more enforce mine office on you.**

(Thank you for the pains that you have taken for me. I do not know how I could pay for your pains.

There is no gain without pain.

All his painful pains to win her heart are of no gain at all.

She, in power intoxication, enforced her office so much on all sub-ordinates that their minds forced them unconsciously and sub-consciously to quit their jobs.

To enforce your office on others is unethical.

What is the difference between 'misuse' and 'abuse'?

'To misuse' is 'to use incorrectly, but 'to abuse' is 'to use excessively or damagingly'.

Abuse is more serious than misuse.

When a drug is misused to the extent of making one fall a prey to drugs, it becomes abuse.

A good administrator neither misuses nor abuses power.

- **Countess: ..................,that's a bountiful answer that fits all questions.**

   **Clown: It is like a barber's chair that fits all buttocks, the pin-buttock, the quatch-buttock, the brawn-buttock, or any**

**buttock.**

The minister just gives the reporters a bountiful answer that fits all their questions.

The teacher resigned his job, as his student gave him a bountiful answer that did not fit any of her questions.

I have moved heaven and earth to occupy this chair. Do not think that my chair fits all buttocks.

I have made this chair for my buttock, not for yours.

You can change or exchange the chair, but not your buttock.

- **Countess: ..............................I will be a fool in question,**

   **hoping to be the wiser by your answer.**

He is a scholar in questions, but a fool in answers.

My questions may be foolish, but my answers are wise.

He is wise in words, not in deeds.

I will be wise in question hoping to become a fool by your answer.

The applicant pretends to be wise, but he is not so either in question or in answer.

Some go on asking questions as they are fools in answers.

- **King: ....I will throw thee from my care for ever....................**

   **.................................both my revenge and hate**
   **..............................in the name of justice.**

You can throw me even from a fast running car, but not from your care.

The girl says, "My boy friend is so careless that he did not care even when I fell down from a fast running car".

You are indulging in unjust activities in the name of justice.

My revenge and hate have earned me aversion and enmity.

The wheels of justice do not run on petrol or diesel.

- **King: Good fortune and the favour of the king**

  **Smile upon this contract;.....................**

Fortune! Do you demand anything for your smile. Victims of misfortunes are yearning for your smile at least once in their life.

The Chairman of the company just smiles at our every contract, but does nothing else.

Many become lazy at the frequent smile of fortune upon them.

All said that smile costs nothing; I smiled at her without expecting that it would cost me more physically than mentally.

When flavour of hard work is left unrecognized before favour of kings and queens, misfortune pathetically smiles at the victims.

The student says, "I do not know when fortune will smile upon my exam paper".

- **Lafeu: Do not plunge thyself too far in anger, .....................**

The word 'plunge' is used both as a verb and as a noun. Students must take a plunge (must plunge) into politics to disprove what Socrates said of politics that it (politics) is the last resort for scoundrels.

The manager plunged himself too far in anger even for trivial matters and went far and far from all his employees.

Anger is also a virtue, but if expressed often, it loses its value and meaning.

Beloved parents plunge into the sea of sadness when their children shout at them.

Just leave that place, when someone uses harsh words against you out of anger, if you are not able to control your anger.

- **Porolles: A young man marriedis a man that's marr'd:**

(Marriage is like cage. Birds inside wish to fly away, and birds outside wish to get in. )

(Life is a jungle as long as you are single. When you become double, you invite trouble. )

Though my friend got married 30 years back, he still remains unmarred.

He is so peculiar that he wants to get married just to get marred.

- **Clown: She is not well; but yet she has her health: she's very merry;**

  **but yet she is not well: but thanks be given, she's very well and wants nothing i', the world; but yet she is not well.**

He is healthy, but he is not well, as he has lost in business all his money.

He is well, but not healthy.

Byron has everything in the world, but he is not well.

Health is wealth.

The patient is not healthy and so his doctor is sure to become wealthy.

- **Helena: I hope, sir, I have your good will to have mine own good**

  **fortunes.**

(Misfortunes are of two types; misfortunes to us and fortunes to others. )

Good will is not on sale anywhere, but it is spontaneous.

Shall I have your good will to have my fortunes?

Her good will may bring you misfortunes, as it comes from her mouth, not from heart.

She says to her husband, "Our business will flourish with my good will and with your good fortunes".

The poor man says, "I have neither good fortune nor good will by my side".

- **Countess: .........................................I have wedded her, not**

**beddedher**

(Wedding is not only for bedding, but for getting together with two minds and hearts. )

Bedding before wedding is a threat to our culture.

He looked manly during wedding, but not during bedding.

She said to him, "You wedded me just for bedding?.Do you think that I am a machine to be operated at your needs and a cog in the machine when not needed?. Is bed the place for exercising male chauvinism?".

(Kannadasan, an outstanding poet in Tamil, writes the following lines in one of his songs as follows

"Kathal enum kavithai thanthein kattilin melay (male voice)

Antha karunaikku naan parisu thanthein thottilin melay...." (female voice) (In Tamil)

I awarded (you) poetry in the bed. (male voice)

I rewarded the mercy in the cradle. (female voice)

- **First Gentleman: .................with the swiftest wing of speed.**

When his girl friend reminded him of marriage, he ran with the swiftest wing of speed without knowing that he would have his mighty fall after marriage.

When his mother calls him for any help, he looks for his wings.

He shows swiftest wing of speed in his plans, but not in actions.

You just fly from pillar to post with the swiftest wing of speed, but in vain.

Only your wings are swift, but not you.

Before the teacher entered the class, his students had run with the swiftest wing of speed.

The international runner, who once had his swiftest wing of speed and brought nation laurels by winning many a Gold Medal, has his wing now slow and swiftless due to old age.

One, who has aspirations and ambitions, must run with the swiftest wing of speed to reach his/her destination.

- **Mariana: I know that knave; hang him!...........................**

  **..............................................Beware of them,**
  **Diana; their promises, enticements, oaths, tokens, and all**
  **these engines of lust, are not the things they go under: many**
  **a maid hath been seduced by them;.................................**
  **I need not to advise you further; but I hope your own grace**
  **will keep you where you are,........................................**

(The girl said to her boy friend, "All your words, greetings, compliments, flowers, promises, enticements, oaths and everything you have given me are of just signs of your lust, not of love. But my own grace has let me know what love is and what lust is. Lust ends, but love continues. As yours towards me is only lust, our love also ends.

Though she knows that he is a knave, she loves him blindly.

(The word 'hang' has two participles 'hung' and 'hanged'. Read the following sentences to learn when 'hung' is used and when 'hanged is used'.

The pictures are hung on the wall. Being found guilty in the murder cases, the criminal was hanged last week.

Hung Parliament – Parliament lacking a majority political party.

How to reduce cases of women being seduced?

There is a difference between 'man of promise' and 'man of promises'. Man of promise is determined, but man of promises does not go beyond promises. At the time of election, let us choose leaders of promise, not politicians of promises, who just promise the sun and the moon, and even a paradise on earth, but does not help people stand even on earth after winning the election.

There is a difference between a statesman and a politician. A statesman is one who is concerned about the next generation, but a politician is one who is concerned about the next election.

In our democracy, promises, enticements, oaths and token have become engines of vote, not of upliftment of the oppressed and the suppressed.)

- **Second Lord:..........................to speak of him as my kinsman, he's a most**

  **notable coward, an infinite and endless liar, an hourly promise-breaker, the owner of no one good quality worthy your lordship's entertainment.**

To live one day as a warrior is better than to live for years and years as a coward.

Dead lion is better than a living dog.

There is a notable coward in your gang, but remains unnoticed by any.

Before truth takes its first step, lie tours all over the world.

One lie leads to many.

I have spoken white lies, but any lie so far. (White lie is that which does not harm any.)

His tongue is the dwelling place for all harmful lies.

He is an expert at spinning a yarn.

How do you rely on him, knowing well that that he is an hourly promise-breaker.

He has broken his love many times by breaking his promises.

He has promised everything to his girl friend, except marriage.

Do you own at least one good quality that deserves human treatment?

None trusts you with any quality, good or bad, because you are an infinite and endless liar.

Till the end of your journey in life, you may come across with endless liars. Be aware of them.

(Once a man came to Prophet Muhammad (PBUH) and said to him, "My three vices are being money minded, being lustful and speaking lies and I wish to give up all my vices, but I can give them up one by one. Which vice must be given up first?". Prophet advised him to give up speaking lies. Then prophet said to his friends, "Lie is the mother of all crimes". )

- **First Lord: That was not be blamed in the command of the service: it**

  **was a disaster of war that Caesar himself could not have prevented, if he had been there to command.**

(Only Caesar could have prevented such a disaster. )

"If mankind must put an end to war, war will put an end to mankind"- Kennedy

War results in disaster. War leads to wars that never end. Peace leads to peace that lasts forever.

She commands as if she were a Caesar.

Where can I find a Caesar to prevent such a disaster?

Whenever he senses some disaster, he doubts everyone around him to be a Brutus.

- **Bertram: If quick fire of youth light not your mind,**

  **You are no maiden, but a monument:**
  **When you are dead, you should be such a one**
  **As you are now,.....................................**

You are not a maiden till quick fire of youth lights your mind.

Your mind can never get lighted even on fire on cylinders and I wonder whether you are a maiden or monument, alive or dead. )

Dedicated teachers must ignite the young minds and make them independent and intellectual thinkers.

- **First Lord: How mightily sometimes we make us comforts of our losses!**

  **Second Lord: And how mightily some other times we drown our gain in**

  **tears! The great dignity that his valour hath here acquired**
  **for him shall at home be encountered with a shame as**
  **ample.**
  **First Lord: The web of our life is of a mingled yarn, good and**
  ill

  **together: our virtues would be proud, if our faults whipped**
  **them not; and our crimes would despair, if they were not**
  **cherished by our virtues.**

(An optimist converts calamities into opportunities;
    A pessimist converts opportunities into calamities. )
    Convert losses into comforts, but do not expect comforts in
losses.
    Too much comforts may land one in discomforts.
    One person's comfort is another person's discomfort, as one
person's meat may be another person's poison.
    One who experiences cannot put up with even an iota of
discomfort.
    He is successful in his business, for he converts his losses into
comforts.
    To drown gain in tears is more painful than to drown pain in
tears.
    ("There is no gain without pain" is a proverb in English.)

- **Parolles: He will steal, sir, an egg out of a cloister; for rapes**
  **and**

  **ravishments he parallels Nessus: he professes not keeping**
  **of oaths; in breaking 'em he is stronger than Hercules: he**
  **will lie, sir, with such volubility, that you would think truth**

**were a fool: drunkenness is his best virtue,................................**

**...............................................................**

**he has every thing that an honest man should not have; what an honest man should have, he has nothing.**

Neelima has every thing that an able administrator should not have; but she has nothing what an able administrator should have.

Many of our politicians are stronger than Hercules in breaking promises.

Hercules (a Roman hero), in classical mythology, is famous for his strength and for his numerous far-ranging adventures.

The nursery school child said to his father, "Dad, am I a Hercules to carry my school bag that contains at least ten books on each subject?)

He is such an expert in stealing that he would steal an egg out of a cloister.

This shop keeper is such a fraud that he may steal en egg out of a cloister.

He drinks, drinks and drinks and drowns deeply in alcoholic ocean. He considers drunkenness his best virtue without knowing that he speaks out everything out of intoxication.

Joe does not drink, but he always speaks as if he were in a state of intoxication.

At the first cup, man drinks wine. At the second cup, wine drinks wine and at the third cup, wine drinks man.

The company changes rules at the drop of a hat and I am afraid that the rules are framed by someone in a state of intoxication

Smoking and drinking are injurious to health.

He smoked away his hard earned money and all his plans to start a business ended up in smoke.

- **Helena: Our wagon is prepared, andtime revives us:**

**All's well that ends well; still the fine's the crown;**
**Whate'er the course, the end is the renown.**

(Hitch your wagon to a star- Aim at high. )

Forget the wound that time present has given you; time ahead will heal your wound.

Time is the best healer of wounds.

Say "All's well that ends well" and see "All's well that ends well".

Do not expect the crown at the first step, but the end must be the renown.

The cunning fellow was not at all known to anyone in the beginning but his end was renown.

- **Lafeu: ......................................................He lost a wife**

**Whose beauty did astonish the survey**
**Of richest eyes, whose words all ears took captive,**

(All eyes are on her, as she is the embodiment/ personification/ paragon of beauty.

Is she an angel on earth?. Is she the physical definition of beauty?

He lost his wife, but not his life.

He lost his life, when he lost his wife itself.

All our ears took captive of the leader's astonishing speech.

The orator has damaged the ears of the audience in his efforts to take captive of them.

- **Bertram: He's quoted for a most perfidious slave,**

('Perfidious' means 'disloyal'. )

You are proud of having slaves in hundreds and fifties, but none of them is perfidious.

Your treatment was slavish and so your slave became most perfidious.

The sheep in the wolf entered my office as an embodiment of humility and I gave him a very good salary, but now he has become a most perfidious slave.

Any slave most perfidious will have to pay for it one day or other.

• **King: Your gentle hands lend us, and take our hearts.**

(Kindness is the language which the deaf can hear and the dumb can speak.)

My mother is the milk of human kindness and my father has his heart in the right place.

One who does not have his/her heart in the right place does not win hearts.

The hands that help are holier than the lips that pray.

Lend your hands to the needy at the time of natural calamities.

I can lend you not money, but my hands and mind.

He does not have a heart, but he considers himself a human being.

The innocent girl says, "He took my heart so warmly, but returned it so cruelly".

# CHAPTER ELEVEN

# MEASURE FOR MEASURE

- Duke (Vincentio):..........................to waste

Thyself upon thy virtues, ...............................
Heaven doth with us as we with torches do,
Not light them for themselves; for if our virtues
Did not go forth of us, 'twere all alike
As if we had them not. ..........................................
Mortality and mercy..........................................
Live in thy tongue and heart.

Tarun who was wasting himself upon his vices, is now spending himself upon his virtues.

Mercy and mortality are only in your words, not in your deeds.

Heart filled with mercy beats even after one's death.

Your tongue pours out mercy and cruelty, but your mind is full of cruelty and immortality.

You are so close to mercy in your words, but so far in your deeds that no one can even dream of nearing you.

(En evil mind is Devils' workshop, isn't it?)

Evil thoughts cannot enter a mind loaded with love.

"Arathirkkay anbusaarbu enba ariyar

Marathirkkum a(h)they thunai"- Thiruvalluvar (in Tmil)
"The unwise deem love virtue only can sustain,
It also helps the man who evil would restrain". (in English)

• **Lucio: .............................Grace is grace, despite of all**

**controversy: ...................................thyself art a**
**wicked villain, despite of all grace.**

Grace is grace, but grace becomes ungraceful in your wicked heart.

All know that you are a wicked villain, but you project yourself as a hero by preaching grace.

He is Mr Grace on the screen, but a wicked villain behind the screen.

Grace is grace and mercy is mercy and love is love, despite all controversy.

He was a wicked villain, but grace made him a hero.

The girl says, "The good heart of a wicked villain is sometimes better than that of a gracious man".

Wicked villains sometimes try their best to project themselves gracious, whereas the gracious, on many occasions, pride themselves of being gracious and become unaware of their becoming worse than wicked villains.

• **Pompey: .................................good counselors**

**lack no clients:**

Good teachers lack no students, good lawyers lack no cases, good counsellors lack no clients, but even bad politicians lack no followers.

By acting as if he were a good counselor, Tony has increased the number of his clients.

Lucy became more mad only after her meeting a good (?) counselor.

The manager is at sixes and sevens after lending his ears too many good counselors.

It is the trust of the clients that brings profit to their counselors.

* **Duke: ……………………………………most biting laws.**

**……………………………………………………**
**………like an o'er- grown lion in a cave,**
**That goes not out to prey.**

Implementation of biting laws in the country has made people like over-grown lions in a cave that do not go out to prey.

Ever after retirement, many, due to personal and family commitments, are working like a Trojan without just staying in caves like over-grown lions.

Ragu asks his son whether he is an over-grown lion to just stay in a cave.

His father is so obsessed with self-respect that he, though an over-grown lion, does not like to stay lazily in his son's cave.

Never think that by enforcing biting laws, you can bring peace on our land.

The laws are not biting, but the ruler.

Laws may be biting, but not the administrators.

* **Isabella: Sir, make me not your story.**

What pleasure do you have in making me your story?

Generally the innocent are being made stories by those who wish to make fun.

You do not know even my title, but you want to make me your story.

He has become a great story writer by making all his friends stories.

You have been making everyone around you your story without knowing that your story will be written by someone one day.

If you talk to Somu just for 15 minutes, he will make you the main character of his own story.

Diana says to her husband, "In order to marry Lucy, you have made me your story".

- **Lucio:** ......................................**All hope is gone,**

**Unless you have the grace by your fair prayer**

All is gone except my hope.

There are some who pray as long as their hopes are wet.

The summer is so hot that I wonder whether the hopes of farmers would get dried along with their lands.

He has no hope at all in life, but surprisingly he hopes to have the grace even by his foul prayer.

She says, "Your prayer is too foul to receive blessings from the above".

It is unfair that foul people, though they pray rarely, wish to unfairly make their prayers fair without knowing that God fairly distinguishes between the fair and the unfair.

- **Lucio:** ...............................**Our doubts are traitors,**

**And make us lose the good we oft might win,**

July says to her husband, "It is your mind full of doubts that is the main traitor to our peaceful life".

His doubts have converted his friends into fiends.

Your doubts have earned you traitors and further vulgarized your vices.

Doubts may be solaceful initially, but harmful when they become traitors.

My doubts have made me lose the good that I had won through storms and fire.

He because of doubts became so a fearful traitor that he lost his beautiful wife and peaceful life.

Sometimes we win, but lose the good; sometime we lose, but win the good.


• **Angelo: We must not make a scarecrow of the law,**


**Setting it up to fear the birds of prey,...........**


The lawyer just makes a scarecrow of the law, setting it up to fear his innocent clients.

As you think, she is not the deciding authority in her work place, but just a scarecrow set up to fear the birds of prey.

I am not a crow to fear a scarecrow, but an eagle to make scarecrow invisible, as my wings are close to the clouds.

By making a scarecrow of the law, the lawyer has made innumerable clients the birds of his prey.

The money minded lawyer confesses the fact that every problem of his every customer is his glittering star.

(Of all birds, eagle is supposed to fly at extreme height.)


• **Escalus: Well, heaven forgive him, and forgive us all!**


**Some rise by sin, and some by virtue fall:**
**Some run from brakes of vice, and answer none,**
**And some condemned for a fault alone.**
Nilofer rose by many virtues, but fell by a single sin.

His too much faith in God has made him a sinner.

It is quite strange that you are commended for vice and condemned for virtue.

He is so innocent that he is most of the time condemned for somebody's faults.

He may be rising on by sins, but will have a mighty fall one day.

I am ready not to rise, but to suffer by sins.

The officer says, "For someone's grave faults, nail is hit on my coffin".

- **Angelo: ........................what benefactors are they?**

 **are they not malefactors?**
(Benefactor- someone who gives a gift, often money to a charity.
Malefactor- a criminal, felon or evildoer)
Is it the environment that converts a benefactor into a malefactor?
A malefactor once, Tom is now a benefactor.
The politician is so cunning that he is a benefactor on the screen, but a malefactor behind.

- **Angelo: The law hath not been dead, though it hath slept:**

 Is there any difference between the law that sleeps and the law that is dead?
The lawyer is arguing on the laws dead.
Criminals are awake when the law is sleeping.
It is unfortunate that law is made to sleep on the oily palms.
People lose faith in law, when it is found either on the pages of books or on bed.
(It is said that judgment delayed is judgment denied.)
Law is not to sleep lazily, but to act swiftly.
Lawyers may sleep, but not law.

- **Isabella: ..................................O! it is excellent**

 **To have a giant's strength, but it is tyrannous
To use it like a giant.**

George looks like a giant, but never behaves like a giant.
The old lady has honey in her tongue, but venom in her teeth.
He has a giant's strength, but a child's innocence.

You may have a giant's strength, but do not use it like a giant.

With children our street hero fights with a giant's strength, but with giants, he fights with a child's strength.


- **Isabella: Heaven keep your honour safe!**


I kept my honour safe, I do not know how it was stolen.

Our manager keeps everything safe, except his honour and self-respect.

The farmer is too poor to save anything, except honour and self-respect.

Honour and self-respect are not available in the market.

The employees have to mortgage their honour and self-respect for survival.


- **Angelo: The tempter or the tempted, who sins most?**


**........................................................**
**Thieves for their robbery have authority**
**When judges steal themselves. ........................**
**..........................................Most dangerous**
**is the temptation that doth goad us on**
**To sin in loving virtue:**


The best way of overcoming temptations issimply to yield to them.

Conscience pricks the tempted more than the tempter.

Though the tempter sins more than the tempted, the tempted is a sinner before law.

Being unable to get tempted, some become the tempters.

Judgment should be neither bought nor sold.

When a judge is bought, judgment is sold.

(It is said that the best way of overcoming temptations is simply to yield to them. However, not falling a prey to temptations keeps one away from troubles. )

- **Duke: Love you the man that wrong'd you?**

  **Juliet: Yes, as I love the woman that wrong'd him.**
  **Duke: So then it seems your most offenceful act**
  **Was mutually committed?**

I wish to love a person, who does not wrong me, even when I am wrong.

She loves the man who wrongs all women, except her.

Law punishes one who wrongs a woman on false charges, thus defaming her name.

It is a shame that the leader is defensive of all his offensive acts.

You are going wrong by loving the man that wronged you.

Suji says, "I can marry a man that is wrong, but not one that wrongs me".

Both Ragu and Lily by wronging each other rightly got married.

- **Claudio: The miserable have no other medicine**

  **But only hope:**
  **I've hope to live, an am prepar'd to die.**
  **Duke: Be absolute for death; either death or life**
  **Shall thereby be the sweeter.**

Hope is my only medicine during my dark days.

Hope is a medicine that heals all.

Death may be more peaceful than life, but is it sweeter than life?

It is life that teaches one more lessons than death, but any lesson that one learns from someone's death teaches one lessons more valuable than what life can never teach throughout one's life.

Birth is the indication of death.

Lessons after death cannot be taught to the alive.

Believers hope that life after death is determined by one's journey from the cradle to the grave.

Grave must be a sinless bed as cradle.

Cry in the cradle is responded by mother, cry in the grave is responded by God.

* **Claud: ...................................................If I must die,**

**I will encounter darkness as a bride,**
**And hug it in mine arms.**

I will not encounter darkness even if I happen to have dark hours in my life.

I wonder why she encounters darkness as a bride and hugs it in her arms even when her life is flushed with prosperity.

Though Arun is pretty young, he has three wives, one in brightness, one in darkness and one in half brightness and half darkness, but it is quite unpredictable whether his life will be bright or dark.

Many of us drown our sorrows, worries and pains in darkness, and stage our smiles in brightness.

You hug her, but without affection and treat her just a bride in darkness.

Vili is an angel in darkness, but a devil in brightness.

Many of us love to light our virtues, but dim our vices.

* **Claud: To be imprison'd in the viewless winds,**

**And blown with restless violence round about**
**The pendent world;...............................**

(pendent- hanging down/ incomplete in some sense)

Tsunami swallows innumerable lives and imprisons innumerable minds.

The innocent people of the village are often blown with restless violence.

She is imprisoned in the viewless wind and I am blown with restlessness.

The poor man says, "Even the viewless winds that blow with restless violence favour the rich, but no wind knows my direction".

- **Isabella: I'll pray a thousand prayers for thy death,**

You don't care to pray even a single prayer for my life, but you say that you will pray a thousand prayers for my death.

The mother prayed a thousand prayers for her son's birth, but now the grown up boy makes her die every day.

The hands that help are holier than the lips that pray.

One prayer involving heart and mind is more effective than thousand prayers involving mouth and tongue.

One prayer keeping God in mind is more effective than a thousand prayers keeping God out of mind.

- **Duke: The hand that hath made you fair hath made**

    **you good: the goodness that is cheap in beauty**
    **makes beauty brief in goodness; but grace, being**
    **the soul of your complexion, shall keep the body**
    **of it ever fair.**

"Beauty lies in the eyes of the beholder".

Let grace be the soul of your complexion.

The hands that are extended to serve the needy make one be good and feel good.

Smile is the soul of my girl friend's complexion.

Grace was the complexion of Mother Teresa.

- **Isabella: ....................................I had rather**

    **my brother die by the law than my son should**
    **be unlawfully born.**

I would willingly prefer to die peacefully than to live unlawfully.

The way he was born may be unlawful, but his birth is not unlawful.

Though Varun is a lawyer, every word and deed of his is unlawful.

What you speak may be lawful, but what you have done is unlawful.

(Law-makers should not be law-breakers.)

- **Lucio: .....................'tis a secret must be locked within**

  **the teeth and the lips;......................................**

She has locked her secret, but given the key to all.

I shall tell you a matter, butyou must keep it on the sly. (on the sly-secretly)

I tried my best to keep my secret within my teeth and lips, but when my teeth and lips were damaged by some rowdies, I had to reveal the secret. (Under threat, the secret was revealed. )

Secret is a secret as long as it is locked within the teeth and the lips.

Do not trust John David with any secret, because nothing will remain within his teeth and lips.

- **Duke: .........punish them to your height of pleasure.**

I can punish them to my height of pleasure, but I have my own height of name and fame in the society.

Better to forgive the evil doers to your height of patience than to punish them to your height of pleasure.

What's the use of punishing such people to your height of pleasure?

To punish her to my height of pleasure is the height of my pleasure.

I love her to my height of love.

He is so greedy of food that he eats whatever he gets to his fullest size of his stomach.

- **Angelo: I should be guiltier than my guiltiness.**

"As long as she was in service, despite her age and experience, she was so cruel and arrogant that she must feel so guilty that she shouldbe guiltier than herguiltiness. And greed". – Steve Madden

"I have too many responsibilities and principles. There's no time for 'guilty pleasures'". –A.R.Rahman

He is quite guilty of his stupidity and arrogance.

When Anitha is not at all guilty, how could she be expected to be guiltier than guiltiness?.

- **Mariana: I'll lend you all my life to do you service.**

I consider it a great boon to lend my agedparentsallmy life to do them service.

(Girl: Will you lend me your life?

Boy: If you do not think of becoming my wife.

Girl: !!!)

You need not lend me all your life. Just come to office every day and do your work.

These volunteers are so mad after their leader that they would lend all their life to do him service.

- **Mariana: ..............best men are moulded out of faults,**

"We rank the best man with his worst performance and the worst man with his best performance"-Dr Johnson

Don't be taken away by the faults of yours, because faults mould and shape one.

Best men are moulded out of faults, but all moulded out of faults are not the best.

(Judge: All faults are yours...

The accused: .....best men are moulded out of faults, Your Honour!

Judge: !!!)


• **Duke: ...................................a willing ear...........**


**What's mine is yours and what is yours is mine.**


( RichFather: Oh my son! Why do you love me so much?

Cunning son: Dad! What's yours is mine and what's mine is also mine. )

The teacher was delivering his lecture though there was not even a single willing ear.

Of all his organs, only his belly is willing and active. (Eagerness to eat?)

My ears are selectively willing.

(Party President: You are welcome to our political party. What is your future objective?

Party man: To make mine of today (service) yours tomorrow and yours of today (properties) mine tomorrow.

Party President: !!!)

Bernard Shaw said, "Politics is the last resort for the scoundrels".

Is politics the best resort for statesmen?

(Politician is one, who is concerned about the next election; a statesman is one, who is concerned about the next generation.)

The orator says, "There are ears in thousands, but unwilling to lend".

The saint says, "Everything is God's but we claim everything is ours".

(Elder brother: What's yours is mine and what's mine is mine.

Younger brother: Mine is mine and yours also is mine.

Saint: After death, nothing is yours. )

# CHAPTER TWELVE

# THE WINTER'S TALE

- **Archidamus: .........I speak it in the freedom of my knowledge:................**


  **.................................................................................. We will give you sleepy drinks, that your senses, unintelligent of our**
  **insufficience, ...............................................................**

(To speak in the freedom of knowledge- perfect knowledge)

(We will offer you drinks which will benumb your senses so that you won't notice our shortcomings.)

The research scholar wishes to share some information with the audience in the freedom of my knowledge.

It is unfortunate that one of my colleagues has extraordinary knowledge but just to swallow and digest, not to share with others, as he has no freedom at all.

It is the freedom of his knowledge that brings many learners close to that VIT professor.

Juli does not speak in the freedom of her knowledge, but with doubts over her own knowledge.

The teacher makes me sleep with his lecture more powerful than sleepy drinks.

(Young girls must avoid sharing their contact Nos with unknown persons and going anywhere alone with unknown persons. It is advisable that they avoid drinks offered by unknown people during travel or while being alone. Should they take drinks offered by unknown persons, they do it at their own risk.)

You always keep senses sleepy without any need for any sleepy drink.

Blind love more than sleepy drinks makes one's senses unintelligent of insufficience.

- **Archidamus: Believe me. I speak as my understanding instructs me, and**

 **as mine honesty puts it to utterance.**

(I speak out of understanding as reason and honesty prompts meto speak.)

The problem with some of us is that we are neither understanding, nor honest.

The minister speaks not as his understanding instructs, but as his wife's understanding instructs him.

His thoughts are as his honesty puts it to, not his utterances.

Babu is on the wrong track as he is instructed by his own understanding.

Mistake me not if anything of what I said is wrong for I told you everything as my understanding instructed me.

It is my understanding that Tom has been terminated from service on some pressure from the higher level.

- **Archidamus: I think there is not in the world either malice or matter to**

 **alter it.**

(Neither malice nor any other cause can change their love for each other.)

(Boy: I think there is not in the world either malice or matter to alter it.

Girl: till you see my sister who is more beautiful than I? )

I think there is none in the world of literature either to define or to describe our love.

There must be either some malice or matter behind her atrocious behaviour.

There is not in the world either malice or matter to alter my profound love for you.

I think there must be either some malice or matter that the rules are being changed at the drop of a hat.

I donot know what malice or what matter prevented the party from giving me a chance to contest the election this time.

The romantic hero of our town will break his love with this girl also without any malice or matter.

He is looking for some malice or matter to break his love with Rosy and to marry Lucy.

- **Polixenes:** ...................................................................**I multiply**

**With one 'We thank you' many thousands more
That go before it.**

"I must write one line of thanks to you for the part you have played........."- a sentence written by Irwin in his letter. (241)

Even Himalayan help can be acknowledged at least with the single word 'thanks', but coming from one's heart.

The ink is sufficient just for a single line of thanks, but my mind has pages full of gratitude.

We request the minister to receive our thanks in multiplication for his kind consent to sanction the amount that we require for our mega project.

My 'thank you' said once now will get multiplied after the work is completed.

Is the utterance of your 'thanks' from your heart or from your lips?

The actress didnot care to say 'thanks' to her fans for their donating blood on her birthday and it might be perhaps her 'thanks' might have stuck to her lipstick.

• **Polixenes: I am question'd by my fears,..............................**

(I am obsessed with fears ....)

(Bacon says, "Men fear death as children fear darkness". There are many amongst us who invite fears through questions. Children at the time of enjoying peaceful sleep at nights with no fear compel their grandparents to tell them stories of ghosts, but with fear they sleep. What creates fear in everyone is Death. Saints say that as they are sure of reaching God or Heaven, they are awaiting death. The peculiar sounds from somewhere, the sound-producing dance of trees at nights and barking of dogs naturally create in one fear. Such sounds raise many questions and the silent answer is Fear.

One of the Tamil Actors cum director K.Baagyaraj received the question from one of the readers of 'Baagya' "How can I overcome the fear of death?", for which he answered, "Death shall not come to you as long as you are alive. When death comes to you, you shall not be alive. So fear not death and live your life till the end of your life without fear".

During the rapid spread of Covid 19, it was the fear of the disease that questioned most of us with more fears than the actual disease. A good doctor cures half of one's disease with pleasing words and the remaining with suitable medicine. Human treatment is as important as medical treatment. Some doctors cure the disease with their efficiency, but kill them to quench their financial thirst. Disease has to wait patiently without harming the patients till currencies fill the cash counters in many hospitals. Nothing is more painful than the acts of squeezing from poor patients as much as money as possible even before the disease is diagnosed. However, dedicated and professionally committed doctors are recognized by patients next to God. The unmatchable and divine services of doctors, nurses and scavengers without being questioned by fears during Covid 19 shall be ever remembered by all. The doctors who lost their precious lives in their sincere attempts to save the life of others without any fear are as great as the great martyrs who lost their precious lives for the sake of a nation.)

The psychiatrist says that the patient's main problem is that she is questioned by her fears and he also says that the problem will get complicated if fears turn out to be doubts.

Fear haunts one when there is any urgent call from a ferocious boss.

The employee could not sleep a wink, as her mind was being questioned by fears.

The innocent girl was questioned by fears at the time of her marriage, but now she is bold enough to supply fear freely to her husband with too many questions.

You cannot take risk or face challenges as long as you are questioned by fears.

It is not the question of fear, but the fear that the decorum of the stage will get collapsed prevents me from questioning him publicly.

- **Polixenes: .........Press me not.....................................**

  **There is no tongue that moves, none, none i'the world,**
  **So soon as yours could win me:.............................**

(None in the world can persuade me as quickly asyours.)

Press me not, else you will get blood pressure.

The manager is bending himself and others under pressure from the top authorities.

Winston is so eloquent that no tongue in the world could win his.

The orator is so fluent that his tongue might be pressed by flood of words.

Shashi Tharoor's vocabulary is so sound that he might press himself wholly and wholeheartedly by all editions of dictionaries and additions in language.

Her tongue is pressed by anger, causing trouble later.

Better to maintain silence than to extend the tongue pasted with communal poison.


- **Leontes: Tongue-tied, our queen? Speak you.............**


(tongue-tied- unable to speak)

Freedom of speech comes to standstill when tongues are tied.

Amir wishes to marry any girl, but with her tongue tied.

Vinoth says, "Better to marry a tongue-tied than to marry a chatterbox".

In many houses, the angry wives punish their husbands by keeping their tongues tied.

(Arise, Awake and stop not till they buy you jewels.)

Some of us are considered saints as long as they speak.

Speak not; for thine shalt be spoken of.

(We come across different types of people in life; some speak and some not; some smile and some not that even; some speak more, some less and some on terms and conditions. Some keep themselves to themselves as they fear that they might meet their trouble by speaking, quite obviously revealing the fact that they do not trust their own tongues. Some successfully reap their harvest by remaining solitary reapers. We cannot scrutinize everyone that we come across in life with X-ray eyes. The drunkards in a state of intoxication generally do not keep their tongues tied, and when they speak, their words also get intoxicated. On many occasions they invite their own troubles by talking whatever their intoxicated minds instruct them to talk. But most irritating among those who do not speak are those who, just because they were born with a silver spoon in their mouth or because they had their education in some leading institutes either by merit or by accident, keep their tongues well-tied in order to make others think that they are unique creatures fit only for an ideal world or fit to sit and chat only with those endowed with more than six senses. This clearly indicates not one's intellect, but immaturity. The education obtained is of absolutely of no use, unless the mind is cultivated constructively and unless the mind attains maturity. But to maintain silence is far better than to hurt one's feelings by speaking.

Between two close intimate friends who speak only between themselves, the world beyond their friendship remains unknown. "Silent spectators are dangerous" is a proverb. When should we speak and when shouldn't we speak? During journeys, careful people avoid speaking to strangers, but when their minds force them to speak; they choose words and develop a conversation. Some, during journeys, judge others by what they speak and how they behave, and then decide over any future acquaintance with them.

In villages, it is quite rare to see people avoiding others, irrespective of their educational and economic backgrounds, but it has become quite common to see educated people sailing in the same boat spending time more with machines than with men. Total avoidance of others means a lot. Some avoid others in order to conceal their ignorance, as it is proverbially said that "To conceal ignorance is to increase it". There are many who prefer to talking with books to talking with humans, but unless they share their knowledge with others, they just unlearn whatever they have learnt. Healthy discussions among academicians irrespective of their level or acquisition of knowledge result in healthy outcome. However, avoiding fellow human beings due to the so called intellectual arrogance is nothing but a sign of immaturity, and when they look back in the evening of their life, they would find their own life full of sound and fury, signifying nothing. Real education shapes one's mind. The boat tied to an anchor cannot move; the person tied to ego cannot improve.

P.V.Narasimha Rao former Prime Minister of India, even though he was considered an experienced and able administrator, was allegedly considered to have used 'silence' as a strategy to find solution to any problem. Mrs Margaret Alva, a former minister of the Congress govt in her autobiography "Courage & Commitment" writes the following out of her association with the then Prime Minister.

"In March 1995, after attending the world Summit for Social Development at Copenhagen with the Prime Minister, we travelled to the airport by bus. There was an interesting discussion on the agenda of the summit and the new areas that the developing world was being urged to 'open up', besides the many commitments we had made for social development.

'Such "opening up" is inevitable', said the Prime Minister. 'We have to be prepared for it'.

'But there will be strong reactions to such moves at home, sir, and elections are not far away. We have to be cautious', I warned.

A.N.Verma, the Principal Secretary to the Prime Minister-as if he were the government's conscience-keeper-said, 'We must be prepared for defeat, if it comes to that. But there is no way liberalization as a policy can be reversed!'

The Prime Minister listened with a grave expression, and pouted.

Later, on the flight, I raised the issue. 'Are we to accept Verma's formula and prepare for defeat? You said nothing to him in reply! Why? I asked

'Win or lose', he said gravely, 'I am not bothered. After all, I will go down in history as the only non-Nehru-Gandhi Prime Minister to last a full term, despite them'. I fell silent.

I had several arguments with him over various issues. 'Why don't you take decisions, sir? You let matters drag on-why? I once, asked.

'Not taking a decision is also a decision', he answered, unperturbed". (276-277)

Is silence a way to solve problems? It is left to the readers' discretion. )

- **Hermione: Our praises are our wages: you may ride's**

  **With one soft kiss a thousand furlongs ere**
  **With spur we heat an acre.**

(Onesoft kiss would do more than a harsh command to us. )

One soft kiss from my mother heals all my mental pains.

One hard kiss of his girl friend made the runner run faster than a well-beaten Arabian horse and win the medal in the Olympic.

A word of appreciation or an award of recognition makes one travel thousand furlongs with a new spirit.

The poor cannot fill their stomachs with your praises as wages, but only with wages given on time. (Prophet Muhammad (PBUH) says, "Give the wages to the coolie before his/her single drop of sweating touches the earth.)

The girl says that she can make her boy friend surrender to her will with a single soft kiss.

Tom says, "It is strange that the iron-hearted girl attracted me with her soft kisses".

- **Leontes: The covering sky is nothing; Bohemia nothing;**

  **My wife is nothing; nor nothing have these nothings,**
  **If this be nothing.**

(The world with all that it contains is nothing. The sky which covers the earth is nothing; Bohemia, nothing! My wife, nothing! All these are nothing..........)

Language is nothing without literature, isn't it?

Absence of literature is making language absolutely nothing.

The boy mad in love says that everything is nothing for him, but his love for her.

Everything has become nothing for him since she left him.

He is so generous that he will give everyone in need something even out of his nothing.

A saint is one who considers everything nothing in this material world.

(Now many so called saints start from nothing and prosper beyond everything!.)

His desire for everything has made him nothing now.

Arul considered his mother nothing because of his blind love for some worthless girl, but now it is his mother who has turned his total nothing into everything of high value.

If you consider everything nothing, why should you look for something?.

Ignorance of everything makes one ultimately nothing.

- **Leontes: I'll give no blemish to her honour,**

(I will not allow any blame to be attached to her honour. )

His son himself is a great blemish to his honour.

Honour is honour until some blemish is attached to it.

The minister retains his honour in spite of being given blemish after blemish.

There are some waiting for every opportunity to give blemish to others' honour.

Our boss has won everyone's trust that none on earth can give blemish to his honour.

(Can one speak as follows on a stage?

Hon'ble Chief Guest! I deem it a great honour to give blemish to your honour. )

- **Polixenes: ........................................I met him**

**With customary compliment, when he**
**Wafting his eyes to the contrary, and falling**
**A lip of much contempt, speeds from me and**

**So leaves me to consider what is breeding**
**That changes thus his manners.**

(customary compliment-usual salutation )

(When he turns his eyes away in other direction and raises his lip in contempt, runs past me and leaves me, I am made to ponder over what might have caused him to change.)

I am not an ordinary administrator to be easily carried away with one's customary compliment.

Her eyes always misguide him and what she conveys through her eyes is contrary to what actually happens.

Our new principal is not taken away by customary compliments.

It is by exchange of smiles and customary compliments, human relationship is developed.

She talks to him but with her lips stuck with much contempt.

He thanks me with a smile but with much jealousy in mind and contempt in heart.

Customary compliments in the morning make the working environment in offices.

They make compliments to their boss just for the sake of custom.

- **Polixenes: Turn then my freshest reputation to**

  **A savour that may strike the dullest nostril**
  **Where I arrive; and my approach be shunn'd**
  **Nay, hated too, worse than the great'st infection**
  **That e'er was heard or read!**

(My royal blood turns into a diseased jelly and my name be for ever linked with Judas, who betrayed Jesus Christ. In that case, let my fairest name so stink that it will affect the dullest sense wherever I go so that my presence be shunned and abhorred more than the greatest infection that wehear or read of.)

How outspoken you are amidst many Judas!

(Boy: Trust me, I won't betray you...

Girl: Even Jesus was betrayed. )

The officer by accepting the bribe has turned his reputation to a savour striking even the dullest nostrils.

If you know of her true colour, you would avoid her, hate her and consider her more infectious than the greatest infection you would have neither heard of nor read.

Forgetting the eared walls around us and the Judas overhearing us, we make our tongues freely roam about, and face the music later.

Shun him, speak not and approach him not, should you consider him worse than Judas.

The old lady's mind is more infectious than any infectious disease.

- **Hermione: I am not prone to weeping, as our sex**

   **Commonly are;.......................**

(I am not prone to weeping, as women are.)

The boy is so sensitive that he is more prone to weeping than a woman is.

Keep a distance from those who are prone to weeping for trivial matters.

A single drop of tear from a woman's eyelids is more powerful than words in thousands from a man's mouth.

Unlike many women, she is not prone to weeping.

She is so fond of and so prone to weeping that she can tearfully contribute to an ocean.

- **Antigonus: ........every inch of woman in the world,**

   **Ay, every dram of woman's flesh is false,**

(I would not trust my wife out of sight and touch. If our queen is false, every woman, every dram of women'sflesh is false. )

The boy is so mad after her that he has written poems in hundreds, describing every part of the girl that he is in love with.

David says that he will marry her after commenting that her flesh is false.

Lust only for flesh is not love for a soul.

Renuha says, "Better to remain unmarried till the end of my life than to marry someone who doubts my flesh".

(A woman can live with any man happily, but not with a doubting Thomas and with one always in the company of 'bottles' forgetting the world they live in. It is the polluted mind and the jaundiced eye that make one doubt his wife. Here the authors are reminded of a scene in a Tamil movie. The villagers gather under a tree, following a charge levelled by a doubting Thomas against his wife. When the panchayat president is about to punish the innocent woman unfairly, the hero K.Baagyaraj, observing the whole scene, will ask the village leaders the question, "Who, among women, come to your mind whenever you think of 'woman of chastity'?. The village leaders would mention a number of names such as Kannahi, and Madhavi. After getting their answers, the hero would tell them they mentioned the names of all women except the names of their mothers and wives. The embarrassed village leaders would get blows from their wives. )

- **Leontes:** ....................................................**Our prerogative**

  **Calls not your counsels, but our natural goodness**
  .................................................................
  **We need no more of your advice; the matter,**
  **The loss, the gain, the ordering on't, is all**
  **Properly ours.**

(My prerogative as king does not need your advice in this matter. I tell you this out of my own natural goodness.........................This matter, the loss or gain from it is my concern and I take the responsibility of its execution and consequences. )

(The word 'counselling' is often mistaken as advice, which, in fact, is not so. The present youngsters have some sort of aversion towards advice being given. It is 'listening' that plays a vital role in the process of counselling. Ears and eyes are and must be more functional than tongues. The more the counsellor talks the less he/she is apprehensive. A good counsellor becomes the counselee and analyses the problem from various perspectives and offers guidance or solution. Psychological and cordial approach facilitates the counselling process. No counsellor with pre-assessment or prejudices can be successful as a counsellor. Counselling is much insisted on in academic institutes, especially where there is a co-educational set up. Some get relief after meeting a counsellor and some get grief after meeting him/her. )

My prerogative calls not your counsel, but our natural goodness.

I am sending you this mail, seeking your appropriate counsel in this matter.

He called his own death after calling for his counsel.

We are enough of your advice and we need no more of that.

We entrust you with the new responsibilities and you are responsible for all gains and losses.

'Blaming others for losses and appreciating self for gains' is highly harmful to any team.

('It is my baby' means 'It is my responsibility'.)

- **Paulina:** .......................................**to lock up honesty and honour**

(To put in prison an honest and honourable lady and to stop her visitors from seeing her.)

By putting him behind bars, you have put behind bars honesty and honour.

It is honesty and honour that I have earned as my great treasures in my decades of experience as a teacher.

She inherited honesty and honour from her parents, and dishonesty and dishonour from her husband.

(New politician: How can I shine as a politician?

Corrupt politician: Lock up all virtues and wear all vices. )

Those who lock up honesty and honour will be locked up one day or other.

Covid 19 locked up the whole world.

Having completely locked up his honesty and honour, our chief guest has come out today to honour us with his visit.

- **Emilia: If I prove honey-mouth'd, let my tongue blister,**

  **And never to my red-look'd anger be**
  **The trumpet any more. ...............................**
  **.................................................................**
  **The silence often of pure innocence**
  **Persuades when speaking fails.**

(If I use sweet words in telling it to him, my tongue may blister, and it may never be the instrument expressing my hot anger...................The silence of pure innocence may be more effective when loudest speechesfail to convince. )

(Woman 1: How did your husband buy you this costly necklace?

Woman 2: I must thank Shakespeare. The silence often of pure innocence persuades when speaking fails.

Woman 1 leaves her silently. )

He is a honey-mouthed scoundrel. It is his honey tongue that makes many girls easily fall into his trap.

The lady says that she can no more tolerate her husband's red-look'd anger.

His face is white but his tongue is red. (white-innocent, red-angry)

Your tongue will blister if you speak even a single ill-word of her.

Whenever my tongue fails, it is with my silence I win.

As he failed as a speaker in politics, he made up his mind to succeed as a silent saint.

- **Paulina: This child was prisoner to the womb,.................**

(The child is innocent.)

(Is Man a prisoner of life? Everywhere the have-nots are living as prisoners of poverty and the haves either as prisoners of hospitals or of ambition and discontent. Those who meet with failure in love are prisoners of intolerable pain. Students who are burdened with assignments are prisoners of the class room or the system. Those who suffer from womb to tomb are prisoners of Fate or Misfortune. "Man is born free but is everywhere in chains.", said Rousseau. A question on this was raised to Mr K.Natwar Singh former minister of the Congress government when he appeared for the Civil Service interview. He narrates it as follows in his autobiography "One Life is not enough". This experience of his will be of some benefit to our young students who aspire to become Civil Service Officers.

"On the appointed day, wearing my best suit, I reached Dholpur House at 10 AM in my brother's Jaguar. I was called in for the interview at around 11 AM. Eight gentlemen sat around a semi-circular table. At the centre sat the Chairman, R.N.Bannerji, ICS, then the Home Secretary.

I sat opposite the Chairman, my heart pounding. The interview commenced with a loaded question, 'In your application you only mentioned the IAS and IFS and not the other services. Are you so sure of getting into either of the two? I answered, 'Sir, I am not sure, but I am confident'.

I was then asked what my plans were if I did not qualify. I told them that I would finish my Tripos at Cambridge and then look for a job. The next question: 'Man is born free but is everywhere in chains. Who said that? My reply: 'Rousseau, sir.' Then: 'In your view, is man in chains?' I said: 'No, sir. I am not in chains.'

I had been warned that at some point a 'trap' question would be asked. Sure enough, the 'trap' was laid with finesse. I was asked if I had read a particular book, which I had not. In nine cases out of ten, the temptation would have been to bluff and say yes, but an affirmative answer would have done me in. But I did not get intimidated and negotiated the 'trap' with some sangfroid. The next question was descriptive essay: 'What are the three events in the last twelve months that have made an impact on you?' 'Can I, sir, be given a minute or two to think before answering?' This, I was later told, had made a favourable impression on the selection board.

The ordeal of the interview was over, I proceeded to Bharatpur. One night, we were about to sit down for dinner when my elder brother, Bhagwat Singh, switched on the radio to hear the 9 p.m. news. Halfway through, the announcer started reading out the names of those who had been selected for the IAS and IFS. My name was amongst them-the first Rajasthani in the country to qualify for the Indian Administrative Service and the Indian Foreign Service". (25-26)

The authors feel that more than reading of books and attending of training classes, it is the association with outstanding and experienced Civil Service Officers that will enable the aspiring candidates to appear for the Civil Service Exams with courage and confidence. )

She is my sister from another womb.

The period of imprisonment of a babe in the womb is 10 months. Many get released even before that.

Life starts with imprisonment?

• **Paulina: That creep like shadows.....................................**

(To walk with silent steps round him.)

The candidate was not selected for he has crept into the interview hall like shadows.

Innumerable doubts on this case creep into the mind of the police like shadows.

The newly wedded couple creep into the room like shadows.

The baby started crying when some insects crept into the cradle like shadows.

• **Leontes: ...............................A nest of traitors!**

The newly married girl considers the house she has entered as a daughter-in-law as a nest of traitors.

A woman from a cultured family converts even a nest of traitors into a home filled with love.

The manager says that the nests of traitors here and there in the company must first be destroyed for bringing it to No 1 position.

I cannot be an inmate in a nest of traitors.

Better to breathe freely under the open sky than to suffocate in a nest of traitors.

It is fate and poverty that has made him an inmate in a nest of traitors.

The political party despite being a nest of traitors easily wins every election.

Can one live like a saint in a nest of traitors for such a long period?

Better to be eaten by worms in my grave than to get my breath polluted in a nest of traitors.

- **Paul: ...........sting is sharper than the sword's;**

The innocent husband says that her every sting is sharper than the sword's.

Sharp swords can further be sharpened by her tongue.

House never becomes Home as long as the inmates' every sting is sharper than the sword's.

Home is not a home unless the hearts in are dry

Better to keep my neck under a sharpened sword than to lend my ears to your red tongue.

She seems to be a saint but stings like a scorpion.

- **Leontes: I am a feather for each wind that blows.**

**Still shall I live on to see this bastard knee!**
**And call me father? Better burn it now**
**Than curse it then.**

(Am I like a feather that blows with the wind? Shall I live to see this bastard grow, kneel and call me father? Better burn it now than I curse it later on.)

He is so selfish that he becomes a feather for each wind that blows for his personal gains.

(Press: Is it true that you, having lost the election, have decided to join the ruling party?

Leader: I am not a feather for each wind that blows. )

The murderer's father says, "Better to be fatherless than to be called father by such a son".

(Girl 1: I am unable to control my anger with the boy who has cheated me in the name of love.

Girl 2: Better burn your love now than curse it then.)

The psychiatrist says that the patient has been carrying all his pains and worries without burning them every now and then. Too much suppression has caused such a curse on his health.

Her survival capacity is so much that she just turns out to be a feather for any wind that blows.

People committed to great ideologies and high principles do not become feathers for every wind that blows.

- **Antigonus:** ......................................**Wolves and bears, they say,**

    **Casting their savageness aside have done**
    **Like offices of pity.**

(Wolves and bears, they say, forgetting their cruel nature, have done such acts of mercy.)

The trials and tribulations of every mother in bringing up her children will move even wolves and bears, casting their savageness aside.

I do not want to keep myself associated with wolves and bears.

Ritu is a saint though he has wolves and bears as friends.

He is a good human being even among wolves and bears.

Robert is such a diplomatic and efficient employer that he can make even wolves and bears do like offices of pity, casting their savageness aside.

One must be careful when wolves and bears cast their savageness aside. ("Calm before the storm" is a proverb in English.)

- **Hermione:** ..................................................**I think had been in me**

**Both disobedience and ingratitude**
**To you and to your friend,................................**

(I should have been guilty of disobeying you, ungrateful to you and to your friend.)

(Kripananda Variyar Swami, a Shaivite spiritual teacher from India and an ardent devotee of Lord Murugan used to highlight the point in his speeches that "One who is ungrateful does not reach God". )

It is most painful that some sons and daughters without an iota of conscience and gratitude leave their aged parents in the lurch. Valamburi John, who was rightly called "Vaarthai Siddhar" for his eloquence in Tamil, used to say that the universities must get back the certificates from those who are ungrateful to their parents, for they are unfit to live in this world, priding themselves in possession of university degree certificates.

In many Tamil families, grandmothers telling stories ending with moral lessons to their grand children is quite common. It is considered one of the reasons for children growing up with values. One of the stories quite commonly told to children is as follows

When two friends were going through a thick forest once, they got frozen in fear on seeing a bear coming towards them. One of them suddenly climbed on a tree, leaving the other. As he did not know how to climb up, he lay down on the floor, acting as if he were dead. The bear came near him, had a smell of him and left. After the bear leaving him, the friend who climbed up the tree came down and asked him what the bear had whispered in his ears. The other said, "The bear came close to my ears and whispered that I should not trust a friend who leaves a friend in danger". Pain becomes intolerable when well-settled sons and daughters are ungrateful to their parents, when a trusted friend becomes ungrateful and when a politician becomes ungrateful to the people of his/her constituency after the election. )

It was his disobedience and ingratitude that kept him away from his own friends.

Obedience and gratitude can neither be supplied nor ordered online.

Despite his disobedience and ingratitude, his parents and teachers love him very much.

The student was very obedient and grateful till he received his Transfer Certificate (TC).

He says that he cannot wail like a dog to prove his gratitude.

"Bayanthookkar seitha vuthavi nayanthookin

Nanmai kadalir perithu". (Thiruvalluvar- in Tamil)

"Kindness shown by those who weight not what the return may be; when you ponder right its merit, 'Tis vaster than the sea". (In English the meaning of the above Thirukkural)


- **Paulina:** .............................................**The tyranny,**


**Together working with thy jealousies,..............**
Your tyranny has shaken hands with jealousy.

Jennifer says that her sister-in-law is not suffering from jaundice, but from jealousy.

John says that he is reminded of Shakespeare's "The tyranny together working with jealousy" whenever his mother and wife face each other.

It is your ever burning jealousy that is converting you into a tyrant.

Revathi is tyrant and her husband is jealous, and they are, by the grace of evil, made for each other.

Our manager is tyrant and our assistant manager is jealous and they will work together to oust all other employees from service.

* **Paulina:** .................................**A thousand knees**

**Ten thousand years together, naked, fasting,**
**Upon a barren mountain, and still winter,**
**In storm perpetual, could not move the gods**
**To look that way thou wert.**

(A thousand knees kneeling together in prayer for ten thousand years, naked and fasting on a barren mountain, in perpetual winter and storms, would not move the gods to take pity on you.)

The drunkard had tortured his wife so much that she would never allow him to enter her life again, even if he kneeled down before her till the end of his life.

God would never forgive the fake saints, even if they kneeled down for ten thousand years, naked, fasting upon a barren mountain.

She says that she will accept my love, if I observe fasting upon a barren mountain when the sun is red with anger.

The mad lover is ready to stoop down to the level of kneeling down, walking naked in public, fasting in hot summer on a barren mountain, and what not, to win her hands.

Even if you kneel down for months, fast on a barren mountain, walk barefoot on the red sands of a desert, can it be compensated with the pain your mother bore when you were in her womb?

("Paradise lies at the feet of one's mother"-Prophet Muhammad (PBUH))

* **Leontes:** ...................................**I have deserved**

**All tongues to talk their bitterest.**

(I deserve worst reproaches from everybody. )

As long as he was a sinner, his tongue misused its full freedom and he, after becoming a saint, says that he deserves all tongues to talk their bitterest.

Those who try to divide people in the name of caste, colour and religion deserve all tongues to talk their bitterest.

Do not think that she is sweet-tongued; in fact she talks ill of everyone the bitterest behind the screen.

The rowdy is such a big nuisance to the public that he deserves all tongues to talk their bitterest.

His heart being warm is unknown to all as his tongue talks the bitterest.

His every word is so bitter that he might have been a bitter guard in his previous birth.

When his true colour comes to light, all tongues will talk their bitterest against him.

His life with her will be peaceful only when his bitter tongue is pasted with some drops of honey.

One cannot become sweet-tongued by eating sugar.


- **Mariner: We have landed in ill time: the skies look grimly**

**And threaten present blusters.**

(We have landed in an evil hour. The dark sky threatens storms to burst soon. My conscience feels that heavens are angry and frowning upon this foul business we have to do. )

Anger will land you in trouble one day or other.

Wherever he goes, the sky above him looks grimly.

The farmer says in pain that he does not know whether he is under the gloomy sky or the gloomy sky becomes his umbrella wherever he goes.

The corrupt politician says, "The unexpected IT raids in my houses, colleges, companies and offices have made the skies above me look grimly and threaten blusters". (There are many corrupt politicians who will find fault even with the sky, if it looks gloomy.

)

The leader says that he could not even imagine that he would landin ill time by joining politics.

She does not mind the sky above her looking grimly, threatening blusters as she is confident that she will land in good time through her hard work.

- **Antigonus: I have heard, but not believed, the spirits o'the dead**

**May walk again:**

(In Tamil, it is said, "Kannal kaanbathum poi; kaathal keitpathum poi; theera visaarippatheymei". It means "Believe not whatever you see; believe not whatever you hear; believe what you see with your own eyes and mind too. )

Heard tales may be false, those unheard may be true and those heard or heard may become either true or false after manipulation.

A good judge does not just believe whatever we sees and hears.

She just believes whatever she hears and that has made her bearer of all such pains.

(Daughter-in-law: Aunty! Were you walking here and there last midnight?

Mother-in-law: No, I was having a sound sleep. Why do you ask me?

Daughter-in-law: I have heard that the spirits of the dead may walk at nights. )

The problem with your boss is that he just believes whatever he hears.

She just hears, but never believes.

It is her love for rumours that has made her ear as big as that of a donkey.

He keeps his eyes and ears open, but keeps his tongue well-tied.

- **Polixenes: ..........................a man, they say, that from very**

**nothing, and beyond the imagination of his neighbours, is grown into an unspeakable estate.**

(A man, they say, is rich beyond the dream of his neighbours, and this man rose to be rich suddenly from a position of absolute poverty.)

The poor mother says to her son, "After your rich father's death, all those who were close to our hearts are now far away from us, and I wish you attained all success beyond their evil expectations of you".

(Husband: what can I get you for your birthday?

Wife: Anything, but beyond the imagination of our neighbour's wife. )

The dull student astonished all his teachers by securing high marks beyond their imagination.

Do not spend money beyond your income.

He has written a poem beyond his imagination for his girl friend.

Being nobody yesterday, you have become somebody today and why can't you become everybody tomorrow?

I am happy that you, from a poor family, have grown into an unspeakable estate.

The kind hearted man takes care of his blind and deaf wife beyond love's imagination.

You got promotion just by projection beyond even an outstanding poet's imagination.

- **Autolycus: …………………………having flown over many knavish**

  **professions, he settled only in rogue:………………………**

(He tried his hand lightly on many dishonest professions and finally adopted the life of a rogue.)

(Interviewer: Have you got any previous work experience?

Candidate: I have flown over many knavish professions, I settled only in rogue.....

Interviewer: !!!)

Titus, having flown over many knavish professions to settle only in rogue, the police have made him settle down in prison.

Though his profession is knavish, he is highly professional in his behaviour.

Some rowdies have been flying over many knavish professions, but they have no idea to land for good.

After having flown over many knavish professions, Mallu now wants to settle down in life as a politician.

"Better to die of hunger than to fly over knavish professions", says the accused.

- **Servant: ...............................He sings several tunes faster than you'll**

  **tell money; he utters them as he had eaten ballads and all men's ears**
  **grew to his tunes.**

(He sings several tunes faster than you can count money; he utters them as if he had eaten ballads, all men'sears are charmed by his tunes. )

Whenever he talks to his girl friend, his words are so poetic and romantic as if he swallowed ballads.

The singer claims to sing several tunes, nothing of which is tune-like.

Bruce issuch an outstanding musician that he can sing several tunes without efforts faster than you can count money.

Confused with several tunes, Tony does not sing even a single tune perfectly.

Her tunes are so sweet that all ears grow to her tunes.

He is such an obedient husband that he dances to his wife's all tunes.

- **Florizel: .................................this hand,**

**As soft as dove's down, and as white as it,**
  **Or Ethiopian's tooth, or the fann'd snow**
  **That's bolted by the northern blasts twice o'er.**


(I take your hand, this very hand, soft and white as dove's feathers, or as white as a negro's tooth,or the snow that is fanned and sifted by the northernwinds. )

Lovers of beauty try all toothpastes and brushes to get Ethiopian tooth and try all beauty creams to get rid of their Ethiopian colour.

Tom loves Dina because her hand is as soft as dove's down, her lips as beautiful as Diana's, and her teeth as glittering as those of the Ethiopians and as white as the fanned snow bolted by the northern blasts twice or thrice.

It is the actresses' Ethiopian tooth that got her plenty of chances in toothpaste advertisements.

He looks like an Ethiopian only in complexion, but he has his heart as white as his (Ethiopian's) tooth.

She always keeps her face and smile as the fann'd snow that's bolted by the northern blasts twice o'er, but her heart is blacker than an Ethiopian's face.

Ethiopians should not be judged by their colours. (Books are not judged by covers. )

Her heart is dark but she made him fall into her trap with her Ethiopian's tooth.


• **Florizel:** ....................................let myself and fortune


  **Tug for the time to come.**


(Let me fight against my fate and try to winit. )

(Those who believe in destiny are fond of using the terms 'fortune', 'misfortune', 'fate' and 'destiny'. Those who do not seek fortunes in life are quite happy when fortunes embrace them. But when hard work is overtaken by fortune, it causes pain. Fortune does not stay with all, all the time and fortune never embraces some. Here the word 'fortune' reminds the authors of an anecdote narrated by former Prime Minister of India I.K.Gujral in his autobiography titled 'Matters of Discretion', which follows in his own words

"I would like to mention how Bansi Lal came to occupy the chief minister's chair. It certainly makes for an amusing story, particularly for those who believe in destiny.

Indira Gandhi did not like Haryana Chief Minister Bhagwat Dayal Sharma who was close to Home Minister Gulzarilal Nanda. She kept applying pressure on Nanda to change the chief minister, but he would not budge. This created a lot of bad blood between them. Finally, Mrs Gandhi asked me to talk to Nanda and persuade him. I then met Nanda at his residence and tried my best for over an hour to persuade him but could not succeed as he kept repeating that there was no other leader as eminent as Bhagwat Dayal Sharma. As I was leaving, Nanda, who was walking me to his porch where my car was parked, casually asked: 'Who can replace him?'

I told Nanda; 'Why annoy Mrs Gandhi? Make anyone you wish'. There were some people in the verandah of Nanda's house. Turning to one lean and rather tall gentleman in crumpled clothes who was sitting on a charpoy (cot), I said: 'kissi ko banaa dijiye. Innhey hi banaa dijiye'. (Make anyone! Make him!.) By the time I reached home, a mere ten-minute drive away, there were two urgent messages from the home minister. When I called himback, he said: "Were you serious about the gentleman that you pointed towards and said make him the chief minister? I was nonplussed. I remember pointing to a backbencher MP-Bansi Lal-but was amazed that Nanda would consider him. I told him that I would get back to him after checking with the prime minister. India Gandhi wanted Bhagwat Dayal Sharma out at any cost and replied: 'I do not care about the successor. Just get rid of Bhagwat Dayal'.

That is how Bansi Lal, to everyone's shock and surprise, became the chief minister of Haryana, and later the defence minister of India during the Emergency. People though that he was close to Mrs Indira Gandhi, who had handpicked him. Few knew that she did not even know who he was or what he looked like. But Bansi Lal never forgot the incident and remained a true and loyal friend of mine all his life". (46-47) Does this anecdote not make us think that Fortune can elevate its favourite one to any position, for which many toil days and nights without food or water? )

It is fortune that can elevate one to the position of chief minister of a state and even more.

A number of fortune sellers (astrologers) have been suffering for want of fortune.

Fortune embraces their close relatives (the lucky) and its trustees (those who trust fortunes) more than the deserving.

Let myself and fortune tug for the time to come.

When fortune embraces one, the wind shows its favour by blowing in one's convenient direction.

Some are so fortunate that even fortune would cry over his continuous misfortune.

- **Autolycus: ....................................................To have an open ear,**

   **a quick eye, and a nimble hand, is necessary for a cut-purse: a good**
   **nose is requisite also, to smell out work for the other senses.**

(It is necessary for a pick-pocket to possess an open ear, a quick eye, a deft hand. It is also necessarythat he should have a good nose, to smell out things in which other senses may be employed with profit. )

This mail of mine is meant for your private ear. (to be kept on the sly)

There are many criminals who keep their eyes, ears, nose open amidst large crowds in order that they might open accounts in banks.

Her nose becomes so smelling whenever she keeps her ears close to the tongues of others.

The pick-pocket is so blessed (or cursed) with open ears, quick eyes, nimble hands and a smelling nose that even the purses of the Scotland police cannot save their pockets.

The innumerable cuts in his own pocket have adversely made him a notorious pick-pocket.

Your nose is really good whenever you go near any non-vegetarian hotel, opened or closed.

How can we talk freely when there are many open ears around us?

"Walls have ears" is a proverb in English.

Biju says, "Walls borrow ears whenever my wife makes comments on my mother".

The walls of his office have been raised with tales whispered within.

- **Autolycus: Though I am not naturally honest, I am so**

  **sometimes by chance;...........................**

He is not honest either by nature or bychance.

The old lady honestly admits the fact that she is not naturally honest, but honest by chance.

There has been no chance to prove his honesty either by nature or by chance.

(Interviewer: How can I trust your honesty?

Candidate: Give me a chance and I shall prove my honesty by chance.

Interviewer: !!!)

Though Herbert is naturally so honest, he sometimes becomes so dishonest by chance.

Do not hesitate to marry me. I might have been, by chance, dishonest when I proposed my love, but by nature I am embodiment of honesty.

Some teenagers are honest in everything, except in love.

The influence of power and money can make even naturally honest people honest only by chance.

- **Shepherd: His garments are rich, but he wears them not handsomely.**

Arun has rich garments, but he does not wear them handsomely.

Even those who are not handsome can look handsome by wearing handsomely.

Her garments are poor, but she wears them richly.

The simplest garment alone does not make one a Mahatma.

His body is too abnormal for any type of garment to fit him well.

Neither with appearance nor with a proper garment, is the candidate able to impress the interviewers.

His true colour is hidden in his garments.

- **Paul: ..................................................Care not for issue;**

**The crown will find an heir; great Alexander**
**Left his to the worthiest, so his successor**
**Was like to be the best.**

(Do not care for an issue; the crown and the kingdom will find an heir after your death. Alexander the great left his kingdom to the worthiest without caring for an heir; and he got a worthy successor. )

Even in democracy, the crown tries to find an heir.

The couple cares not for anything, but for a happy issue.

A clown came to the throne as the crown was missing.

Is he an Alexander to find another Alexander to be his successor?

All cannot get worthy successors as Alexander the great got.

The politician is not Alexander the great to leave his own heir in the lurch, and look for the worthiest?

(Husband: As Alexander left his kingdom to the worthiest, I wish to leave my properties to our neighbour's son the worthiest.

Wife: Your soul will leave your body before you leave our house.

Husband: !!!!)

(Student: Sir, as Alexander left his kingdom to the worthiest, you can leave the class to...........

Teacher: !!!)


• **Gentleman: Ay, the most peerless piece of earth, I think,**

**That e'er the sun shone bright on.**

(She is peerless in beauty, unsurpassedin beauty. )

What a beautiful piece of literature she is! How beautifully written poems her eyes are! What a beautiful, but not carved, statue she is! What a peerless piece of earth she is! Even if the red sun dries her skin for 16 summers, she is such a snowy flower that never fades and falls.

Many girls are beautiful and peerless pieces of earth before marriage, but their life, after marriage, is torn into pieces because of heartless and intoxicated husbands.

Which shines brighter?-the sun or the face of the girl I am in love with?

I am reminded of the morning rose, whenever I see her face in early mornings.

The girl I am going to marry is as bright as the sun, as sweet as honey in words, though not blessed by Aphrodite.

It is her peerless beauty that induces me to compose peerless music.


• **Leontes: Your father's image is so hit in you,...................**

(You bear the image of your father so truly)

Your father's image is so hit in you, but every act of yours just damages his image.

In love your mother's image is so hit in you, and in discipline your father's image is so hit in you.

Neither the image of your father nor that of your mother is so hit in you.

He has his father's image in him, but only in appearance, not in character.

She looks like her mother to a 't'. (exactly)

"Just because your efficient father's image is so finely hit in you, we cannot consider you fit for this job", said the interviewer to the candidate.

(Is it true that 'each' seven persons in the world look alike? )


• **Camillo: My lord, your sorrow was too sore laid on**

**Which sixteen winters cannot blow away**
**So many summers dry.**


(Your sorrow was much too sorely felt and borne; even sixteen winters have not blown away the burden of your sorrow, not sixteen summers could heal. )

I am ready to wait for any number of summers, any number of winters to enjoy my spring with her.

Many summers have dried me; many winters have frozen me; still the girl I am in love with is not ready to warm my heart.

She loves him so much that she becomes the gentle breeze of his summers and warm blanket of his winters and on the whole she is the spring of his entire life.

How can I marry you when you are not ready to wait for me at least for a single summer and a single winter?

How can I get my dad's consent to marry you when he is hotter than the sun of the hottest summer?

Your father is the only 'all time summer' to our spring love.

Your sorrows of summer will become the joys of spring. So do not worry.

Many summers and winters just pass on like clouds in his life, but his sky is not yet clear and his spring is not visible.

He is so unconscious that he neither feels the heat of summer nor blown away by winter.

The student has crossed sixteen winters and sixteen summers, but he has not cleared a single paper. His stay on the campus is full of countless summers and winters and his academic record is full of arrears.

The girl warms him with her kisses in summer and burns him with her words in winter.

The poor farmers toil hard in summer from womb to tomb without a spring in their own life.

# CHAPTER THIRTEEN

# THE TEMPEST

- **Boatswain: None that I more love than myself.**

Moses loved July more than himself once and now he is afraid of loving himself.

Toru does not know what 'love' means for he loves none, but himself.

One who does not know how to love others cannot love himself/herself.

Is there any that he more loves than himself?.

(Mother's love pours from heart.

Father's love is even in anger.

Lover's love appears in eyes.

Govt's love is in action.

God's love is in creation.

Baby's love is in smile.

Love for literature is in love for language. )

So selfish Niru is that that there is none on earth that he more loves than himself.

- **Sebastian: I'm out of patience.**

('Blessed are the meek, for they shall inherit the earth' is a proverb. )

The patient is so out of patience that he doesnot care to listen to what the doctor says.

He is out of success, as he is out patience.

Good decisions may not be taken when members of the team are out of patience.

Do not meet the boss when he is out of patience.

Whenever our professor is out of patience, we are out of class.

- **Prospero: .................................................having both the key**

**Of officer and office,.......................................**

The Cleopatra of our office operates the whole world of industry, because she has the key of officer and office.

Offices are there everywhere, but the remote is in the officer's hands, but when the officer is at someone's hands?..............

The old arrogant lady is so powerful and so cunning that she can change both the officer and the office within one day.

Peter is only a lock, but the key is in his wife's hands. (Is he out of power at home?)

The officer says that he is unable to keep even the key of his mind.

The Romeo of our college often loses the key of his heart.

How can you convince your executive officer who has locked her mind and lost the key too?.

Our new manager claims himself to be the superior officer, but he is not trusted even with his office key.

- **Miranda: Your tale, sir, would cure deafness.**

My grandmother's excessive telling of tales last night made all of us deaf.

The patient says to the doctor, "Your tale is not a medicine to cure my disease".

Your tale is so interesting that it will cure one's deafness.

The young and innocent girl became deaf, after lending her ears to your tale.

My life is a tale of unbearable agonies that it can be told either to the deaf or to the dead.

The speaker is so deaf that he can't hear what he himself says.

I do not want to become deaf by listening to the tales of all Toms, Dicks and Harrys.

I came to you in the hope that your tale would cure my deafness, but now I have lost my ears.

- **Miranda: Good wombs have borne bad sons.**

The actress is so arrogant that her own mother wonders whether her womb had been filled with arrogance during pregnancy.

Parents seek admission in leading English medium schools even for babes in wombs.

Nathiya is my sister but from someone's womb.

Nothing is decided in wombs.

It is, whether a child grows good or bad, in the hands of his/her mother.

There are some bad wombs, but having borne good sons.

- **Prospero: I find my zenith doth depend upon**

   **A most auspicious star,…………………………**

My zenith depends not upon any auspicious star, but upon the grace of God.

He is in search of some auspicious star to become a film star.

Even the star I was born under is not auspicious to me.

The lazy are looking at the auspicious stars in the sky without toiling on the land.

Toru is working like a Trojan, but his auspicious star is not visible to his eyes.

So lucky my neighbour is that he has all auspicious stars over his head.

• **Ariel: .............................................'Hell is empty,**

**And all the devils are here'.**

(Here the authors are reminded of a proceeding in Tamil Nadu Assembly during Mr M.G.Ramachandran's tenure (MGR). Mr K.Rajaram was then the Speaker. A member recalled the issue of exporting monkeys that was discussed on the floor the previous day. Minister Kulandaivelu said how Ramarajyam could be formed without monkeys. The Speaker replied that the members need not worry about the monkeys that already left, as the State still had plenty of monkeys. Here the leader of the Opposite Party Kalaignar Karunanidhi made all members, including the Chief Minister, roar with laughter, commenting that the Speaker did not mean 'the members in the Assembly by the statement that "the state has plenty of monkeys".)

Heaven is empty, and all angels are here.

I think all devils have been transferred from hell to heaven.

Even a heaven shall become a hell if such devils are accommodated there.

It is strange that heaven is empty without good angels and hell is empty without devils.

The teacher says, "Class room is empty and all the devils have gone on a tour".

• **Ariel: Remember I have done the worthy service,**

**Told thee no lies, made no mistaking, served**
**Without grudge or grumblings.**

Roja has served this institute for quite a long period without any grudge or grumbling.

Some husbands tell none lies, except their wives.

The worse lie of many liars is that they aver often that they never speak lies.

Those, who do worthy services, must be fittingly recognized.

Lucy has done all worthless services, told maximum lies possible, made nothing, but mistakes, served only with grudge and grumblings.

Worthy services must be remembered. Thiruvalluvar says,

"Ennanri kontaarkkum vuivundaam; vuivillai

Seinan(t)ri kontra maharkku". (In Tamil)

"Who every good have killed, may yet destruction flee;

Who 'benefit' has killed, that man shall ne'er scape free". (in English)

- **Prospero:** ...........................................thy groans

**Did make wolves howl, and penetrate the breasts
Of ever-angry bears.**

So inexplicable are your groans that they would make wolves howl, and penetrate the breasts of ever-angrybears.

Do you think that the harsh words you used would not have hurt me? They would have penetrated the breasts of ever-angry bears.

Your kind words will melt the breasts of even angry bears.

Your heart melts with unbearable groans that can make wolves howl.

She says that her groans could penetrate the breasts of angry bears, but not even touch the stony hearts of the so called human beings.

(Nurse: The patient howls like a wolf out of pain.

Doctor: Show him the bill. He will trumpet like an elephant. )

- **Prospero: Fill all thy bones with aches,.................**

Better to be boneless than to live with aching bones.

She has filled my bones with aches and mind with pains.

He is so fond of eating that he fills even his bones with food stuff.

My heart, my mind, my bones and even my liver is filled with aches.

The pain in his mind is severer than the aches he has in his bones.

The doctor says, "The patient has no bone at all, how could he fill his bones with aches?".

The old man says, "Better to fill my bones with aches than to fill my mind with agonies and worries".

- **Prospero: Thy nerves are in their infancy again**

  **And have no vigour in them.**

Your sinews are as weak as they were in your childhood, and are almost benumbed.

The nerves of the aged are in their infancy again and have no vigour in them.

The infant in their hands about 25 years ago has now forsaken his aged parents with their nerves being in infancy again without any vigour.

My nerves may be in their infancy again and I might have lost my vigour, but my mind is strong in possession of self-respect.

His vigour is not in his body, but in his mind.

- **Ferdinand: ............................All corners else O'th' earth**

  **Let liberty make use of;...............................**

Let every bit of space on the earth be kept for free-men.

The drunkard says that he has no liberty even in a corner of his own house.

The bricks, pillars and all corners of the world I live in enjoy the breeze of liberty.

"Man is born free but is everywhere in chains", said Rousseau

There are many who feel being chained even when free air blows in every direction they turn.

It is the mind that makes one breath the air of liberty.


• **Miranda: My father's of a better nature, sir**

**Than he appears by speech.**


Do not judge a book by its coverand so my father by his speech.

My father by action is of a better nature than he appears by speech.

Verbal honey flows freely on the tongues in romantic intoxication.

She is not as good by acquaintance as by her appearance and speech.

Many politicians appear better by speeches than by promises.


• **Prospero: ..........................................Thou shalt be as free**

**As mountain winds,.......................................**


The aged parentsareworried about their only son being with absolutely no sense of responsibility as free as mountain winds.

He drowns his worries, concerns and disappointments by making his mind as free as mountain winds.

The king is so cruel that he thinks of blocking even the free flow of mountain winds.

Before marriage, her mind was as free as mountain winds.

My grandmother lived a long and healthy life, for her mind was as free as mountain winds.

I can compose poetry, when my mind is as free as mountain winds.

The minds of employees under stress and pressure shall not be free, even if they stand on the top of mountains with gentle breeze blowing in all directions.

- **Gonzalo: How lush and lusty the grass looks! How green!**

(lush- beautiful, sexy, mellow, soft, amazing, cool
Lustful- beautiful, pleasant)
To look at the lush, lusty and green grass in the chill mornings delights my mind and heart.
Even at the age of 85, my grandmother's memory is as green as the morning grass.
He looks like the lush and lusty green grass, but he is hiding his groans in dark clouds.
The teacher says, "I love to teach you as your faces are as lush and lusty and green as the grass in all my classes".
(Two friends during a wedding
Friend 1: The bride's face looks lush and lusty like the green grass.
Friend 2: The summer has not yet started. ) (Life after marriage is as hot as summer? )

- **Antonio: If but one of his pockets could speak, would it not**

   **say he lies?**

(Once a man met Prophet Muhammad (PBUH) and told him that he was in possession of three sins; committing adultery, drinking alcohol and speaking lies. As he could not give up all these three at a time, he sought Prophet's advice on which of the sins be dropped first in his efforts to drop all the three sins, but one by one. Prophet Muhammad advised him to give up the habit of speaking lies. Getting annoyed at Prophet's suggestion on giving up speaking lies, which seems to be not so sinful as committing adultery and consuming alcohol, the followers (Sahaba's) asked Prophet

Muhammad about this, for which the prophet replied that the other two sins would disappear, if the habit of speaking lies was given up. The mind filled with concocted lies is a devil's workshop.)

If one of his pockets spoke, it would say that he is aliar.

I think he is carrying lies in his pocket.

One lie leads to many.

Only when she was washing her husband's shirt, she found out that even the shirt pocket of his contained plenty of lies.

He may go to the extent of telling the lie that he was pushed out of plane for ticketless travel.


- **Gonzalo: ....................our garments are now as fresh as when**

**we put them on first...............................**


He has been using this garment for the past ten years, but still it is as fresh as he put it on first.

Your garments are as fresh as when you put them on first, but your mind is impure with evil thoughts.

His face is as fresh as the garment on his body.

During an interview, your garment must look as fresh as when you put it on first.

He wants such a white collar job that he expects his garments to look as fresh as when he puts it on first in the evenings of hot summer.

(The garments of our politicians these days are always as fresh as when they put them on first, when there are many in the nation without a garment. Winston Churchill called Mahatma Gandhiji "a half-naked fakir". Without a full garment, he garmented our nation and saved it from naked eyes. Once when he visited a school, a student, seeing his simple dress, asked him whether he could bring him a new dress. Gandhiji replied that he was in need of garments in thousands. The boy could not understand what he said. Gandhiji said, "How can I wear good dresses, when there are many too poor to wear a good dress?". )

- **Sebastian: I think he will carry this island home in his pocket**

  **And give it his son for an apple.**

(Mr R.Venkatraman former Presidentof India in his book "My Presidential Years" makes a mention of one Mr Kinnock, when he met him in England.

"Kinnock was the next caller. He had met me earlier in India and exchanged views with me. He was ebullient and full of confidence and spoke as if he had the next prime ministership of England **in his pocket**". (315)

Corrupt politicians wish to do all what they can do to carry the whole country in their pockets, leaving nothing for subjects.

(Even if their nation dies, they live in their currency. Mahatma Gandhi is fated to smile on the currency notes accepted as bribes? Former Chief Justice of the Supreme Court Mr V.R.Krishna Iyer in his book "Leaves from My personal Life" writes that "Who lives if India dies? Perhaps every V.I.P., be he public official, legislator servant of the people, will privately say; "I live even if India dies because I have made enough and it is in Switzerland...............The oldpatriotism has died down and India Private Limited is comingto stay". (16-17) )

The so called saint is carrying an island in his pocket.

I may enjoy my life in an island, but I am aware that I am surrounded by sea water.

- **Gonzalo: The truth you speak doth lack some gentleness,**

  **And time to speak it in. you rub the sore**
  **When you should bring the plaster.**

He is rubbing the sore without applying ointment. (He is complicatingthe problem. )

Rub not the sore till you get a plaster.

You speak the truth, but it lacks gentleness.

The sore is not healed just by rubbing. (The problem is not solved just by discussing or negotiating.

The nation has been just rubbing the sores all these years. (When solution?)

You speak but it lacks gentleness and you speak, but when the time is not ripe.

You rub not only your sore, but also those of others. (You poke your nose into the affairs of others. )

There are many among us who speak lies genuinely and speak truths gently.


- **Gonzalo: All things in common nature should produce**

  **Without sweat or endeavour;.....................**

Nothing worthwhile can be achieved without sweat or endeavour.

Can aspirations and ambitions be fulfilled without sweat or endeavour?

The candidate wants to get his PhD without sweat or endeavour.

Love just blossoms without sweat or endeavour.

Our forefathers did not get freedom for the nation without sweat or endeavour.


- **Alonso: ........................................I wish mine eyes**

  **Would, with themselves, shut up my thoughts.**

Prasanth judges everyone and everything by what he eyes.

You are misguided by your own eyes and your own ears.

Unless your senses are blind to your eyes or your eyes blind to your senses, you will face the music.

I wish my eyes would shut up my thoughts.

Her eyes, I think, are blind to her thoughts.

Samuel never thinks at all and there is no question of his eyes shutting up his thoughts.

- **Sebastian: It seldom visits sorrow; when it doth,**

  **It is a comforter.**

(comforter- a great healer)

Sorrow is a comforter in love failure.

It is strange that he is burdened with joys and comforted with sorrows.

One gets acquainted with sorrow at its being a regular visitor.

I do not open my doors when sorrow is the visitor.

When sorrow breaks my doors, I consider it my fate.

She says, "Sorrow! Be thou my comforter".

She says, "My mother is the comforter, whenever my mother-in-law becomes my sorrow".

- **Antonio: My strong imagination sees a crown**

  **Dropping upon thy head.**

You said that your strong imagination saw a crown dropping upon our party leader's head, but he is in prison now.

My strong imagination sees a girl of paragon beauty winning your hand and heart.

My strong imagination sees your father becoming a butcher on seeing your progress card.

You are strong only in your imagination.

My strong imagination saw a sword of Damocles hanging on his head.

- **Antonio: ..........................so high a hope that even**

  **Ambition cannot pierce a wink beyond,.........**

His hope is so high that even ambition cannot pierce a wink beyond.

Standing always on the surface, he keeps his hopes high.

Ambition without efforts is like a bird without wings.

He is so hopefully ambitious and ambitiously hopeful that he sleeps not a wink these days.

He is so hopeful that even ambition cannot pierce a wink beyond.

• **Antonio: The man i'th' moon's tooslow till-newborn chins**

**Be rough and razorable;...............................**

The time for him to take any decision is more than the time for the new born chins becoming rough and razorable.

The MLAhas not visited the constituency, though the newborn chins have become rough and razorable.

Many can wait till a newborn baby's skin becomes razorable, but cannot wait till their wives finish their make-up even before going to market.

You speak as though you were my great grandfather even before your newborn chin become rough and razorable!

(Son: Dad! Give me my share. I cannot wait till my newborn chin become rough and razorable.

Dad: I can make it rough and razorable with my blows now.

Son runs away. )

His newborn chin has not yet become rough and razorable, but he has an old head on young shoulders.

• **Antonio: .................................................it was the roar**

**Of a whole herd of lions.**

Uncle Tom's snoring is the resemblance of the roar of a whole herd of lions.

My friend's wife is so bold that she will enter the cave that echoes the roar of a whole herd of lions.

Even the roar of a whole herd of lions can go unheard when you snore during sleep.

Yours is not a sound sleep, but sleep with sounds.

That rowdy roars like a lion everywhere, but mews like a cat at home.

Whenever his boss roars like a lion, he barks like a dog and howls like a fox. Ultimately, the office suffocates due to animal smell.

- **Caliban: All the infections that the sun sucks up**

  **From bogs, fens, flats, on Prosper fall, and make him**
  **By inchmeal a disease!**

(May all the diseases that the sun draws up from marsh and morass and lowland fall on Prospero and make him sick inch by inch.)

(Saint: What is your prayer?

Daughter-in-law: All the infections that the sun sucks up from bogs, fens, flats, on my mother-in-law fall, and make her by inchmeal a disease.

Saint: ???)

Your words are more infectious than all the infections that the sun sucks up from bogs, fens and flats.

More than the spread of Corona virus, it is the fear and rumour that make most people sick inch by inch.

All the infections that the sun sucks up from bogs, fens and flats cannot infect her as her mind is more infectious and poisonous than anything else.

- **Trinculo: ......................................Misery acquaints a man**

  **With strange bedfellows!**

(Misfortune forces a man to keep company withstrange people. )

Misery drowns one into disappointments and acquaints him/her with strange bedfellows.

Strange fellows get acquainted at the time of misery and those close to heart just disappear.

Better to bear with misery than to get acquainted with strange bed fellows.

His misery is nothing but his acquaintance with strange bedfellow.

• **Stephano: ...............................If all the wine in my bottle will**

**Recover him, I will help his ague.**

(ague-an acute or intermittentfever)

Many drown their frustration in alcohol.

Jose does not wish to get recovered as the bottle is empty without wine.

His ague cannot be helped even if all wine bottles are emptied.

I can help his ague only with all the wine in my bottle.

He cannot help my ague even with all the wine in his bottle.

• **Stephano: ...............................my stomach is not**

**constant.**

Neither his mind nor his stomachis constant.

Not his mind, but his stomach is constantly thinking.

He can speak well on any stage, but his stomach is not constant.

When he was talking constantly, his stomach was constantly troubling him.

• **Caliban: Hast thou not dropped from heaven?**

Lekha walks and talks as if she were dropped from heaven.

Raghu is so saintly that people wonder whether he would have been dropped from heaven.

She walks with her nose in the air and behaves as though she were dropped from heaven.

My angel is so beautiful that anyone would think that she would have been dropped from heaven.

(Girl: I was dropped from heaven.

Boy: That's why your mind is full of injuries. (You are very arrogant. Or your mind is full of evil thoughts. )

Has she been dropped from hell for every word of hers reminds one of Lucifer?

- **Ferdinand: ..........he's composed of harshness.**

(He is made up entirelyof harshness. )

Our leader seems to be cool, but is composed of harshness.

Nitheesh once composed of humility is now of harshness.

Though he is composed of harshness, his heart is in the right place.

Though composed of harshness, our house owner has won many hearts.

Many are composed of harshness till marriage, but fate makes them become world class sadhus after marriage.

- **Caliban: .........................Let me lick thy shoe. I'll**

**not serve him; he is not valiant.**

(valiant-courageous)

He claims to have been born under a lucky star, but his lucky star has made him lick everyone's shoe for every elevation in life.

Better to serve a valiant than to serve a coward.

You may be my boss, but do not expect me to lick your shoe.

His mad love for power and wealth has made him madly lick one's shoe.

The poor man says, "There is no need for anyone to lick anyone's shoe under any circumstances".

The poor father is licking many shoes just to get bread for his children.

(In the Tamil movie, "Siraichalai" (Imprisonment), the trials and tribulations experienced by the freedom fighters in the Andaman prison are clearly portrayed. One of the scenes in which an atrocious British officer with his head made of pride and arrogance would ask an Indian to polish his shoes by licking. The atrocities exercised on the freedom fighters make us realize that that we did not get freedom over night or by cook or crook. Mohan Lal hailing from Kerala is the hero of the movie. )

- **Stephano: .................keep a good tongue in your head.**

(Speak politely, if you are rebellious.)

How can a tongue be kept in an evil head?

Good heads sometimes invite their own ruin by unreliable tongues.

The speaker's good head was broken because of his bad tongue.

His evil head can never be identified because of his good tongue.

His virtues just remain unidentifiable because of his bad tongue.

- **Caliban: ............................knock a nail into his head.**

Nail can be knocked into his head, but not knowledge and wisdom.

His head is so strong that any number of nails can be knocked into it.

Even if all answers were knocked into his head, he won't answer.

The professor said, "I cannot knock the lesson into your heads. Listen carefully".

His head is so corrupt and devilish that even the new nails knocked into his head would rapidly get rusted.

- **Stephano: .........................................I'll**

**turn my mercy out o'doors and make a stockfish
of thee.**

(I shall throw away all mercy and beat you as a dried codis beaten before it is boiled. )
Many of us are living turning mercy out of doors.
The so called rules and regulations sometimes throw away mercy out of doors.
Anyone can knock at his door, except mercy and love.
I shall turn my mercy out of doors and make a stockfish of you.
Mercy is mercilessly turned out of doors.

- **Ariel: ...................................I and my fellows**

**Are ministers of fate. The elements,
Of whom your swords are tempered, may as well
Wound the loud winds....................................................
.........................................If you could hurt,
Your swords are now too massy for your strengths,
And will not be uplifted.**

(my fellows-my comrades, ministers of fate- agents of fate)
(You might inflict wounds upon the invisible air. If you could hurt, your swords are now too heavy for you to lift, and there is no use tryingto use them.)
The Chief Minister says, "I and my cabinet ministers of fate tender our resignation, owning responsibility to the fatal incident in the state".
The day of marriage is the day of joy for some, day of sorrow for some and the day of fate for many.
He is such a coward that he inflicts wounds upon the loud winds, but runs back shouting loudly at the very sight of his enemies.

Verathi is so harmful that she might wound even the wind that gently embraces her.

- **Ferdinand: ...................................shall never melt**

   **Mine honour into lust..........................**

Honour gets lost when it melts into lust.
   My honour shall never melt into lust.
   Keep your cool honour away from hot lust.
   His honour got burned into the ashes of lust.
   It is the uncontrollable lust that melt one's honour.
   I would not give up, even if my honour got melted into lust.
   It is the uncontrollable lust into which the so called saint has his honour melted into.

- **Ferdinand: The white cold virgin snow upon my heart**

   **Abates the ardour of my liver.**

(The virgin purity of love in my heartlessens the heat of passion.)
   Even the white cold virgin upon my heart cannot abate the ardour of my liver.
   The ardour of his liver cannot be abated as his heart is filled with dark bushes.
   The white cold virgin snow upon his heart cannot abate the ardour of his liver as he is suffering from jaundice now.

- **Prospero: ...................................our little life**

   **Is rounded with a sleep.**

(Human life ends in a sleep. )
   His grandfather has lost his sleep, as his last sleep is fast approaching.

Our little life is rounded with a sleep, but we make many sleepless in life.

His life became little because of long sleep.

The student goes rounds everywhere actively, but is rounded with a sleep in classes.

Many of us are rounded with trials and tribulations before we are rounded with the last sleep.

Many of us attain maturity and become saints when rounded with the last sleep.

(A guest once visited a professor of English, who was noted for his love for literature and frequent use of literary expressions. When the guest took leave of him, the professor found what Robert Frost said quite appropriate, and said, "Miles to go before I sleep and miles to go before I sleep". Unable to understand what the professor said, the guest innocently asked the professor when he would sleep. )


- **Ariel:** ...............................**they were red-hot with drinking,**

  **So full of valour that they smote the air**
  **For breathing in their faces,**

(They were flushed with drinking and they were so pot-valiant (courageous by drink) that they beat the air for blowing intotheir faces....)

He gets his physical valour from bottles and mental valour from books.

They are so intoxicated that they smote the air for breathing in their faces.

His face is red-hot with drinking and his tongue is hot with philosophy.


- **Caliban:** ................................................**If he awake,**

  **From toe to crown he'll fill our skins with pinches,**

(If he wakes up, he will fill your whole body with pinches from head to foot. )

From toe to crown your skins are safe, for your rival is fast asleep.

Shall I wake him up by fillinghis skins from toe to crown with pinches?

His courage goes to sleep, when his wife wakes up.

Mr Cunning is earning money by filling from toe to crown the customers' skins with pinches in the name of massage.

- **Ariel: His tears runs down his beard like winter's drops**

  **From eaves of reeds.**

(Tears run down his beardlike melting icicles from a thatched roof.)

When he heard of his beloved daughter being tortured by her husband, his tears ran down his beard like winter's drops from eaves of reeds.

When the earnest and enthusiastic poor girl was denied admission in the institute of her dream, tears ran down her cheek and chin like winter's drops from eaves of reeds.

The farmer's tears runs down his beard like winter's drops from eaves of reeds, as he is too poor to reap the harvest.

Even in hot summer, tears runs down Mr John's beard like winter's drops from eaves of reeds because of his son's arrogant and indifferent attitude.

- **Prospero: ..........................The rarer action is**

  **In virtue than in vengeance.**

The old lady's mind works faster in vengeance than in virtue.

Your action is rarer in virtue than in vengeance.

His heart is so stony that he cannot differentiate between virtue and vengeance.

You can find virtue in her words, but vengeance in her thoughts and deeds.

Her face is the same both in virtue and vengeance.

The newly married girl says, "My mother-in-law speaks of virtue, but delights in vengeance".

- **Sebastian: The devil speaks in him.**

Some devil has occupied his whole body that he speaks and acts likea devil.

You donot speak, but the devil in you.

Mouth is his, but every word is devil's.

The devil in you grows by the words that you are using.

All devils stay in him, but never speak in him.

The devil speaks in him, even when he is fast sleep.

How he, without even an iota of conscience, pours out venom verbally! Has she swallowed devils that make him speak like that?

- **Prospero: .........................................to call brother**

**Would even infect my mouth, ...................**

To forget one's fault is human and to forgive is divine.

Your harsh words have infected your mouth.

I am not a saint to forgive your rankest fault.

To call you my friend would infect my mouth.

Your mouth won't get infected just because you call her your mother.

- **Prospero: Their eyes do offices of truth, their words**

**Are natural breath.**

His eyes speak the truth and his breath is natural.

Your eyes do offices of truth, your words are natural breath only now, but you are in the evening of your life.

Varun is such a liar that even his breath is not natural.

He breathes naturally only when he speaks lies unnaturally.

His eyes are contradictory to his utterances.

(We must always speak the truth. Lies may delight and even benefit us, but when conscience pricks us, nothing can be more painful than that. Justice V.R.Krishna Iyer in his book "98 Not Out" highlights the value of speaking Truth by quoting Mahatma Gandhiji, who was insisting uncompromisingly to his client. "Yes, tell me the truth, the whole truth, but nothing but the truth, this without reservation. Gandhiji has another unspoken undertaking from his client that he has the freedom to tell the court the truth and the whole truth. Even if parts of the truth were adverse to his client and the opposite party would take advantage of it". (1) He also writes in his book that "The Mahatma won his way after all, facts were ¾ of the law and the court was satisfied that Gandhiji would speak only the truth. They would hear him and tell the opposite lawyer we have heard the facts. You need only argue the law. Thus the judge found it easy to reach the foundation of facts and decided on the truth of the case. Therefore the reputation of the Mahatma as a Veracity Attorney rose so high that he became a prosperous popular lawyer speaking and practising only the truth. Gandhiji rose in stature before the judges. No false cases, no false witnesses, bare facts made the court hall a Mahatma in action and every litigation proved to be a moral exercise and experimental truth". (2)

- **Ferdinand: I have cursed them without cause.**

Many curse others without cause and some look for causes to curse others.

Mother-in-law curses her daughter-in-law with or without cause; daughter-in-law in turn curses her mother-in-law with or without cause and her husband (mother-in-law's son) causes himself without cause.

I cannot look for causes to curse my fellow human beings.

His cursing others without cause has become the only cause for others to curse him.

There are causes to curse him, but there are no apt words to curse him.

- **Prospero: Let us not burden our remembrances with**

**A heaviness that'sgone.**

We should not load our memory with a sorrow that is past.

Sweet remembrances delight us and the bitter ones disappoint us.

I do not know why she pulls forward a heaviness that's gone!.

There is no use burdening your remembrance with a heaviness that's gone.

Do not unnecessarily burden your mind and heart with bitter remembrances.

- **Gonzalo: I have inly wept,.......................**

(inly- inwardly, within, internally, secretly)

(Sir Charles Spencer Chaplin, popularly known as Charlie Chaplin was an English comic actor. His screen persona "The Tramp" gained him name and fame and made him a worldwide icon. He made the audience roar with laughter through his comic acts. The actor who made all laugh was inly weeping, as his personal life filled his heart with grief, sorrow and misery. Unable to bear, he met a doctor. The doctor, without being able to identify him, advised him to go and watch the comic scenes of Charlie Chaplin in order that his grief might find a great relief. He replied innocently that he was none, but Charlie Chaplin. )

There are some who, after marriage, are inly weeping, but outwardly laughing.

Joy that is shared gets doubled and sorrow that is shared gets reduced.

- **Alonso: Let grief and sorrow still embrace his heart**

Grief and sorrow embrace the farmers when their demands fall on deaf ears.

When his wife embraced him, he felt grief and sorrow embracing his heart.

My heart is free from grief and sorrow.

Better to die of heart attack than to live with a well-functioning heart, but full of grief and groan.

No cardiologist can cure a heart full of grief and sorrow.

(Mr Anna Durai, former Chief Minister of Tamil Nadu said, "Ethaiyum thangum ithayam vendum". Herat that bears anything (pain/grief/failure) is needed. )

Grief and sorrow can never embrace my heart, for my heart is not with me.

- **Boatswain: .................................range and several noises**

**Of roaring, shrieking, howling, jingling chains
And more diversity of sounds, all horrible,........**

He says that he need not go to any jungle to hear the noises of roaring, shrieking,howling, jingling chains and more diversity of sounds, but just an oral fight between his mother and wife will do.

He is so fond of non-vegetarian items that even his human sound has become like roaring, shrieking, howling and more diversity of sounds.

He is so mad after non-vegetarian stuff that he wants even his dining hall to echo strange and several noises of roaring, shrieking, howling, jingling chains and more diversity of sounds.

I think there must be a heavy fight between husband and wife because the house is full of strange and several noises of roaring, shrieking, howling, jingling chains and more diversity of sounds, all horrible, but quite enjoyable.

- **Prospero: His mother was a witch, and one so strong**

   **That could control the moon,...............**

The arrogant old lady used to speak as if she could control the sun and the moon.

He is so strong that he can control the agitating waves of the sea at the time of tsunami.

She says to her friend, "Your father must be a saint as your mother is a witch".

The hot sun will get back its firing rays at the very sight of such witches.

If William Shakespeare saw the old lady, he would include her as one more witch in his "Macbeth".

She is a witch, and one so strong that could control the moon, but not her own tongue.

Hari says to his wife, "First control your tongue. Then you can think of controlling the moon".

# Reference


Nehru, Jawaharlal. 2004. *An autobiography*. Penguin India.

Nehru, Jawaharlal. 2008. *The discovery of India*. Penguin India.

Nehru, Jawaharlal. 2004. *Glimpses of world history*. Penguin India.

Chaudhuri, C. Nirad. 1964. *Autobiography of an unknown Indian*. Jaico Publishing House.

Venkataraman. 1994. *My presidential years*. Collins Publisher.

Iyer, V. R. Krishna. 2010. *Leaves from my personal life*. Gyan Publishing House.

Iyer, V. R. Krishna. 2015. *Dynamic lawyering*. Universal Law Publishing – An imprint of LexisNexis.

Iyer, V.R. Krishna. 2007. Sublime footprint. Gyan Publishing House.

Iyer, V. R. Krishna. 2015. *To work is a pleasure*. Universal Law Publishing Co Ltd.

Iyer, V. R. Krishna. *Up till now*. Universal Law Publishing Co Ltd.

Iyer, V. R. Krishna. *98 not out*. Universal Law Publishing Co Ltd.

Singh, K. Natwar. 2014. *One life is not enough*. Rupa and Co.

Singh, K. Natwar. 2004. Heart to heart. Rupa Publications India.

Tharoor, Shashi. 2020. *The battle of belongings.* Aleph Book Company.

Churchill S. Winston. 2002. *Never give in: the extraordinary character of Winston Churchill.* Cumberland House Publishing, US.

Vairamuthu. *Aayiram padalkal - tamil.* Thirumagal Nilayam.

Pope. G. U. 2017.*Thirukural: English translation and commentary.* Createspace Independent Pub.

Shakespeare, William. 2020. *The comedy of errors.* Fingerprint Publishing.

Shakespeare, William. Barbara A. Mowat (Ed.). 2004. *The taming of the shrew.* Simon and Schuster.

Shakespeare, William. Gupta N. K. Das. (Ed.). 2016. *The winter's tale.* Laxmi Narain Agarwal.

Shakespeare, William. Pinto Xavier. (Ed.). 2020. *The merchant of venice.* Beeta Publications.

Shakespeare, William. Sen. S. (Ed.). 2020. *The tempest: a critical evaluation.* Unique Publications.

Shakespeare, William. Sen. S. (Ed.). 2021. *As you like it: a critical evaluation.* Unique Publishers India Private Limited.

Shakespeare, William. 2012. *A midsummer night's dream.* Maple Press.

Shakespeare, William. 2014. *The merry wives of Windsor.* Dover Publications Inc.

Shakespeare, William. Hart .H.C. (Ed.). 2010. *The works of Shakespeare: measure for measure.* Nabu Press.

Shakespeare, William. 2016. *Two gentlemen of Verona.*

Shakespeare, William. 1993. *All's well that ends well.* Cambridge University Press.

Shakespeare, William. Sen .S. (Ed.). 2020. *Twelfth night: a critical evaluation.* Unique Publications.

Shakespeare, William. 2013. Much ado about nothing. Maple Press.